T0244144

BATTLE ELEPHANTS AND FLAMING FOXES

BATTLE ELEPHANTS AND FLAMING FOXES

AND

ANIMALS IN THE ROMAN WORLD

CAROLINE FREEMAN-CUERDEN

For James
and for my brother, David.

A special thank you to Xander Freeman-Cuerden for being my reader and critic.
Love and thanks to Poppy and Alice, to Dad and Janet for their encouragement,
and to Susan Hanson, Kate Hickling and Lara J. West for their support.

First published 2023

The History Press
97 St George's Place, Cheltenham,
Gloucestershire, GL50 3QB
www.thehistorypress.co.uk

British Library Cataloguing in Publication Data.
A catalogue record for this book is available from the British Library.

ISBN 978 0 7509 9961 8

Typesetting and origination by The History Press
Printed and bound in Great Britain by TJ Books Limited, Padstow, Cornwall.

Trees for LYfe

CONTENTS

Introduction 7

PART ONE: A Bit of a Bestiary 9
The Elephant 11
The Wolf 27
The Horse 33
The Dolphin and the Whale 47
Birds 55
Insects and Arachnids 68
The Dog 78
The Cat: Big and Small 92
The Snake 101

PART TWO: Animals in the Roman World 109
The World of the Chariot Horse 111
Animals in the World of Fashion and Beauty 135
Animals in the Amphitheatre 147
Animals on a Platter: Food 171
The World of Science and Health 184
Pets 200
Animals in Religion and Philosophy 211
Animals in the Military 223
The World of the Battle Elephant 239

Epilogue 259
Appendix: Roman Authors 262
Bibliography 272
Index 275

INTRODUCTION

T he story of Rome's birth does not revolve around a goddess or a god but around an animal. It's the she-wolf who takes the starring role, and the wolf who became the symbol of Rome's foundation.

Animals bellowed, trumpeted, growled and roared through every avenue of Roman life: in ships transported across oceans, on battlefields, in temples, in palaces and homes, in books, in amphitheatres, on racing tracks. Their bones were turned into ash for medicine, their sinews wound onto catapults, their skins pulled tight over battering rams and shields. Chariot horses thundered around the packed Circus while spectators in their thousands hollered and cheered. Animals became the symbols of Roman legions, chickens were consulted to predict the future, and oxen were sacrificed to the sound of music and the smell of incense.

The first Roman emperor, Augustus, kept a seal skin near his side to protect against thunderstorms. The emperor Commodus (strangled to death in his bath by a wrestler) chopped the heads off ostriches in a grand display of his hunting skills, while the dog-loving Hadrian wrote a poem to his favourite horse.

If you wanted rid of a tattoo on your body, you needed only apply pigeon poop mixed with vinegar. If you fancied an aphrodisiac, you would just dry out a few horse testicles, grind them up and pop the powder into a drink.

When Roman armies were faced with the might and terror of the war elephant on the battlefield, they had to learn how to defeat this unknown enemy, even if it meant using pigs as an anti-elephant weapon. Spectacular shows in Roman arenas across the empire saw the slaughter of thousands and thousands of animals for entertainment, and animals became the executioners of unfortunate human victims condemned to punishment and death by beast attack in the arena. Over 100 days, 9,000 animals were killed at the games of Titus in AD 80, and some thirty years later, another 11,000 in games to commemorate Trajan's conquest of Dacia. The Romans watched these slaughters and were even responsible for the extinction of the North African elephant, *Loxodonta africana pharaohensis*, but – if they were wealthy enough – left gravestones to their dead pet dogs and recorded the achievements of the most celebrated chariot horses on monuments.

Roman philosophers wrote about eating animals, not eating animals, about animals being here solely for the use of humans, about animals having feelings and about our duty to be kind to them. Horses are engraved on nearly every one of the 600 gravestones for the Roman guard, the bones of dogs have been excavated from the ruins of Pompeii gardens, and animals left their paw prints on Roman tiles – archaeological finds to be dug up 2,000 years later.

The Romans wrote poetry about humans transforming into birds, a spider, a weasel, a stag and a cow; they wrote verse for a courageous lion's performance in the amphitheatre, guides on how a cavalryman should train on his horse, and books on how to fatten up your dormice for a posh dinner or how to choose your dogs and the best names to give them. The great writer Cicero, whose head and hands were nailed to the rostrum at Rome after his execution, wrote about the elephants who caused a rebellion in the crowd at the mighty colosseum in Rome. *Felicula*, meaning 'Kitty', was a pet name for girls; a lazy man was a *cuculus*, a cuckoo, and the Romans used the surname *Mus*, as in 'Mr Mouse'. While we let sleeping dogs lie, if a Roman 'held a wolf by the ears', it meant they were in trouble – but not as much trouble as a siege soldier down a tunnel after a swarm of bees had been released as a chemical weapon against him.

Once we start looking at the animals in Roman society, we see the Romans themselves more clearly. How did animals fit into the Roman war machine, their love of entertainment and a show, or the quest for luxury? By looking at the words left to us, the uncovered bones and gravestones, every animal tells a story and shines a light on the history of Rome itself.

PART ONE

A BIT OF
A BESTIARY

THE ELEPHANT

Elephantus

Out of all the animals in the Roman world, it is the elephant that ancient authors wrote about the most. They appeared on coins and mosaics, they became the symbol of a courageous legion, their tusks were crafted into sword hilts and statues, and the African war elephants who lined up in battle during Rome's civil war even played their part in dimming the light of the Roman Republic and aiding the ascendency of Rome's most famous dictator, Julius Caesar. The battle elephants of the Roman world line up in an entire chapter to themselves later, but we can't parade through a bestiary of Roman elephants without mentioning at least one example of their part in the ancient theatre of war. And so, let's begin in the first century BC at Thapsus in North Africa.

JULIUS CAESAR AND KING JUBA'S BEARD

North Africa, 46 BC. The armies of Julius Caesar and Quintus Metellus Scipio prepare to fight one another in what is to be the decisive battle of the Roman Civil War. Caesar's old friend turned enemy, the Roman general Pompey, has been defeated at Pharsalus less than two years earlier, but now the Battle of Thapsus is on the horizon. Pompey is dead, assassinated in Egypt, but his father-in-law, Scipio, fights on in his name; Scipio and his fourteen legions prepare to do battle with Caesar and his army of eight legions of veterans. Enter the elephants.

It's a Roman policy to allow African rulers to keep their own elephants, and King Juba I of Numidia has a huge number of the animals. Unfortunately for Julius Caesar, he is not one of Juba's favourite people,

11

not since an incident in a court case against Juba's father. The young Julius Caesar got so worked up in arguing his case that he went beyond mere words, reaching over and pulling on Juba's beard. What with all the beard tugging, when Scipio needs a contingent of war elephants in his army, it's no wonder that Juba is happy to loan sixty of them to an enemy of Caesar. The Roman legions on both sides of this civil war don't know it, but the battle elephants at Thapsus are not only going to lead to the deaths of thousands of men, they will lead to the death of the Roman Republic itself.

Elephant Preparation for the Battle of Thapsus

Scipio's elephants have to be trained for what they might face on the field of war. The last thing the general wants is for the animals to turn on their own men if they come under fire. To combat this, the animals have been lined up, and stationed right in front of them are slingers – men skilled in using hand-held slings to fire deadly stone bullets. A hail of stones is catapulted at the elephants and, as they turn away from the airborne missiles, they are attacked by another line of slingers placed behind them who fire a second round, forcing the elephants to wheel around and face their original enemy again. Scipio does not want his war elephants to run from enemy missiles when it comes to the actual battle, and hopefully this training will stop them turning and trampling their own troops in any assault from Caesar's slingers.

Scipio has also used the animals in a psychological tactic designed to intimidate and spread panic amongst Caesar's troops. Dressed in full battle array with men atop the towers on their backs, the elephants have been led to the front line of Scipio's camp and positioned in full view of Caesar's army. The plan is that these live weapons of war will terrorise both Caesar's men and his horses.

Successfully subduing the elephants will be crucial to any victory. Two of Scipio's spies are sent into Caesar's camp to find out what is being planned: have any anti-elephant traps or trenches been built in front of the camp? What are Caesar's strategies in facing the elephants in the upcoming battle?

Caesar knows that dealing with the elephants is vital to his military success, and that his army's morale depends on diffusing the awe and fear that the animals could inspire in his men. We know Caesar's tactics from an eyewitness soldier, possibly a centurion in his army, who described Caesar's anti-elephant strategy in the Roman military commentary *The African War*:

> [H]e had ordered elephants to be transported from Italy, so that the soldiers could get to know and recognise the appearance and abilities of the animal and which part of its body was most easily wounded by a missile and, when an elephant was in battle dress and armoured, which part of its body was still left exposed so that missiles could be fired there. On top of this, so that they wouldn't be terrified of them, his horses should get used to the smell, trumpeting and appearance of the beasts. Caesar benefited greatly from these techniques: for the soldiers handled the elephants and became acquainted with their slowness, the cavalry threw blunted javelins at them and the passive nature of the beasts led the horses to feeling comfortable around them. (*The African War*, 72)

Caesar knows that Scipio wants to destroy his men's morale. But Caesar has his Fifth Legion and he believes these veterans have the spirit to deal with enemy elephants. Singling the legion out for special elephant training, he issues them with specific instructions to get into their formations when the elephants attack. These are soldiers who have proven themselves in battle; they are the ones who have the spirit and courage to face the terror of charging war elephants.

The Battle Begins

Scipio faces Caesar's troops, deploying his elephants up front and on the left and right wings. Positioned here, they should intimidate the enemy, weaken morale and throw the Caesarean legionaries into chaos when they charge. Along with more reinforcements from Juba, the animals number more than sixty and Caesar's army can see every intimidating one of them.

With about 480 men to a cohort during this period, Julius Caesar divides his ten cohorts of the Fifth Legion, positioning them opposite each side of the enemy elephant wings. He then walks amongst his veteran legionaries and works up their spirits for the battle to come. *Remember how bravely you have fought before? You've made a name for yourselves! You have achieved glory before and now you will do it again!* To those new recruits about to have their first taste of battle, he boosts their spirits by telling them how they could now emulate the proven bravery of the veterans.

As the elephants charge, the Fifth Legion move into action. From the right wing, Caesar's veterans bombard the elephants with missiles. As the lead 'bullets' and stones hit the animals and the hissing sound of the flying missiles terrify them, the elephants turn and begin to rush into their own troops, trampling men as they stampede. The Moorish cavalry, who have been stationed alongside the elephants, now lose their protective body-guard of animals and turn, fleeing towards the gates of their camp while the remaining animals battle the ten cohorts on the left and right wings of Caesar's army. This was the mission of Caesar's Fifth Legion; the veterans have been told this will be their last battle, and they stand firm against the charging elephants. The fighting is fierce and bloody with elephants using their trunks against men, and the Fifth Legion hurling their javelins and slashing at the animals.

Caesar's men do not let him down. Here, at Thapsus, these men facing Juba's war elephants will take their place in Roman military history. One soldier, in particular, who helps a civilian merchant who is being crushed to death by an elephant, has his story recorded:

It doesn't seem right not to mention the courage of a veteran of the Fifth Legion. For an elephant on the left wing, inflamed by the pain of a wound, had attacked an unarmed sutler,[1] pinned him underfoot, and then knelt on him. With its trunk erect and swinging from side to side, trumpeting loudly, it was crushing him with its weight and kill-ing him. The soldier could not bear this; he was an armed professional – he had to battle the beast. When the elephant noticed him coming towards it with his weapon raised, it abandoned the dead body, encir-cled the soldier with its trunk and lifted him into the air. The soldier, realising that he had to act quickly in this kind of danger, with as much strength as he could slashed over and over into the trunk that encircled him. Driven by pain the elephant threw the soldier down, turned and with loud trumpetings charged at speed back to the rest of its herd. (*The African War*, 84)

---

1 A 'sutler' is a civilian who travels with an army and sells provisions to the soldiers.

As the elephants are neutralised, turning and crashing into their own men, Caesar's legionaries push on until, overpowered, the Pompeian army falls back in defeat. Juba's war elephants have not held their line and their chaotic retreat into their own men is a defining point in the battle. Caesar captures Scipio's elephants and takes sixty-four of them — armoured and with towers on their backs — onwards to the city of Thapsus. Scipio and King Juba go on to take their own lives. The Roman civil war is at its end, the Roman Republic is in its final days and Caesar is ready to take his place as dictator of Rome.

Julius Caesar's Herd

Marching back into Rome, Caesar takes part in a splendid triumph, leading the celebrations with an escort of forty elephants — probably Juba's captured animals — each carrying a torch in its trunk. He displays them at the Games, where two 'armies' of 500 men, thirty horses and twenty elephants on each side stage a battle for the entertainment of the crowds, along with a fight between men sitting atop forty elephants.

What happened to the elephants then? It seems they were not killed in the arena. Caesar's herd of captured elephants was supposedly still breeding in Rome fifty-eight years later when Augustus was emperor.

Julius Caesar used the elephant on a coin he struck in his own military mint. Historians still argue about what the elephant on the front of the denarius[2] coin symbolises. Is it Caesar advertising his own power? The elephant's trunk is raised into the air and the animal is ready to trample what seems to be a snake. Perhaps people looking at the coin would have seen it as the mighty Julius Caesar triumphing over evil. However, some historians think this is an example of Caesar using the elephant to ridicule his civil war nemesis Pompey. You'll read later how Pompey had a bit of trouble with elephants and this coin could very well be Caesar attacking a political rival by poking fun at Pompey's failures — think of it as the ancient equivalent of a GIF on Twitter posted to mock a politician.

---

2 The denarius was a standard silver Roman coin.

The elephant denarius coin from 49–48 BC, struck by Julius Caesar not long after the great civil war had started. Circulating a new coin was a great way to advertise your successes. (The Metropolitan Museum of Art, New York)

THE WISDOM OF ELEPHANTS

The elephant is the closest to man in the capacity for feeling. In fact, it understands the language of its country, obeys orders, remembers duties that it has been taught, is delighted by affection and by praise. Indeed, it has those virtues which are rare even in man: honesty, intelligence, a sense of justice, and also a reverence for the stars and a respect for the sun and the moon.

(Pliny, *Natural History* VIII.1)

First-century Roman Pliny[3] not only recorded how clever these animals are and how they have memories, he told us that they show affection, care for their young and grieve for their dead friends. Sadly, it didn't matter that the Romans noted the elephant as the gentlest and most docile of nature's creations; none of this ancient knowledge protected the animal from being used by Romans in any way they wanted.

3   Also referred to as Pliny the Elder. He is more commonly known simply as Pliny, which is the name you'll see from now on. He was not only an author, historian and scientist but an army and navy commander too. His is the Roman voice you're going to hear most from in this book. Turn to the appendix for more on this fascinating Roman nobleman.

Elephants fitted into the Roman world in all sorts of ways: killed for their ivory and for entertainment in the arenas, they were also used as impressive symbols of the power of Rome in triumphal processions, as well as intimidating weapons on the battlefields – mainly attacking Romans, but used occasionally by the Roman military itself.

HOW TO CAPTURE OR KILL AN ELEPHANT

Mad elephants can be tamed by hunger and blows.

(Pliny, *Natural History* VIII.9)

If you were in the animal export business, you wouldn't have found better customers than the Romans: they had the money, they were organised and they liked a show, whether it was a lion in the arena or a lovely show-off table with ivory legs.

The Romans used both Indian and African elephants, although the African ones were not the huge bush elephants we see on wildlife programmes today. They were the smaller forest elephant *Loxodonta africana pharaohensis*, which was a much easier elephant to handle and train.

Ancient writers tell us that in India tamed elephants were used to help capture wild ones. An elephant rider – a *mahout* – would ride out on a domesticated elephant and hunt down a lone wild animal. If the elephant wasn't alone, the *mahout* would try to separate it from the herd. The method was to flog it, keep on flogging it until the elephant was tired out and then climb on its back.

This sounds pretty dangerous to me. Perhaps the African method was less dramatic: dig your own elephant traps and capture the animals with pit falls. Get to any elephant trapped in a pit fall before the herd finds out that one of their own is in trouble as, 'when a straying elephant falls into one of these, the rest of the herd immediately gather branches, roll down rocks, build ramps and try with all their strength to get it out'.

Once in a trench or pit, the elephant can be starved into submission. You can test if the elephant is broken by holding out a branch to it and seeing if it will gently take it from your hand. To get the elephant to trust you, give it a bit of barley juice alongside the starvation method. If you're after ivory and don't need a live animal, you can bring an elephant down with a few javelins to the feet (Pliny, VIII.8).

HOW AN ELEPHANT CAN HELP WITH YOUR STATUS: IVORY

Nowadays there's no pleasure for rich men at dinner; neither his turbot nor his venison have any flavour, his unguents and his roses no scent, unless a huge, gaping leopard of solid ivory supports the wide legs of his dining table.

(Juvenal, *Satires* XI.120–4)

There is no doubt that the Romans were greedy for ivory. They couldn't get enough of it and their quest for it gradually contributed to the extinction of certain species of elephant. Where did the Romans get their elephants from? Let's go to Africa first.

Unfortunately for the elephants who lived there, the kingdom of Askum (in ancient Ethiopia) was the main supplier of African ivory to the Romans. Exporting their goods from the bustling commercial Red Sea port at Adulis in present-day Eritrea, this Aksumite kingdom traded across the ancient world, from India to Persia to Egypt, selling every kind of exotic animal (after all, Rome was always looking for something special for its arenas). For the Aksumites, ivory, rhino horn, tortoise and turtle shell were big business. So much so, that by the first century AD there was a real shortage of African ivory and it wasn't until the third century that the ivory trade with Rome got back to a thriving business again.

The voyage across the Red Sea was not an easy one. Here's the first-century BC Greek writer Diodorus Siculus describing elephant transport along the coast of these waters.

The ships, which carry the elephants, being of deep draft because of their weight and heavy by reason of their equipment, bring upon their crews great and terrible dangers. For running as they do under full sail and oftentimes being driven during the night before the force of the winds, sometimes they will strike against rocks and be wrecked or sometimes run aground on slightly submerged spits. (Diodorus, *Library of History* III.40)

Indian ivory came overland and by sea. At one point, over 14,000 tusks per year were shipped into the Roman Empire from India. Ivory imports were good news for the Roman treasury because with all the tax contributions, they provided a great source of revenue.

For years now, furrow-browed historians have been hunched over a document called the 'Muziris papyrus'. This piece of ancient paperwork reveals fascinating information about particular products on the trade route between India and Roman Egypt, specifically details from the second-century AD cargo list on the trading ship the *Hermapollon*. Travelling from India, the vessel was packed with goods, which included the following:

- 80 boxes of nard – a plant that produced an expensive perfume
- 167 elephant tusks, weighing more than 3 tonnes
- Half a tonne of ivory shards and fragments

There would have been a hefty customs tax for this ivory, sailing its way to Roman Egypt and then being sold off all over the empire.

Never mind the *Hermapollon*: at the Horrea Galbae warehouses of ancient Rome, excavations dug up a store of ivory shards big enough to make up about 2,500 elephant tusks.

Part of the 'Great Hunt' mosaic from Piazza Armerina in Sicily, fourth century AD. (Funkyfood London, Paul Williams/Alamy Stock Photo)

Neither my dice nor my counters are made of ivory, even my knife handles are bone. (Juvenal, *Satires* XI.131–4)

If you were a wealthy Roman, there were lots of ways to show off just how rich you were: have your own aviary, build yourself giant fishponds that no one else has, or – if you're the emperor Caligula – build your favourite horse an ivory stable. When he wasn't writing books or tutoring Nero, the philosopher Seneca was involved in the ivory business and had 500 tables made from citrus wood, all with ivory legs. The elephant produced a high-status material and even the tiniest ivory shard could elevate the smallest item into something special.

During the Republic, ivory was found in the decorated chairs of the *curules* (government officials), but the ostentatious days of Empire that followed had far more elaborate plans for ivory than decorating the chairs of a few magistrates.

Such was the prestige of ivory that it was used for religious statues and decoration in temples. Great tusks were sometimes dedicated to gods and carried in processions. If parents were rich enough, their children's dolls might be made of ivory. By the first century AD, some cunning craftsmen were whitening elephant bone to pass off as this valuable material. Here are some of the products the Romans decorated with the real thing – from using the smallest shard to building with chunks of ivory – if you were sufficiently wealthy:

- Tables
- Dice
- Flutes and lyres
- Book covers
- Hair combs
- Brooches
- Writing implements
- Chests
- Medicine boxes
- Plectrums

- Sword hilts and scabbards
- Inlay on beds and couches
- Back scratchers
- Chariots and carriages
- Staffs and sceptres
- Floors
- False teeth[4]

It wasn't common, but Pliny says that the Roman penchant for luxury led to another reason for loving the elephant: chewing on the hard skin of an elephant trunk. Why? For no other reason than it feels 'like munching actual ivory'.

Roman dice made of ivory.
First to third century AD.
(The Metropolitan Museum
of Art, New York)

---

4 The Romans weren't alone in this. Throughout history, people have used animal bone, ivory and actual animal teeth filed down into false teeth for a human mouth. US president George Washington famously had ivory in his dentures.

WHEN AN ELEPHANT WAS
TOO BIG FOR ROME'S BOOTS

I told you that the Roman general Pompey had a bit of trouble with elephants. Well, here's an example. More than thirty years before that Battle of Thapsus with Julius Caesar, the young Pompey (apparently he was too young even to grow a beard yet) had achieved great military success in Africa. Returning to Rome from Africa, Pompey entered the city in a traditional Triumph – a great procession to celebrate the power of Rome and the achievements of those who had secured it. (Imagine a modern-day football team after winning the FA cup: the victors in the top of a bus, driving through the streets in celebration but with animals, chariots and a whole lot more pomp.) Animals were a great symbol of lands and people conquered, and Pompey had brought back with him several of Numidian King Hiarbas's elephants. Imagine the impact of these animals carrying a general of Rome into the city. What an impressive sight it would have been to enter the gates of Rome in a chariot drawn not by horses but by four magnificent elephants!

This show of power was not to be: the team of elephants were too big to fit through the gates of Rome. With a quick backstage change, Pompey had to shrink his ego and his animals and revert to the usual horse-drawn chariot for his triumphal display. (Poor old Pompey's bad luck with elephants continued, as you'll read when elephants trumpet their way through the arenas later.)

YOU CAN'T TEACH AN
OLD ELEPHANT NEW TRICKS

If elephants weren't having parts of their bodies turned into tables or dolls, being poked by a javelin to force them to enter a Roman amphitheatre or having their legs hamstrung by a sword in a battlefield, they got to perform tricks like tightrope walking for the Roman crowds – just as they, sadly, still tightrope walk in some regions across the world today.

In the first century AD, the emperor Augustus loaned some of his imperial herd to Germanicus (Roman general, twice a consul of Rome and father of future emperor, Caligula) for just such a performance.

The elephants went down a storm and Germanicus's popularity rose, because there's no better way to ingratiate yourself with the public than a group of elephants on a tightrope:

> At the gladiatorial show of Germanicus Caesar, some of them even performed crude movements, like dancers. It was common for them to throw weapons through the air and to perform gladiatorial contests with each other or play together in a high-spirited war dance. Afterwards, they walked on tightropes, four elephants even carrying one in a litter who was acting like a woman in labour. (Pliny, *Natural History* VIII.2)

In AD 59, when Nero was hosting a festival in honour of his mother (whom he went on to murder, by the way), the crowd was thrilled by an elephant being led up to the highest point of the theatre and the animal walking back down on ropes.

The history books give us a description of a certain posh elephant banquet, which delighted its Roman audience. The sand of the theatre was scattered with mattresses, pillows, cushions and embroidered throws, and the scene set out for a high-status dinner: expensive goblets, silver and gold bowls full of water, and citrus wood and ivory (the irony) tables laden with meat and bread. In came six male elephants dressed up in men's clothes and six females decked out in women's garb. They sorted themselves into pairs and, at the signal, reached forward with their trunks and began to eat. Finally the silver and gold bowls were placed in front of each elephant and the animals drank up the water with their trunks and squirted the attendants standing near them.

Humans seem to love seeing elephants drawing with their trunks and it was the same in Roman times. Just as elephants have been trained to paint pictures today, captive Roman elephants appeared to write letters in the sand with their trunks. Late second-century writer on all things animal, Aelian, had his doubts though.

> I have actually seen an elephant writing letters on a tablet in a straight line with its trunk. However, its trainer's hand was placed on the trunk and guided it to the shape of the letters; mind you, when it was writing its eyes were paying such attention you would have said the eyes were trained and knew the letters. (Aelian, *On the Characteristics of Animals* II.11)

HOW TO TRAIN YOUR ELEPHANT

After their journeys from Africa and India, elephants were housed as state- or municipally owned herds in *vivaria* (enclosures) near Rome. It wasn't just Julius Caesar who had his own state herd: the emperor Augustus and the emperors who came after him all kept herds in the days of Empire. From here, the elephants would lumber to their different destinies, marching in grand processions, facing the violent world of the Roman amphitheatres or performing tricks in the theatre.

Roman writers recorded how once you'd tamed an elephant, it was such an incredibly gentle animal that you could induce it to do whatever you wanted. One poor Roman elephant, described as 'slow witted' in the ancient records, just couldn't perfect the trick it was being taught. After it had been 'punished with repeated beatings' it was found in the night practising on its own.

If you're feeling sad after all the elephant beating, this might put some animal handlers in a (slightly) better light: one elephant trainer in Rome at least included *some* kinder methods in his training techniques when he took on the instruction of several young elephant calves. Recorded for us by Aelian, here are some of the teaching methods he followed:

- Be quiet and gentle with the elephants in your approach.
- But also, get them used to loud sounds – they're going to have to face large crowds and you don't want them to go wild at the sound of flutes, the banging of drums, the beating of marching feet or the singing of the masses.
- Give them tasty treats and good food; when you add treats to the gentle approach you have a better chance of taming them and 'enticing them to abandoning all trace of ferocity'.
- Train them to be charmed by the pipe and to get used to discordant notes; they should not burst into rage if required to move in time to music.
- Make sure they are not afraid of large groups of men; they must get accustomed to crowds above all.
- Get them used to the odd blow; they shouldn't get angry if you have to hit them.

The same trainer's elephants performed an act that was recorded by several Roman authors, including Aelian. Twelve of the animals entered the theatre from right and left, costumed in flowered dresses. They wowed the crowd with a dainty dance, 'swaying their whole body in a delicate manner'. With one word from the conductor, they got themselves into a single line, moved into a circle then sprinkled the floor with flowers while their feet stamped to the rhythms of the music. (Aelian, II.11)

SOME SMALL FACTS ABOUT BIG ELEPHANTS

The first time any Romans encountered elephants was in 280 BC when King Pyrrhus (of Epirus in ancient Greece) invaded Italy. It was here that Rome had its first taste of war elephants, at the Battle of Heraclea in the district of Lucania. From then on, the Romans called elephants the *Luca bos*: the Lucanian cow.

How about elephants coming to Rome itself? A few years later, in 275 BC, four of Pyrrhus's elephants were captured at the Battle of Beneventum. These four were brought to Rome and paraded in a triumphal procession, where the sight of such exotic animals would have thrilled the crowds and celebrated just how great Rome was.

A couple of decades later in 251 BC, the Romans captured 100 African elephants after a battle with the Carthaginians at Panormus in modern-day Palermo in Sicily. These animals were put on rafts, taken across the sea to Rhegium in southern Italy and transported all the way up to Rome. The elephants were exhibited in all the towns they passed through and must have caused a great stir. When they got to Rome, they were taken to the Circus Maximus where crowds of Romans watched as the animals were poked by blunt javelins and driven across the sand.

The tomb of an imperial freedman has been found, its inscription proudly bearing his job title: *procurator ad elephantos* – 'elephant keeper'.

The great Carthaginian general Hannibal once put on a bit of entertainment with some unfortunate Roman prisoners of war he had captured. Forcing them to fight one another to the death, the surviving soldier was then pitted against one of Hannibal's elephants; if he could kill the animal, he would be a free man. Facing the great beast in the arena, the soldier fought and won, slaying the Carthaginian's elephant. This wasn't the result Hannibal had expected. He really needed his enemy to fear the elephant and realised that his battle animals' reputation was now at stake. As the Roman soldier left with hopes of freedom, Hannibal sent horsemen to cut him down and cut short the story of a single man being able to bring down one of his mighty battle elephants.

The emperor Claudius is said to have shown off the power and glamour of Rome when he brought an elephant over the sea during his invasion of Britain.

And finally, here is Pliny in a simple, unromantic description of elephant behaviour, which makes us wonder at these animals in their ancient world of tightrope walking, battlefields and beast hunts:

> It's told that the elephant's gentleness towards those less strong as themselves is so great that if it encounters a flock of sheep it will move any that get in its way with its trunk so as not to accidentally trample on them. (Pliny, *Natural History* VIII.7)

THE WOLF

Canis Lupus

W hen King Amulius ordered the death of Mars's twin sons, Romulus and Remus, the babies were abandoned on the banks of the River Tiber. The god of war wasn't going to put up with this fate for his offspring. The woodpecker, the bear and the wolf were all sacred to Mars, and the wolf was one of the animals the god called on to help rescue his children. A she-wolf took the babies and raised them herself, suckling them like one of her own cubs until she handed their care over to a shepherd and his wife. Romulus went on to become the legendary founder of Rome and the she-wolf became forever entwined with Rome's identity. She took her place on funeral vases, the scabbards of Roman swords, sarcophagi and, along with the bull, became the symbol of Julius Caesar's *Legio VI Ferrata*: the Sixth Ironclad Legion. A coin showing a Roman emperor on one side might show a she-wolf on the other, because this animal was all about the founding of something powerful and enduring: Rome itself. Aligning yourself with an animal as significant as the she-wolf was a great bit of imperial marketing to the masses.

Even today, the she-wolf is still the official symbol of Rome and any tourist can see images of the animal around the city, from the famous Capitoline Wolf statue with its representation of the she-wolf suckling Romulus and Remus to the image of a wolf on the front of a park's rubbish bin. The she-wolf has featured on Italian stamps, including one issued during the Second World War with the image of the animal nursing Mars's abandoned babies. If you're a football fan, you might be familiar with the image of the she-wolf as the symbol of Italian football club A.S. Roma.

From AD 117–192, a bronze Roman coin from Turkey, showing Romulus and Remus and the famous she-wolf; an animal that has kept its place as a symbol of Rome for well over two thousand years. (Gift of William F. Dunham, The Art Institute of Chicago)

WOLF STORIES

Unlike so many other animals, the wolf seems to have dodged the fate of appearing in the Roman amphitheatres. Were they too difficult to catch? Surely not, given that the Romans could capture the ferocious lion or the fleet-footed ostrich. Perhaps the symbolism of the wolf protected it from being used as entertainment for the people.

Not only did wolves escape the arena, but there are stories of them being left unharmed after loping into towns or military camps. Here's one from the first-century writer of Roman history Livy, describing an incident of a wolf entering the ranks of the Roman army just before a battle with the Samnites and the Gauls.[5]

As Livy tells it, the Romans and their enemy had drawn up their battle lines across a plain. Suddenly a hind, chased out of the mountains by a wolf, bounded across the fields that lay between the two armies. The animals swerved, the hind fleeing towards the Gauls, the wolf running in the direction of the Romans:

---

5 The Samnites were a warlike tribe from southern central Italy and the Gauls were fierce warriors from large areas of central Europe, including what is now most of modern-day France. By the end of the first century BC Gaul's glory days were over and it was divided up into Roman provinces.

The ranks made way for the wolf; the Gauls speared the hind. Then a Roman soldier stationed by the army standards on the front line said, 'Over there, where you see the animal sacred to Diana lying dead, flight and slaughter will ensue; here the conquering wolf of Mars, whole and unharmed, reminds us of our founder and that we are of the race of Mars.' (Livy, *History of Rome* X.27)

Sadly for the wolf, its great connection to Roman history did not protect it entirely. We know that in the middle of the second century BC, the Roman *velites* – light infantry – sometimes covered their helmets with wolf skin. As well as giving them a bit of extra protection, it marked them out in battle so that any officers could judge whether a particular soldier was fighting bravely or not. As you will read later, wolf parts, if you could get them, were suggested in medical cures and even in the odd spell. (Victim of a spot of black magic? Hang a wolf muzzle outside your door.) But whatever you do, don't lock eyes with a wolf who has never seen a human before. It has the power to take away your voice.

HOW TO PROTECT YOUR FLOCK

If you were a shepherd, then the symbolism of the wolf was not a priority, but looking after your sheep was essential.

First-century Roman and retired soldier Columella wrote twelve books on agriculture. Here are two of his tips for shepherds:

- Choose white dogs to protect your flock. This way you won't mistake your dog for a wolf in the half light of dawn or dusk and are sure to bludgeon the right animal if you have to wade in to protect the flock.
- Your sheep dog should be good at picking quarrels, strong enough to repel a wolf and long, slim and fast enough to chase it and make it drop your stolen prey.

(Columella, *On Rural Affairs* VII.12, 3–5)

ANCIENT WEREWOLVES

When the sensible Roman author Pliny heard tales of people changing into wolves, he thought very much like us: pull the other one. But there was so much folklore about werewolves that, as Pliny put it, 'the belief of it has become firmly fixed in the minds of the common people'. The Romans had a word for someone who could change themselves into a wolf or werewolf: *versipellis*, which means 'changing the skin' or 'turn skin'. Interestingly, you didn't have to look like a wolf to be called a *versipellis*; ancient medical writers used the word for people who were mentally unwell enough to believe they really were a wolf and Romans used it for anyone who had gone through a major change in their personality.[6]

Here's a werewolf story from Petronius, first-century writer and darling of emperor Nero's court. He didn't stay the darling, sadly, and after someone whispered in Nero's ear that Petronius was plotting against him, Petronius took his own life before he could be killed. Petronius's novel, *Satyricon*, includes a famous scene at a Roman dinner party and this is where we find his character Niceros telling a tale to the dinner guests. Who doesn't love to be frightened? Niceros does his best to spook the guests with a werewolf story. In this tall tale, Niceros invites a guest in his house to take a moonlit stroll with him. This walking companion is a soldier 'as brave as Hell' and, as was the custom in Roman times, the road they walk along is lined with graves:

So we piss off around daybreak: the moon was shining like midday. We're amongst the gravestones: my man went off to do his business at the tombstones, I sit down, full of song and count the gravestones. Next thing, I looked round at my mate. He's undressed himself and put all his clothes down at the roadside. My heart was in my mouth, I stood there like a dead man. He pissed a circle round his clothes, and suddenly turned into a wolf. Don't think I'm joking, I wouldn't make this up for any fortune. But as I was saying, after he'd changed into a wolf, he began to howl and legged it into the woods. At first, I didn't know where he was, then I went off to snatch up his clothes – but they'd turned to stone. I could have dropped dead with terror. Still, I drew my sword

---

6 Pliny, VIII.34.

and slayed shadows as I made my way to my girlfriend's house. In I went like a ghost, almost out of my mind, sweat flying down my crotch, eyes glazed; you could hardly revive me. My Melissa was surprised I'd gone out walking so late and she said, 'if you'd come home earlier, at least you could have helped us. A wolf got into the house and let the blood of the whole herd of sheep just like a butcher. He didn't get away with it mind you, even though he did run off; for our old man pierced his neck with a spear.' When I heard this I couldn't ignore what was happening, but at daylight I fled to our Gaius's house like a pub landlord who's been robbed and when I came to the place where the clothes had been turned into stone, I found nothing but blood. Honestly, when I got home my soldier was lying on the bed just like an ox, and a doctor was seeing to his neck. I realised that he was a werewolf. I couldn't sit down for a meal with him after, not for the life of me. Let other people think what they like about this; but may I feel the fury of your guardian angels if I'm telling a lie. (Petronius, *Satyricon* 62)

WOLF SLANG

Here are a few words the Romans connected with the Latin for wolf, *lupus*. You may sense a theme to them.

- *Lupa*: slang for a sex worker
- *Lupor*: someone who hung around with sex workers
- *Lupanar*: a brothel
- *Lupula*: a 'little wolf' or slang for a witch

On a floral note, the flower lupin gets its name from the Latin for wolf.[7] And on a literary note, now you know why J.K. Rowling's Professor Lupin had the perfect name for a human who could change into a wolf. *Lupus* was also a Roman surname: Mr Wolf.

---

7 Was this because certain lupins grow in wild and rough earth – just the kind of land that wolves roam? Some say it is because of the wolf-shaped fang in the centre of the flower, others that lupins can deplete the soil like a predator. In fact, lupins help rough soil by putting nitrogen back into the earth.

The animal loped into a number of animal proverbs too; the Roman saying 'on this side the wolf, on that side the dog' is a bit like our 'caught between a rock and a hard place'. Another, 'the wolf in the tale' is equivalent to our 'talk of the devil'.

Finally, we are back with Romulus and Remus at the beginning of things. From the *Life of Romulus*, founder of Rome, a few lines from Greek philosopher, biographer and historian Plutarch:

> Our birth is said to have been secret, and our nursing and nurture as infants stranger still. We were cast out to birds of prey and wild beasts, only to be nourished by them – by the dugs of a she-wolf and the morsels of a woodpecker, as we lay in a little trough by the side of the great river. (Plutarch, *Parallel Lives: Life of Romulus* 7)

THE HORSE

Equus

[T]he man experienced in war chooses his horses in one way, and feeds
and trains them in one way; the charioteer and circus performer chooses
another way: the criterion is different for the person who breaks horses
for the saddle or trains them for the carriage than it is for the man concerned with military matters, since they want to have spirited horses
in the army, but on the contrary, they prefer placid ones for the roads

(Varro, *On Agriculture* II.7)

The horse galloped through the whole Roman world: across the Empire
in Roman military camps and round the Circus tracks; it travelled on
ships, transported goods, pulled carriages and lived on farms. Some horses
became superstars at the Circus, some live on forever in literary works,
some have their images on military gravestones, others had their own
funeral processions or carried emperors on their backs and thousands were
wounded in wars just like the humans they shared the battlefields with.

How do you know if your horse is a good Roman horse? According to
Columella this is what you should look out for:

As soon as a foal is born, it is possible to judge its nature immediately.
If it is cheerful, if it is bold, if it is not shaken by the sight or sound of
something new, if it runs at the front of the herd, if it sometimes sur-
passes its peers in playfulness and liveliness and running in a race, if it
jumps a ditch and crosses a bridge over a river without hesitation – these
are the marks of noble character. (Columella, *On Rural Affairs* VI.29)

ENEMY HORSES

In battles against enemies such as Syrian King Antiochus or Mithridates, King of Pontus,[8] the Romans had to face a Persian invention: the *quadrigae falcatae* – the scythed chariot. These chariots only worked well if they were rampaging across level ground, and at top speed the horses could be difficult to control. Any obstacle beneath the wheels of the chariot or the hooves of the horses could stop this enemy weapon literally in its tracks, with horses being killed or equine casualties falling into Roman hands. Here's the fourth-century writer and military expert Vegetius on how the Romans faced these Persian horse-drawn war chariots:

> The Roman military disabled them with this strategy: when battle began, they immediately scattered caltrops[9] over the whole field, and the horses that pulled the chariots, galloping head-on at them, were destroyed. (Vegetius, *On Military Matters* III.24)

SEA HORSES

With Rome marching its way across the known world, transporting horses across the ocean would have been a necessary part of Rome's expansion. Did the horses get seasick? The journeys could certainly take the strength out of the animals. Due to the fact that horses have a tight oesophageal sphincter, food and fluid can make its way into the stomach but it can't come back up: seasick horses can't vomit like seasick humans. With journeys taking much longer in ancient times, it is no wonder that horses often arrived at their destination weak and drained.

When Julius Caesar's army arrived in Africa during the civil war, Caesar's enemy Pompey took full advantage of Caesar's horses' seasickness.

---

8 Antiochus III, Roman enemy of the second century BC, and Mithridates VI, King of Pontus, who battled the Romans in the first century BC.

9 For those readers not familiar with devices designed to seriously injure people and animals, a caltrop is a piece of iron with four spikes poking out. Three of the spikes stick into the earth, while the final spike sticks up ready to trip, wound and hopefully kill enemy horses or men.

After Caesar had sent his men out on a mission to gather grain supplies, Pompey attacked his cavalry. A lot of Caesar's soldiers were killed in hand-to-hand fighting; their cavalry was debilitated and unable to spring into action at full power since the horses hadn't had enough time to gather their strength and recover from the sickness of their journey.[10]

According to Aelian, the best friend of the horse was the terrestrial bird the bustard: 'It spurns all other animals grazing in any meadows or valleys, but when it catches sight of a horse, full of happiness it flies right up to it and stays near its side, just like men who love horses'. (Aelian, II.28)

A Roman bronze figurine of a horse. From the second century AD, the statuette is only about 17cm x 24cm but shows all the ornamental trappings on the horse's body. (The Metropolitan Museum of Art, New York)

10   See: Cassius Dio, *Roman History* XLIII.2.

ASHES TO ASHES

When Mount Vesuvius erupted in AD 79, the ash from the volcano preserved a treasure trove of Roman history for archaeologists. The ancient town of Herculaneum, which lay buried beneath ash and pumice for millennia, was preserved even better than its famous neighbour, Pompeii.

We know from excavations at Herculaneum that a Roman soldier lost his life down near the shores of the sea. A study of his preserved body told experts he was around 37 to 40 or so when he was killed. He was found with his sword and his military belt, with gold and silver decorating the belt and ivory on the hilt of his sword. Clearly, this Roman was more than just a regular soldier; researchers have argued that he may even have served in the elite Praetorian Guard and the thinking is that he was part of a rescue party, sent by boat to save the lives of those caught up by this huge natural disaster. He was well built, his bones showed he had led an active life, but the skeleton had the marks of an old stab wound to the left leg and revealed three teeth missing through violent blows rather than decay.

What has this victim of Vesuvius got to do with the horse? Marks on his body show us how much the horse was part of Roman life. Right next to this military man's knees were enlarged tubercles – nodules – which showed that he had spent a lot of time on horseback. Here was a Roman whose life and career as a soldier was bound up with the horse, an animal which clearly played a role in his military journey. A journey that ended in disaster and violence on the shores of Herculaneum where, 2,000 years after his death, this horse-riding, sword-bearing Roman was to bring the past back to life and give us a view into history.

As for horses themselves, about 9 miles from Herculaneum, fourteen skeletons were excavated from Pompeii, all of them killed in the volcanic eruption. Historians believe some of these might have been left behind by fleeing humans as the thick layers of ash became too much for the horses to be of any use pulling carts or carrying people. Five horses were found in one building, all of them looking as if they had died in panic in their stalls. The animals may have been shut in their stables and simply had no chance of escape before they were overcome.[11]

---

11   If you want to know more, *The Natural History of Pompeii*, edited by Wilhelmina Feemster Jashemski and Frederick G. Meyer, has all the details on this soldier and the horses and mules of Pompeii.

Cast of a horse excavated from the ash of Vesuvius's eruption. An expensive harness was found with it, suggesting the animal was a high-status breed. It may have been saddled up and ready to go but was killed before any escape plan could be put into action. (Marco Cantile/Alamy Stock Photo)

HORSE PLAY

In the second century AD, during the reign of emperor Commodus, a certain Sextus Condianus heard that he had been condemned to death. How could he escape this fate? By faking his own death. A horse, a hare and a ram became his tools to freedom in a plan of action. He drank the blood of the hare but didn't swallow it. Holding the blood in his mouth, he mounted a horse and 'accidentally' had a dramatic fall, crashing to the ground. The fall looked serious because Sextus began to 'vomit blood' and was carried up to his room.

He must have been a great actor because things looked so bad that word got round that Sextus had died from the fall. The ruse continued when a ram's body was placed in his coffin and burnt. Sounds implausible? After all, who would be fooled by a dramatic fall from a horse and a spurt of blood from the mouth? But Roman historian Cassius Dio tells us that Sextus escaped, became a fugitive and avoided his death sentence, unlike the hare, the ram, or the many men taken to be him and whose heads were brought to Rome as proof of capturing the escapee. (Dio, LXXIII.6)

FAMOUS HORSES

No one but Julius Caesar was allowed to ride Julius Caesar's favourite horse. When Genitor was born (the name means 'the creator' or 'sire'), his strange hooves caught the attention of the soothsayers, who said that whoever became master of this horse would become master of the world. This is the kind of prediction a future dictator can't ignore, and Caesar broke the horse in and raised it himself. Genitor's hooves were described as 'remarkable' by the Roman historian Suetonius, as they were apparently divided into five toes like a human foot. When Genitor died, Caesar dedicated a statue to him before the Temple of Venus Genetrix in the Forum of Caesar, and the horse has gone down in history.

Pliny tells us of another famous horse, Bucephalus, who accompanied Alexander the Great into battle. Bucephalus was bought for Alexander from the herd of Philonicus of Pharsalus (modern Farsala in Greece) while Alexander was just a boy, as he was so struck by the horse's beauty. Just like Julius Caesar's horse a few hundred years later, Bucephalus wouldn't stand for anyone but Alexander riding him. During Alexander's attack on Thebes, despite being wounded, Bucephalus fought on and would not allow himself to be replaced. When the animal died, Alexander held a funeral procession for his horse, built it a tomb, built a city around that tomb, and called the city Bucephalus.[12]

In fact, a picture of this fourth-century BC horse is hanging over my twenty-first-century fireplace. The picture is a copy of part of a Roman floor mosaic found at the House of the Faun in Pompeii. This image, preserved by the eruption of Mount Vesuvius in AD 79, is still being admired thousands of years later. Even a volcano can't dim the bright star of a horse as famous as Bucephalus.

The emperor Hadrian (AD 76–138) didn't build a city for his trusty steed, but the horse (whose breeding was from a Sarmatian tribe called the Alans) has lived on through a poem the emperor wrote for the animal after

---

12   Situated in modern-day Pakistan, on the banks of the Jhelum River. Bucephalus is thought to have been buried in Jalalpur Sharif near Jhelum, Pakistan.

Alexander and his horse Bucephalus at the Battle of Issus (333 BC), from the Alexander Mosaic. (Adam Eastland/Alamy Stock Photo)

its death. Hadrian loved hunting and he loved his own personal animals. Here's his elegy to Borysthenes, his great hunting horse who chased those wild boar alongside his emperor without ever succumbing to a wound:

> Borysthenes the Alan
> Fleet hunting horse of Caesar
> Wont to fly o'er the ocean and marshes
> Across the Etruscan hills
> You chased Pannonian boar.
> Not one glittering tusk
> Was bold enough to harm you
> Nor did the foam from any mouth
> Sprinkle even the tip of your tail
> As it is wont to happen.
> But your day came.
> Killed in the flower of your youth
> You lie, unwounded and whole
> Buried here, in this field.

HOW TO PROTECT YOUR HORSE

If you had anything to do with horses, from mucking out a stable to facing an elephant on horseback in a battlefield or breeding expensive chariot horses, then you would have been familiar with Epona, the 'Great Mare' and goddess of the horse. Originally a Celtic goddess, the Romans did what they loved to do and absorbed her into their own culture. Epona was the protector of horses, mules, donkeys and asses, and her icon could be found in stables around the Empire, especially in Gaul and Germania where Roman soldiers worshipped this horse-loving goddess.

For members of the *equites singulares Augusti*, the emperor's horse guard, your horse was your status, your career and no doubt your special companion. (Nearly all of the 600 graves at the horse guard cemetery in Rome portray the men's horses.) Epona was a special favourite of these horsemen, the goddess who looked out for your horse and its rider. What would the Roman Empire have been without its horses? The military might need these animals to perform well in battle, so caring for the animals was paramount to Rome's power. Epona was believed to be part of that care, protecting her horses and protecting the men who rode them, so it's no surprise we've found hundreds of inscriptions and artefacts to her.

HORSE MEDICINE

Remember Columella, the Roman who wrote about all things agricultural? He offered the following advice on caring for your horse:

- If your horse is weak, give it roasted wheat – it's better than roasted barley – and also give it wine to drink.
- If your horse starts bleeding from the nose, extract some juice from a bunch of green coriander leaves and pour into the animal's nostrils. (Columella knew his stuff. Even *The Times* has listed coriander leaves in its top ten natural cures for nosebleeds. Apparently, it balances the pressure of blood in the blood vessels and bottles of coriander oil nasal drops are sold as an instant aid to a nosebleed.)
- Horses should be rubbed down daily. Massaging your horse's back will do it more good than if you were to give it a load of food.

- Build your stable floor of hard wood boards and sprinkle it with chaff. You want the stable to be as dry as possible to keep horses' hooves in good condition, and the harder the wood, the more your horse's hooves will toughen up.
- Just like we have mosquito nets today, Columella advised covering the stable with netting to protect horses from flies and mosquitoes.
- These things will wear your horse out: the heat, the cold and spurring them into a gallop when they've been standing for a long time. If they do become worn out, give them a drink of oil or fat mixed with wine and let them rest. (You can use a *cornu*, or curved horn, to pour the drink down your horse's throat.)
- Remember those seasick horses? To alleviate nausea in your horse, give it a head of garlic mixed with wine.
- If you want your horse to conceive a male foal, you should tie up the stallion's left testicle with a flaxen cord. If you want a female horse, tie up the stallion's right testicle. (Good luck with that.)

(Columella, VI 28, 30, 34)

HORSE DOCTORS

Battles could be lost and won depending on your cavalry, so keeping your horses in tiptop condition was good military strategy. The Romans couldn't just rely on a figurine of Epona to look after their horses. Any Roman camp with a fair few cavalry units would have had its own vet to care for them and academics have deduced that these Roman veterinary teams were better than any set-up the enemy had. Here are a few of the roles in this military vet practice:

- The *veterinarius*. Not a vet but more akin to what we know as a farrier – someone who took care of the horses' hooves.
- The *medicus veterinarius*. This was the actual vet, which in a military setting was most likely an officer. His job was not only to treat animals but to take care of the food supplies.
- The *strator* – groom. The *strator* mucked out the stables, saddled the horse and kept guard. From the word *strator* we get the Latin *stratura*, which meant a layer of manure, and *stratus*, which was a horse blanket or covering.

- The *strator consularis*. This was the big boss of the stable, who oversaw the grooms and the running of the stables.
- The *marsus*. Part of the team that cared for horses (and people), the *marsus* was a field medic who treated snake and scorpion bites.[13]

COMMON HORSE INJURIES

There were a whole load of injuries waiting on the racetracks for horses who took part in the explosive chariot races of Rome and they are dealt with later. For horses in the military, a *medicus veterinarius* would have dealt with all the usual horrors of a battlefield: missiles embedded in the flesh, blood loss and infected wounds. First things first, he would have covered the horse's head to calm it, and then used a rope, a yoke and a pole to keep the animal as still as possible.

What did the Roman vet use to treat injured horses? When you read the items in the list below, they might not sound like a huge help to the horses. However, a little research into contemporary science proves that most of the tools used to treat the animals make good sense.

- Herbs. For example, henbane was used as a sedative and painkiller. Henbane was also known as 'soldier's herb', 'soldier's tree' and, worryingly, 'insane root'. Hemp was another painkiller used for surgery, as was the powdered bark of the white willow tree, *salix alba*, in oil, which also worked to bring down fevers. *Mandragora* – mandrake – or 'Circe's root', was a well-known narcotic, again used as a sedative and pain relief for surgery. (The Carthaginian general Hannibal once used mandrake as a military tactic, mixing the root into wine, retreating from his enemy and leaving the jars of wine behind. Once his enemy had glugged down the drugged wine, they were stupefied and in no state to fight. Hannibal returned and took an easy victory.)
- Food stuffs, such as vinegar, honey and leeks. Honey and vinegar were used as antiseptics and anti-inflammatories. (There is plenty of modern-day medical evidence on the antibacterial qualities

---

13 Scuttle to the chapter 'Insects and Arachnids' or slither on to 'The Snake' if you want to know just what these treatments involved.

of honey.) Vinegar – acetic acid – could be used in cleaning out a wound, although any horse or soldier must have had to take a lot of herbal painkillers and sedatives before that kind of treatment.

- Oils, grease and pitch. These were put onto wounds and covered with linen bandages. Olive oil has been proven to have some wound healing properties in modern research, and putting oil on the horse's wound and wrapping it in a bandage would have kept the affected area moist and acted as an anti-inflammatory.
- Hipposandals. As the Greek for horse is *hippos*, you can guess what these were. If a horse needed a dressing to protect an injured foot or keep healing medication in place, *soleae spartae* – hipposandals made of straw or broom – were placed over dressings to keep them secure.

SHOES FOR HORSES

It is said that he never made a journey with less than a thousand baggage carts; his mules shod with silver, and the drivers dressed in the finest Canusian cloth.

(Suetonius, *The Twelve Caesars: Nero* 30)

For longer-lasting hoof-wear than the shoes made from straw or broom, and less extravagant than the emperor Nero's silver-footed animals, the Romans made *soleae ferreae*, metal horseshoes, which weren't nailed on like modern horseshoes but kept in place with leather straps or cords. Modern researchers have tried these out on horses and the coverings come off at any speed remotely rapid. Still, they would have protected horses or mules at a walking pace over difficult ground. Some even had nails banged through the shoe with the point facing out, like modern-day crampons, to be used in icy conditions.

HORSES FOR SALE

Let's pick up the reins and gallop a few hundred years into the Roman Empire now, racing more than 300 years past Julius Caesar and leaving emperor after emperor behind us.

In AD 301 the emperor Diocletian issued an edict on prices, giving the maximum price allowed for everything from a Roman soldier's sword to a cabbage. A *mulomedicus*, who trimmed the hair and hooves of horses and mules, had his wages capped at 6 denarii per animal. Here are some more horse-related prices from Diocletian's edict:

- War horse, first class: 36,000 denarii
- Racehorse: 100,000 denarii
- Leather military horse saddle: 500 denarii (a soldier had to buy his own)
- Donkey for riding: 15,000 denarii
- Donkey, baggage animal: 7,000 denarii
- Breeding donkey: 5,000 denarii (let's hope it never saw the price of a racehorse)[14]

DEAD HORSES

How did the Romans treat equines at the end of their lives? Parts of dead horses were used by the military (more of that later), but we do know that the Romans were not at all keen on eating horse flesh. The Roman historian Tacitus gives us a couple of examples of soldiers being forced to eat horses to avoid starvation, one instance being when Roman ships had gone down and soldiers were washed up on remote islands with no human inhabitants and little to no sustenance. Most of the legionaries died but a few survived by eating the dead horses who were washed up on the same island. When Tacitus writes about besieged Roman soldiers during the reign of Vespasian, he makes it clear that only the direst of circumstances could excuse eating horsemeat.

> Loyalty on the one side and desperation on the other, tore the besieged between honour and disgrace. Hesitating on what to do, their food supplies, both the usual and the unusual, ran out, for they had eaten their baggage animals, their horses and all the rest of their animals, something which, although profane and disgusting, they had been forced to do by necessity. (Tacitus, *Histories* IV.60)

---

14   All prices from Diocletian are taken from *An Edict of Diocletian, Fixing a Maximum of Prices Throughout the Roman Empire AD 303*, YA Pamphlet Collection, Library of Congress.

WHAT TO DO IF YOUR HORSE
FALLS IN LOVE WITH ITSELF

At last, here's the answer to a problem that all horse lovers need answering. Columella does admit that this condition didn't happen often, but here's his advice on how to make a narcissistic horse fall out of love with itself.

> It is rare but acknowledged that there is a certain madness which comes over mares if they have seen their reflection in water. They are seized by a vain passion; all thought of food goes from their mind and pining away with love, they die. There are signs of this type of insanity: the horses gallop about the pastures as if they were being goaded on, continually looking about them, searching for something, longing to find it. This delusion is broken if you raggedly cut off the horse's mane and lead her down to the water. Then, gazing for a while at her own ugliness, the memory of what she fell in love with is destroyed.
> (Columella, *On Rural Affairs* VI.35)

HOW TO MAKE THE
WORST OF A GOOD ANIMAL

The writer Plutarch gives us a story, which sounds like the worst ever episode of *Dragons' Den*. Set way back in Roman history, it stars a cruel despot called Aemilius Censorinus, who liked nothing better than discovering new ways of torturing people. To this end, he would reward inventors of any new and exciting torture device.

A certain Arruntius Paterculus decided to put his creative talents to use by devising a novel way of making people suffer. He would invent something appalling, take it to Aemilius and pitch it to him. Never mind the Trojan wooden horse, how about a bronze one? The idea was that a person could be shoved inside and set alight. After presenting his bronze equine to the torture-loving tyrant, Paterculus found himself on the receiving end of his invention when Aemilius decided to test the cruel device out and used its inventor as the guinea pig. After being thrown into his own horror horse, Paterculus was then dragged from its burning bronze innards and hurled from the Tarpeian Rock – a cliff on the Capitoline Hill in Rome that was used for executions.[15]

THE LITERARY HORSE

Let's put this chapter out to pasture with a famous literary horse from Virgil's *Aeneid*. The wounded Mezentius is grieving for his son, Lausus, who has been killed by Aeneas. He turns to his beloved horse, Rhaebus, and tells him they will avenge Lausus's death together, even if it means dying. In fact, both Mezentius and Rhaebus will later die side by side on the battlefield. The mighty warhorse is speared and killed by Aeneas, falling on top of his master, who is dispatched with a sword to the throat. With Rhaebus lying dead next to him, Mezentius's last request is that he might be buried with his son, Lausus. Here's Mezentius talking to his faithful horse, Rhaebus, before both ride out together to meet the bloody fate that awaits them in battle.

So saying, he raised himself up on his wounded thigh
and although his deep wound ebbs away his strength and hinders him
he is not cast down but orders them to bring forth his war horse.
His pride, his comfort, from every battle it had brought him home.
He spoke thus to the sorrowing beast:
My Rhaebus, we have lived long
if anything is long for mortal creatures
Today you will bring back in triumph the bloodstained armour and head of Aeneas
and be, with me, the avenger of the pains of Lausus;
or else if I am vanquished you will fall beside me.
For, my brave steed, you would never suffer, I know, the commands of a stranger
or bend your knee to any Trojan masters.
(Virgil, *Aeneid* X)

---

15 The author of *Parallela Minora* (*Parallel Stories*), from which this story is taken (section 39), has been the subject of debate. Academics now believe the writer is not Plutarch the great philosopher and author, but a 'pseudo Plutarch' who could have been one person or several.

THE DOLPHIN
AND THE WHALE

Delphinus et Balaena

THE DOLPHIN

Only to the dolphin has Nature bequeathed that excellent quality, so much sought for by the best of philosophers: to love for no advantage.
(Plutarch, *On the Intelligence of Animals* 984)

Plutarch wrote how the dolphin is the only animal on earth that loves humans for their own sake, and it's this love for us that makes the dolphin so beloved of the gods. We all know the ancient stories of dolphins helping and befriending people, and Romans would have known of these tales of dolphin–human friendships. After all, they were familiar with the mythical story of the Greek Arion and his rescue by a dolphin from pirates, earning the animal a place in the stars as the constellation *Delphinus*.

It wasn't just dolphin tales that the Romans were interested in. They also took note of dolphin behaviour, recording how dolphins (and whales) suckled their young, looked after them for a long time after birth and showed affection for their offspring. What a relief to know there is no Roman record of a dolphin being hunted like other animals were. In fact, the poet Oppian calls the hunting of dolphins immoral – why would you pollute yourself by hurting these kings of the ocean?

There is, however, a record of a Roman dolphin in distress. The dolphin was caught by the king of Caria (a Roman province of Asia) and kept tied up by him in the harbour. Were the public happy with this? Not at all. Crowds of people in distress begged for pity to be taken on the dolphin and the king released the animal back into the ocean.

What's So Good About Dolphins?

Here are some Roman reasons for loving a dolphin:

- They have no fear of humans.
- They are friendly, they race with ships and even pass them when ships are under full sail. In fact, the dolphin is 'swifter than a bird and moves sharper than a javelin'.[16]
- Dolphins love music, are soothed by singing and especially love the sound of the *hydraulus* (water organ).
- The god Cupid is associated with dolphins. Cupid riding a dolphin was a popular and playful image, one which we can see in Roman figurines, mosaics and in paintings that survived the eruption of Vesuvius at Pompeii.
- What friendlier animal could accompany you on your journey from life to death? The dolphin was used as an image on funerary art where the animal leaps and swims across the ocean guiding the dead on their journey.
- They had a cute nickname: *simus*, meaning 'snubnose', which was said to be the name the dolphins loved the most.
- There is nothing more divine than a dolphin. They were once men, living in cities until Dionysus turned them into fishes and they exchanged the land for the sea. The human spirit that still lives in them means they are filled with human thoughts and human actions.
- Everyone loves good parenting and dolphins clearly love their children.
- They are gentle and understand human hearts since their hearts are so similar.

(Pliny, IX.7–10 and Oppian, *Halieutica* I & V)

---

16   Pliny, IX.7.

From a second-century AD mosaic found at Fishbourne Roman Villa in Chichester. The deity Cupid takes a playful ride on the back of a dolphin. (Nikreates/Alamy Stock Photo)

Dolphin Workmates

Why do all the work yourself when nature has provided you with skilled dolphin helpers? There are Roman records of fishermen using dolphins to bring in their catch of mullet.

Pliny wrote of one such animal encounter happening in the Roman province of Gallia Narbonensis (modern-day Languedoc and Provence in the south of France). Whenever this occurred, locals would gather to watch, standing on the shore and calling out, 'Snubnose! Snubnose!' The dolphins would soon appear and get into position, ready to give their help.

After blocking the passage out to sea, the dolphins would drive the red mullet into the shallows, where the fishermen cast their nets around them and brought the fish in. It was a sight worth seeing, with dolphins leaping and darting about, the sea glittering with shoals of mullet and an audience gathered on the shore. At the end of the work, apart from getting a reward of fish, the dolphins were given a naughty treat of bread mash dipped in wine.

The same type of dolphin fishing also happened at night with the help of lit torches. The dolphins turned up when they saw the light and would corral the fish for the humans. With the catch all herded together by the dolphins, the fishermen got to work. Each boat had its own dolphin and the fishermen hand-fed their own dolphin with a reward of fish. (Pliny, IX.9 and Aelian, II.8)

Just stories? An identical method of fishing is practised today in Moreton Bay, Australia, as well as in Africa, India, China and Brazil. The fishermen in Laguna, Brazil, even catch exactly the same kind of fish as the ancient Roman fishermen: red mullet. We don't even have to shut our eyes to picture this happening 2,000 years ago – you can see this same human–dolphin partnership playing out today on YouTube videos or on *Human Planet* with David Attenborough. Instead of people standing on the shore shouting 'Snubnose!', there are film crews and photographers recording this voluntary working partnership between animal and human. As for the ancient Roman dolphins helping at night, we now know that certain types of plankton are attracted to light, and dolphins are attracted to the plankton – that's why those ancient dolphins followed the torchlight. So, simply a myth? No! The Roman descriptions were right: dolphins really can help humans to fish.

Stories of Dolphin Friendships with Humans

Nowadays, there are plenty of stories of wild dolphins befriending humans. There are even records of dolphins protecting humans from sharks, corralling swimmers and circling them for up to forty minutes until the shark has disappeared.[17] The Romans recorded their own stories of dolphin encounters and, as Pliny says, *nec modus exemplorum* – 'there are countless examples'. Here's a story about a dolphin that lived during the reign of Augustus (63 BC–AD 14).

This encounter happened at the Lucrine Lake in southern Italy. A young boy, who went to school every day across the lake in Pozzuoli, befriended a dolphin, which had swum into the lake. He would call out to it – 'Snubnose!' – and feed it little bits of bread. Eventually, the dolphin

---

17   For example, see the article by Sam Jones, 'Dolphins Save Swimmers from Shark Attack', *The Guardian*, 23 November 2004.

came to know him and would swim out of the depths to see the boy every day until, bit by bit, the boy began to swim with the dolphin, eventually gaining such trust with the animal that he could hold onto it across the bay to Pozzuoli. This went on for a few years until the boy died from a disease. The dolphin returned again and again as if it were looking for the boy and it too died, no doubt – said the Romans – from grief. (Pliny, IX.8)

The Famous Dolphin of Hippo

Another dolphin, from the first century AD, became quite the star of the Roman town Hippo Diarrhytus on the coast of northern Tunisia. Pliny the Younger (who left us a series of letters and was nephew of Pliny the Elder) wrote to a poet friend to tell him that he'd heard of a friendly dolphin, which was becoming the subject of dinner party chat. He said that the story might sound like a fairy tale, but it was, in fact, entirely true and from a credible and trustworthy source.

The story went that there was a lagoon close to the town where people used to go to boat, swim and fish. The lagoon led onto an estuary, which flowed out to the open sea. A dolphin had befriended a boy swimmer who had swum out to sea, playing around him and swimming alongside him back to shore.

The people of Hippo were so charmed by this that they stood on the shore to watch every day while the boy swam out and the dolphin swam and leapt alongside him. The dolphin got so friendly with humans that it could be fed out of people's hands, and it didn't mind being stroked or played with. Eventually, it even allowed the boy to cling to its body and be swept along as he held onto the dolphin's back. Other boys would swim around the pair, shouting out, and another dolphin even joined them (although this one kept its distance).

Though it is hard to believe, admitted Pliny the Younger, the friendly dolphin even swam up and out onto the shore, rolling itself back into the sea when it became too hot. The dolphin became so popular that it got special Roman treatment: the Roman governor Octavius Avitus put on a bit of a show by smearing the animal with perfumed essential oil when it was lying exposed on the shore one day. After its unwelcome anointing, the dolphin took itself back to the open sea where it disappeared for several days before showing up again quite listless and weak. After getting its strength back, it was up to its usual tricks and friendliness and still wowed the people of Hippo. This was the dolphin's downfall.

Hippo had been a quiet and peaceful place, but now it was full of people wanting to see this unusual animal. The expense of hosting official visitors started to outweigh the benefits of having a celebrity dolphin. What to do? Sadly, the people of Hippo decided to quietly kill the dolphin and the town went back to normal. (Pliny the Younger, *Letters* IX.33)

Should we believe these dolphin stories? Bear with me while we skip forward two millennia to see if the Romans were just being creative or telling the truth. *Dolphins*, by Antony Alpers, describes towns that have had modern-day encounters with dolphins. Alpers points out that the parallels between these modern dolphin–human interactions and Roman dolphin stories suggest that there may be some truth in the ancient tales.

I hope you'll forgive a story from the 1950s shouldering its way into a book on Roman history. However, the details from the following description of a modern-day dolphin encounter contain facts which are so similar to Pliny the Younger's recounting of the ancient Hippo dolphin that we can't help feeling that the story was based in truth, not fiction.

In 1956 in Opononi, New Zealand, a lone female dolphin – given the name Opo by the town residents – began befriending locals in boats and started to swim around the town's shore close to the beach. Just like the Roman dolphin from Hippo, Opo eventually allowed herself to be stroked and petted, and even played with a ball.

She was especially friendly with children, her favourite being a 13-year-old girl. The dolphin swam with people and, just like the dolphin in the Hippo story, allowed children to cling onto her back as she carried them around the waters.

When news spread – just as it had in Hippo – the town became jam-packed with visitors flocking to see this friendly animal. Cars, trucks, vans and buses parked half a mile or more on the road into town, which became overwhelmed with dolphin watchers. A protection order was about to come into effect for Opo when she was suddenly found washed up in a small crevice between rocks near the town's harbour. Just as the Hippo dolphin was likely burnt by the sun when the Roman governor smeared oil all over it, the autopsy on Opo showed that she had died of sunburn after becoming trapped when the tide went out.

When we look at the inscription the people of Opononi left for their friendly dolphin, we can imagine the dolphin of Hippo and the feelings the town had for it. (Yes, I know they killed their dolphin, but still ...) It reads: 'Opo the dolphin. Who came in from the open sea and lived along this shore becoming so tame that children could ride upon her back. 1955 – 1956.' These ancient dolphin stories might be grounded in mythology, but the twentieth-century story of Opo and other dolphins like her validate Roman stories like Pliny's of human encounters with these special animals.

THE WHALE

There amidst the waves dwell the sea-blue gods:
Sweet singing Triton and ever-changing Proteus;
Aegean pressing with his arms
the monstrous backs of whales.
(Ovid, *Metamorphoses* II.10–14)

The Romans were not big on simply staying home and sticking to the boundaries of their own country. In fact, as my Scottish mother might say, they were 'wee stoppy outs'. A penchant for adventure and expansion meant the Romans came across animals they would never have seen if they'd stayed put with their feet up in Italy. Conquering Britain meant spotting the odd *ballaena Britannica* – British whale – in the North Sea, as well as the sperm whale in the sea around Gaul. Pliny describes sightings of this huge marine mammal in the Bay of Biscay, with the whale 'rising up like an enormous pillar higher than the sails of ships and belching out a kind of deluge'.[18]

Sailing to India to trade in the East introduced the Romans to even more wonders of the ocean depths. The Greek geographer and historian Strabo, author of major work *Geographica* on the world known to him at the time (he died in AD 24), described how huge humpback whales in the Arabian Sea would swim close to Roman ships, which were travelling to

---

18   Pliny, IX.3.

India for trade. The whales would spray the ships with water from their spouts, but the Romans soon learnt that they could scare the animals off with loud trumpets and shouts so that the creatures never attacked them or appeared in large groups. (Strabo, *Geographica* XV.2.13)

Claudius and the Whale

The emperor Claudius is responsible for a Roman whale becoming beached in the history books. Remember the dolphin tied up in the harbour by the King of Caria? The one who was set free after grief-stricken people begged for a bit of compassion? Well, this story is nothing like that.

During Claudius's reign (AD 41–54), a ship with a cargo of leather hides was wrecked in the harbour of Ostia, Rome's sea port. Some of the animal skins had fallen overboard and into the sea, and a whale, attracted by the hides, swam into the harbour, where it stayed for a few days. Unfortunately for the whale, the waves created mounds in the sand and it ended up trapped in the harbour with its back sticking up out of the water, looking like the capsized keel of a boat.

Being a Roman emperor, Claudius decided to put on a spectacle for the people and the beached whale was going to be the star of the show. Nets were stretched across the harbour mouth and the emperor's own elite troop of personal bodyguards – the Praetorian Guard – hurled their lances at the whale from ships, attacking it until it was killed. If it makes you feel any better, during this bloody show one of the guards' boats was sunk by the unlucky whale. (Pliny, IX.5)

BIRDS

THE EAGLE

Aquila

> Of all the birds we know, the eagle is the most honourable and the bird of the greatest strength.
>
> (Pliny, *Natural History* X.3)

In a little nook in my kitchen is a small figure of Jupiter, lightning bolt in hand – and there, at his feet, is an eagle. As Jupiter's armour bearer, this great bird of prey was considered the highest of heavenly birds: not even the god's own thunderbolts or lightning strikes could harm it.

Eventually becoming the symbol of Rome's military standards, it was the majestic eagle on whose wings Roman emperors would ascend to the heavens as they became deified after death. If you should find yourself standing on the Via Sacra in Rome, look up at the arch of Titus and there you will see an image of the emperor carried on the wings of an eagle up to his rightful god-like place in the heavens. By the second century AD, the eagle had become an emblem on funeral reliefs, even if you weren't an emperor.

When the Greek historian Herodian wrote about the funeral and deification (in AD 211) of the Roman emperor Septimius Severus, he described the great structure of the emperor's funeral pyre and the live eagle that flew from it: soaring out of the flames from the uppermost part of the funeral pyre, the eagle ascended as if from a high battlement. Here was the soul of Septimius Severus, carried on the eagle's wings from the earth up to the heavens, where the emperor would be worshipped evermore alongside the rest of the gods. (Herodian, *History of the Roman Empire* IV.2.11)

An ancient story from Pliny sees an eagle on another funeral pyre. This time, the eagle is the loyal companion of a young girl who has hand-reared the bird from a chick. The bird brought the girl birds and other prey to show its gratitude for her kindness, and when its young human companion died, as her funeral pyre was burning, the eagle is said to have thrown itself upon the flames and was burnt together with her body. (Pliny, X.6)

Here are a few eagle-related facts you might like:

- With the Latin for eagle being *aquila*, you can see where we get the description of an 'aquiline' profile from. Also known as a 'Roman nose', that large curved nose, as noble as an eagle, has its roots in Jupiter's bird of prey.
- Plutarch wrote that while the Romans liked to call ignorant or stupid people 'fish', certain powerful men liked to be called after birds; King Pyrrhus, enemy of Rome, liked to be called 'eagle'.
- 'Aquila' was also a Roman 'cognomen' – a name used like a nickname would be today. If a Roman was called Aquila, there must have been something eagle-like about them. It could be that they had a large nose or, considering how the eagle was an important symbol for the military, it could mean Aquila was quite the soldier.

If you want to see the eagle in all its martial glory, turn to 'Animals in the Military' to see just what an important symbol this bird of prey was to the Romans.

Hunting Birds with Birds

We are used to hearing about dogs being used to hunt other animals, but history tells us that birds can work alongside human hunters and become part of the chase too. Pliny was aware of sixteen species of hawk and recorded how the varieties could be differentiated from one another by the way they hunted for their food: hawks that only took prey from the ground, hawks that took birds perching on tree branches, and others that hunted birds in flight. If you were thinking of tying the knot, it was said that the *aegithus* species of hawk, when lame in one of its feet, was an excellent omen for a marriage contract. However, it was the hawks that hunted those birds in flight which, Pliny tells us, had a most interesting *societas* – partnership – with humans. These skilled birds of prey worked alongside fowlers, who used them to drive down birds from woods and reed beds. The hawks would fly amongst the birds and signal to the men by their screeching and the manner of their flight that the time was right to seize the quarry. Catching their prey in bags, the hunters would share their prize with the hawks.

The hawk wasn't the only bird recorded as helping humans to hunt. Pliny tells the story of Crates, a man who had trained several ravens to help him catch his prey. With a raven perched on the crest of his helmet and others on his shoulders, we can picture Crates as he walks into the forest and his birds take off, soaring into the sky and driving out the game for him. Wild ravens would circle the kill too – handy for the hunter, as they marked out, in the sky, the land below where the game had been killed. If you're wondering whether a raven could actually bring down a mammal of any size, an article some years ago in a British newspaper featured flocks of ravens that were causing a problem for farmers by attacking and killing sheep, lambs and calves.[19] (Pliny, X.9–10 & 60)

A Famous Roman Raven

Put the image of flocks of ravens pecking a lamb to death out of your mind. Here's a much better raven story from the first century AD, when Tiberius was emperor.

In the Roman forum, a brood of ravens hatched on top of the Temple of Castor. One of the young birds flew down and landed at a cobbler's shop. Hanging out at the cobbler's, bit by bit the raven started to pick up words. Off it would fly to salute the statues of Germanicus and Drusus Caesar *nominatum*, 'by name', chatter to the passersby and then wing it back to the cobbler's.

Now, if you find the idea of a talking raven hard to believe, you need only google 'Mischief raven' or 'Fable the talking raven' to see and hear ravens speaking. They are incredible at mimicking sounds, and Fable's keeper says that her bird has learnt up to fifty words so far and can even talk in short sentences.

It's no wonder, then, that back in ancient Rome, the cobbler's talking raven attracted a lot of attention. Who wouldn't want a chatty bird to

---

19   Paul Kelbie, 'Flocks of Ravens in Killing Spree', *The Guardian*, 4 May 2008, www.theguardian.com/environment/2008/may/04/wildlife.

entertain them while they waited for their sandals to be repaired? Over the years, the raven became quite a wonder to the people. Unfortunately, a rival cobbler, whose own birdless business was likely suffering from a lack of customers, decided to get rid of the main attraction and killed the raven. But you can't just bump off a popular talking animal and not expect a bad reaction. The cobbler was driven out of his district and then killed. People were so upset and disturbed by the loss of this tame and talkative bird that the raven was given its own public funeral.

On 28 March in AD 36 (yes, this raven was so popular that 2,000 years later we even know the date of its funeral), the bird was carried on a draped bier through crowds of followers on the shoulders of two Ethiopians. A flute player led the way to the funeral pyre, which had been built on the right-hand side of the Appian Road. Pliny tells us that this bird's cleverness was considered justification for the punishment of a Roman citizen and an entire funeral procession. Clearly, you don't mess with a talking raven in ancient Rome; the murderous cobbler should have stuck to mending shoes. (Pliny, X.60)

THE WOODPECKER

Picus

Who doesn't know that the children were fed on milk
From a wild animal, and that a woodpecker often brought them food?
(Ovid, *Fasti* III.1.53)

Who would have thought the woodpecker was up there with the noble eagles and portentous owls of the ancient world? But this bird winged its way through the origin story of Rome, alongside the she-wolf. It may have been a wolf who provided Romulus and Remus with milk, but it was a woodpecker who brought food to the two babies after they had been left to die. Just as the she-wolf was sacred to the babies' father, Mars, so too was the woodpecker, which was known as *martia avis*, the bird of Mars. When it came to auguries – the signs that predicted the future – the woodpecker took its rightful place near the top of the tree for omens.

There was a famous Picus in ancient times, said to be the son of Saturn and the first king of Latium. He was great with horses and skilled at reading omens. His favourite bird to do this with was the woodpecker. Out hunting one day, Picus was accosted by the enchantress Circe, but Picus only loved one woman and that was his wife, Canens. The problem was, you just couldn't turn down a minor goddess without consequences. In revenge for spurning her, Circe transformed Picus into a woodpecker.

> Then twice she turned to the west
> and twice she turned to the east;
> three times she touched the young man with her wand,
> three incantations did she speak;
> he fled, but in wonder at his unaccustomed speed
> he saw wings upon his body
> and soaring high to the Latian woods
> angry at this new and sudden bird
> he struck the wild oaks with his hard beak
> and full of rage dealt out wounds to the long hanging branches;
> his wings took on the purple colour of his cloak;
> the broach pin which had held fast his golden vesture
> turned to feathers, and a golden yellow circled about his neck;
> nothing was left of Picus as he was before
> Except his name.
> (Ovid, *Metamorphoses* XIV)

THE GOOSE

Anser

You might imagine that the animal attributed to Juno, wife of Jupiter, might be a tigress, a lioness or a fierce she-wolf, but it was the goose that was associated with the queen of the gods. I hope Juno won't mind if I introduce my uncle Lenny to the story of the goose, since he once kept one as a pet, which he said was better than any dog when it came to alerting him to visitors to his property. In ancient Rome, this animal's skill as a loud and reliable watch-bird and guardian earned it a special ceremony and a place in the history books.

A Short Story about Smug Geese and Dogs in the Doghouse

The Romans owed a lot to Juno's bird. In 390 BC, when the Gauls were attempting a night attack by storming the ramparts to the city, the dogs slept on while the sacred geese kept in the Temple of Juno honked and hissed an alarm, alerting the inhabitants to potential barbarian danger. These feathered watch-birds saved the skins of the Romans and were thereafter celebrated in an annual ceremony during which a goose decorated in purple and gold and nestled on a cushion was carried on a litter. The name of this ceremony was the *supplicia canum* – 'the punishment of the dogs' – and you would be right in thinking this doesn't sound too good for the dogs.

While the goose was borne in ceremonial and elevated comfort, the unfortunate canines who slept through the attempted attack were punished by a dog being crucified and carried, suspended on a cross of elder, from the Temple of Juventas to the Temple of Summanus. On top of this, the sacred geese of the Capitol could feel even smugger as feeding them became a contractual obligation for the city *censors*, or magistrates. (Plutarch, *Morals: On the Fortune of the Romans* 12)

THE PIGEON

Columba

Some interactions between animals and humans never change: Aelian describes pigeons massing around people in cities, completely unafraid and quite tame. It seems pigeons got under people's feet 2,000 years ago, just like they do today. In fact, Aelian says the more humans the better, as a crowd gives the pigeons *tharros* – courage. Too few people, and the birds get nervous and fly off. (Aelian, III.15)

Ancient Messenger Pigeons

Pigeons were put to human use too. In 43 BC, during the siege of Mutina (modern Modena in northern Italy), Decimus Brutus – famed assassin of Julius Caesar – managed to send messages tied to the feet of pigeons to his consul Hirtius, who had sent birds over with despatches for Brutus. Brutus's enemy, Mark Antony, thought he had things covered, but he hadn't counted on trained pigeons: 'What use to Antony were his rampart and his watchful besieging army, and even the nets spread across the river, when the message was winging its way through the sky?' (Pliny, X.53)

First-century Roman soldier, engineer and author Frontinus gives us more details on these pigeons. He describes Hirtius shutting the pigeons

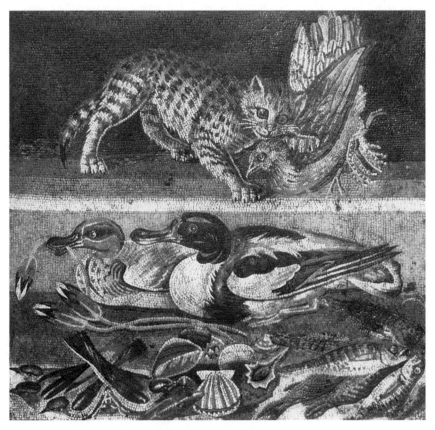

A cat paws a Roman hen; below are four small birds and two ducks. Part of a mosaic excavated from Pompeii. (Prisma Archivo/Alamy Stock Photo)

up in the dark, starving them for a while and then attaching messages to their necks with a hair. The birds were then released as near to the besieged city as Hirtius could get. Searching for food and light, the birds flew to the highest buildings where Brutus had scattered food out for them.

We also know from Frontinus that Hirtius had managed to get some soldiers across the river with messages inscribed on thin lead slabs tied to their arms. This is likely how Brutus knew about Hirtius's plan to use pigeons to communicate during the siege and about the strategy of leaving food out in particular places. How can a tiny hair be used to tie messages on a bird? This technique had been picked up by the Romans from the East. The message was wrapped around the hair, then the hair was pulled around the pigeon's head so that it and the message were concealed in amongst the pigeon's neck feathers. In Roman Egypt, it wasn't the pigeon's neck or the feet that messages were tied to, but the tail feathers.[20]

Roman pigeon fanciers were *insaniunt* – crazy – for the birds. The biggest pigeons were from Campania and the best birds could cost a pretty penny. Fanciers would build pigeon lofts on the roofs of their houses and chat about the best breeds of birds and what pedigree their own were. (Pliny, X.53)

How's this for a distraction at the theatre? People would take their pigeons or doves to a show, hold them close to their chest, then let them loose – safe in the knowledge that their birds were trained to fly home.

How to Look After Your Pigeons

Your pigeons needed looking after, whether you were keeping a few as a hobby or 5,000 of them in your country pigeon houses to be sold and served up on someone's table. When he was about 80, the Roman scholar

---

20   This insight is from the work of George Jennison, late author and superintendent of the now closed Belle Vue Zoological Gardens in Manchester. You can read more in his wonderful book *Animals for Show and Pleasure in Ancient Rome*.

Varro wrote a whole work on agriculture. Here are his top tips for caring for your pigeons and doves:

- Make sure the walls of your pigeon house are made of the smoothest possible plaster (mixed from marble dust). Keep the edges of the windows plastered, too. If you keep this maintained, you'll keep mice and lizards out. Because, don't forget: *Nihil enim timidius columba* – 'Nothing is more timid than a pigeon.' (Unless, of course, it's a city pigeon, remember?)
- Nests should be round, placed side by side in a row.
- The entrance and exit holes for each nest should be just large enough for the pigeons. And under each row of nests you should have a board, two palms wide, to make a nice little walkway for the birds.
- These birds like to keep clean; make sure there is a flow of water for them to drink and bathe in, and muck out the pigeon house every month. Don't waste the pigeon poop – use it as fertiliser for your crops instead. It will generate a lot of heat and warm the ground up nicely. If you're one of these Romans with thousands of pigeons and are looking to make a profit, all of this pigeon waste could actually be a great fertiliser business for you.
- To protect your pigeons and doves from hawks, find two twigs, cover them with lime – sourced, of course, from limestone – and stick them in the ground leaning towards one another. Find an animal a hawk likes to hunt, tie its legs and leave it between the two twigs. The hawk will go for the bait, become smeared with the lime and then you can catch it and kill it.

(Varro, *On Agriculture* III.7)

CAGED BIRDS

The first person to establish aviaries for caging all kinds of birds was Marcus Laenius Strabo, a man of equestrian rank from Brundisium. From him, we began to imprison behind bars animals to whom nature had assigned the sky.

(Pliny, *Natural History* X.72)

You needed money to have your own aviary, but as the Republic began to fade and die and the Empire began to stretch its legs, people had to find something to do with their wealth. Having a personal aviary was a great way to display just how well off you were. Some of these aviary birds were kept for the dinner table or for the food business, but others were there for show, the sound of their song and the benefits they had on mental health.

The great Cicero's brother had an aviary built in one of his villas in 54 BC, and Varro, who wrote about country life, had huge gardens at his estate at Casinum, with colonnades of trees, fishponds, ducks and an aviary full of songbirds. No wonder Varro wrote that keeping birds like this was good for the *anima causa* – 'for the sake of the mind'.[21]

SOME FLEETING FACTS ABOUT BIRDS

He throws four vultures. I grab the dice, invoke my lucky charm Hercules and throw a winner.

(Plautus, *Curculio* II.3.78)

- The lines above are taken from a play called *Curculio – The Weevil* – by the writer Plautus. They don't mean that someone has chucked four birds of prey across the room, but they do mean someone was enjoying a bit of a gamble. The Roman dice game *tali* was played with dice made from the ankle bones of sheep or goats. Very unlucky for the animals whose leg bones were used to make the dice, but lucky for players who threw the right combination of numbers. Players threw four *tali* with thirty-five possible named ways the dice could land. Venus was the best throw, which was when all the dice were different numbers to one another; if you threw four identical numbers, it was called the *vulturius* – the vulture. But not every identical number was good. If your four identical numbers happened to land on the number one, you were in trouble. The rule was that all four dice landing on the number one was the worst throw of all and called *canis* – the dog.
- Talking of vultures, Aelian wrote how these birds were known to follow armies, understanding by instinct and experience that a battle meant corpses. (Aelian, II.46)

21   *On Agriculture* III.5, 8.

- Pliny tells us about migrating quails being troublesome to sailors. He described huge numbers of the birds taking a rest and massing together on the sails of ships during the night. According to Pliny, the combined weight of the birds could sometimes cause ships to sink. (Pliny, X.33)
- The Latin word for an ostrich is *struthiocamelus*, or sparrow camel.
- While the purple coot was thought to be prone to jealousy and the peacock a right show-off, the crow was given a better report: believed to be incredibly faithful, they were said to keep their partners for life and love them intensely.
- The emperor Alexander Severus (r. AD 222–235) loved his aviaries on the Palatine Hill and filled them with peacocks, pheasants, hens, ducks and partridges. All of these birds helped him forget about his *sollicitudines publicas*, or 'cares of state', his favourite being the thousands of doves he kept. As he didn't want the cost of their food to affect the grain supply (a food dole handed out to the poorest residents in Rome), he had slaves who sold eggs and baby birds to provide the income for bird food. At Severus's banquets, he liked to have tiny birds flying about amongst the guests as well as partridge fights and – every dinner guest's favourite amusement – puppies playing with little pigs. (*Augustan History: Alexander Severus*, XLI.5–7)[22]
- As sailors set out to sea, watching the flight of cranes could tell them whether it was a good idea to keep going or not. If the pilot of a ship looked skyward and saw cranes turning in the sky and flying back the way they had come, it was a signal of oncoming storms. Aelian tells us that, in this way, cranes passed their knowledge on to mankind, and that learning from the birds' instinct saved the lives of sailors and protected the ships they sailed in. (Aelian III.14)
- If you were keeping birds for profit, Varro advised only having a few windows in your birdhouses. Why? If the birds can see trees and other birds flying free, it will give them a terrible feeling of longing and make them grow quite thin. By keeping the light low, your birds can see food, water and perches but not much else. You should also have some shelves inside your birdhouses, where your bird keeper can put the dead birds – he will have to account for every bird to his master, after

---

22 The *Scriptores Historiae Augusta* (*Augustan History*), a collection of biographies, is a debating point for academics. The date it was written as well as the author/s are still disputed.

all. As for the healthy birds, when it is time to take them to market, put them in the *seclusorium* – the smaller bird coup. This lighter room is where your bird keeper will kill the birds ready for sale. It's a good idea to kill them like this, out of sight of the birds in the main birdhouse, as it prevents the birds who aren't due for the market yet from going into a state of misery and dying at an unsuitable time. (Varro, III.5)

- Flies annoying you? Try a fancy fly flapper made of peacock tail feathers. Here's the punchy poet Martial describing just such a fly swatter in his list of doggy-bag gifts to hand out to dinner guests:

That which prevents filthy flies from licking your dinner, was once the proud tail of a distinguished bird. (Martial, *Epigrams* XIV.67)

BIRD CALLS

So call me your little sparrow, your chicken, your quail,
your little lamb, tell me I'm your little kid or your darling calf,
take me by the ears, join your lips to my lips.
(Plautus, *Asinaria* 3.3.78)

Just as we might say that someone's swanning about in their budgie smugglers, sticking their beak in and acting a bit of a goose, the Romans used bird terminology in creative ways too. Here are some bird-themed terms of endearment:

- *Pullus*: my chick
- *Mea columba*: my dove
- *Coturnix*: my quail
- *Passer*: my sparrow, my darling

But avian nicknames weren't always affectionate. Writer and philosopher Seneca recounted how a certain Cornelius Fidus was seen crying in the Senate because he'd been called a *struthocamelum depilatum* – a 'plucked ostrich'. Here are a few more tweets from the language of birds:

- *Passer* and *passerculus*. Meaning 'little sparrow', these were naughty references to the penis in various poetry and plays. There is still an argument whether the *passer* in Roman poet Catullus's poetry is literally his girlfriend's pet sparrow or innuendo for her clitoris or her boyfriend's penis.

- *Strutheus*. Latin for 'sparrow-like' and also slang for a penis.
- *Turturilla*. 'Little turtle doves' and soldiers' slang for a brothel.
- *Gallina*. A 'hen'; a term of endearment but also slang for a sex worker.
- *Vulturius*. A 'vulture', used just as we do today for someone who is greedy or grasping.
- *Cuculus*. If you called someone a 'cuckoo', you were calling them a fool.
- *Ala*. This means 'wing' and, as if it were a bird of prey ready to swoop, *ala* also referred to the wing of an army. It was also the word for an armpit.

And here are a couple of phrases the Romans used that we still say 2,000 years later:

- *Pinnas incidere alicui*: to clip a person's wings
- *Extendere pinnas*: to spread one's wings

How about a few flighty Roman surnames?

Aquila wasn't the only bird to turn up in Roman names; you might have also come across these avian-themed folk on the streets of ancient Rome:

- Corvus: Mr Raven
- Buteo: Mr Hawk
- Racchus: Mr Jackdaw
- Merula: Mr Blackbird
- Pavo: Mr Peacock
- Falco: nickname for someone who was pigeon-toed

Birds took up a lot of space in the Roman world, so there is more to come. Owls and chickens are perching over in 'Animals in Religion and Philosophy', while other birds are being fattened up for the pot in 'Animals on a Platter'.

INSECTS AND ARACHNIDS

THE SCORPION

Scorpio

> They are a terrible plague, poisonous like snakes except that they cause
> an even more painful torture with a slow death that takes three days ...
> their tail is always trying to sting and at no moment does it stop threat-
> ening to strike in case it should ever miss its chance.
>
> (Pliny, *Natural History* XI.30)

In AD 116, during the long Parthian Wars between Rome and the Persians,
the emperor Trajan besieged the wealthy town of Hatra (south of Mosul
in Iraq). The city was built in the middle of miles and miles of desert,
and was protected by a huge fortified wall. Anyone not used to desert
conditions was in for a tortuous time: water supplies were an issue, and
the exhausting heat caused heatstroke and disease. Trajan failed, and two
years and a new emperor later, Septimius Severus tried again, not once
but twice.

How could one city resist Roman attack like this? Hatra had left Severus
with scores of wounded men, dead legionaries and siege engines burnt to
ashes. The defeat gnawed away at Severus and he couldn't give up.

He targeted Hatra again, returning with siege engines galore and large
stores of food supplies. The same intolerable conditions were waiting for
the Roman army: the desert, heatstroke and attacks from Arabian cavalry every time they went out foraging. The Romans were bombarded by
arrows and missiles and, as they besieged the city's wall, the Hatrenians
hurled naphtha (a form of chemical fire) at them, burning up the soldiers
and siege engines below.

If you think this all sounds terrible for the Roman soldiers, it gets worse. Imagine storming a high city wall and seeing pots launched down at you. For a few seconds, you're confused. Compared to arrows and fire, who cares about a hail of clay pots? But as the pots descend, creatures begin to fall from them; down through the air they fly, legs spread as if they are soaring on wings, and onto faces and arms land hundreds of scorpions. They crawl into any part of the body that is unprotected and begin to sting.

These poisonous grenades were an effective terror weapon against the Romans: Septimius Severus's second attempt failed. Scorpions played their part in resisting the Roman Empire and the Romans retreated.[23]

The Scorpion Symbol

The emperor Tiberius had a new camp built in Rome on the Viminal Hill specifically for his Praetorian Guard, the elite bodyguards of the emperor. Tiberius's sign of the zodiac was Scorpio, and from then on the scorpion became the official emblem for the Praetorian Guard, lurking on shields and standards. The scorpion was unique to the Praetorians and no other Roman legion used it, so if you see a Roman relief and the soldier is wearing a helmet with a scorpion etched on the side, you know it's a Praetorian Guard.

Ancient Scorpion Deterrents

To avoid being stung by a scorpion, our ancient natural historian Aelian tells us this advice was picked up from the people of Roman Libya:

- Wear high boots.
- Keep your bed away from the wall.
- Put the feet of your bed in containers of water.

---

23 In 2014, newspapers reported how the Islamic State of Iran and Syria, ISIS, were employing the exact same scorpion tactic that the Hatrenians used against the Romans two thousand years previously. ISIS targeted civilians in Iraq and blasted canisters filled with scorpions into towns and villages in order to create panic and fear.

- Put some aconite on a scorpion's back and it will shrivel up for a while (hellebore has the opposite effect and revives the scorpion).[24]

Faced with a whole land full of scorpions, you would need to send out the equivalent of ancient Rentokil to get rid of them. Persian kings knew that travel across their scorpion-infested desert regions could be a deadly affair. The whole area would be off bounds if something wasn't done, as scorpions were lurking under every stone and lump of earth. Orders would be sent out that several days before a journey started, everybody was to go out and hunt the scorpions – whoever caught the most would receive a reward.

Scorpion Sting Tactics

Scorpions will go to extreme lengths to sting a person:

1. One scorpion dangles from the roof with its stinger hanging down.
2. A second scorpion crawls down over it and hangs onto the first scorpion's tail.
3. A third, and a fourth, and a fifth, and so on, do the same thing.
4. Scorpions follow until the whole scorpion chain leads down to the target.
5. The last scorpion stings the sleeping human.
6. This scorpion crawls back up.
7. The rest follow and the chain is disconnected.

(Aelian, VI.23 & IX.27)

How to Deal with a Sting

If you think that sounds bad, Roman writers recorded how this 'plague of Africa' could be blown by southerly winds to give the appearance of actually taking flight. There was a Roman superstition that if you saw a scorpion and said 'two', the scorpion would not sting you.

---

24 Why would you want to revive a scorpion? If you were using them as a weapon like the ones hurled onto the Roman soldiers besieging Hatra, you would have to collect them first and using a spot of aconite would certainly make this easier. Dropping some hellebore into your clay pots would have revived the numb and subdued scorpions ready for war.

If, for some reason, this didn't work, you needed only burn a scorpion, mix its ashes with wine and drink it back for a cure. The good news was that once stung by a scorpion, you would never be stung by hornets, wasps or bees.

The last words go to the scorpions. *Scorpius*, the Latin word for scorpion, had a few different meanings. Apart from a deadly stinging arachnid that could send your body into convulsions, a *scorpius* could be any of the following (you'll notice that all of them involve spikes, pain or pointy-shaped objects):

- A military engine for hurling missiles (more on that later)
- A prickly sea fish
- A prickly plant known as scorpion wort or scorpion grass
- A heap of stones forming a point at the top and used as a boundary marker
- An instrument of torture.

THE BEE

Apis

But amongst all the insects, the first place goes to the bees, which are quite rightly the most admired, as out of this species they alone have been born for the sake of man.

(Pliny, *Natural History* XI.4)

The Business of Bees

There was money in honey and bees were a profitable business; even Roman taxes could be paid in honey or wax. Honey was used in food and medicine, and as if bees weren't busy enough producing all the honey, Romans also used the *propolis* that bees produce. Bees make this gummy bee-glue from tree sap and use it to close up any chinks in their hives, and the Romans used it for medical treatment. Been stung by a bee? Remove the sting with propolis. Got a foreign object stuck in your flesh? Propolis.

We've got loads of detailed advice from Roman writers like Varro, Pliny, Columella and Virgil on beekeeping:

- If your bees are fighting with each other, sprinkle them with honey water and they'll be too busy licking the water to kick off. Or, even better, sprinkle them with mead and they'll lap it up and become quite stupefied.
- The best beehives are made from bark. Cork from cork trees makes excellent beehives as cork hives don't get too hot in summer or too cold in the winter. Failing this, you can use fennel stalks or willow woven together to make hives. If you have to, you can make hives from wood hollowed out or cut up into boards. Some people suggest hives made of dung (but don't forget, these can catch fire) and then there are brick beehives. Hives made of horn or *lapis specularis* – a type of transparent stone – will let you get a glimpse of life inside the hive. The worst hives are earthenware as these will be affected by the heat and the cold.
- In the spring and summer, check your beehives about three times a month; get rid of vermin, smoke the hives gently and clean out any dirt. In the winter, some people use dead birds to keep their bees warm. Take out the birds' intestines and pop the birds in the hive where the bees can find a little gentle heat amongst their feathers.
- The bigger and rounder a bee is, the worse it is, and the worst kind of bee of all is a fierce bee. If your bees are not too bad natured, you can soothe any moody temper in them with plenty of handling, since the more you handle them the tamer they become.
- The best crop to grow for your honeybees is wild thyme. In fact, you can grind up thyme in a mortar, soak it in warm water and then sprinkle the herbal concoction on the land you are going to have your hives on. Honey produced from thyme is the best. The absolute worst? Farmhouse honey from vegetables and dung-covered grass.
- Things to keep away from your bees: frogs and toads, wasps and hornets, spiders, moths, sheep (bees can get tangled in their wool) and the smell of crabs being boiled.
- Bees hate bad smells (hence the crabs). Make sure your beehives are not kept near the stench of the toilets, the smell of mud from a marsh or the stink of a bathroom or dunghill (difficult if your hive is made from dung).

- If bees become scattered, they can be brought back together by the clapping of hands or the beating of cymbals.[25]

How to Warm up a Bee

What if your bees are knocked down by heavy rain or get too chilly? If your bees are lying around looking dead, collect them up in a vessel and put them in a warm spot under cover. The next day, burn some wood from a fig tree and gently dust your bees with the warm fig ashes. Don't touch the bees yourself but carefully shake the vessel, and then put them out in the sun to revive. (Varro, III.16.37)

Wax

If you were Roman, you wouldn't just loves bees for their honey, but might wax lyrical about beeswax too. Here are some of the places wax would turn up in Roman life:

- If you were a soldier, it was important to keep your armour in good shape. Wax was just the product for this job, protecting against rust and naturally inhibiting corrosion.
- Wax writing tablets. A wooden frame filled with melted wax that had been left to set was used with a pointed writing utensil called a *stylus*. Pick up your *stylus* and write in the hardened wax.
- Musical pipes. The *syrinx* or panpipe instrument was made of reeds held together by wax.
- Varnish for wall paintings. A thin coating of wax was applied over the finished painting as a layer of protection against things such as dust.
- For decoration. Does your terracotta or marble need some colour? Paint pigments were added to heated wax in a technique known as *encausticus* – encaustic or hot wax painting. To make black, add ashes of papyrus to your wax. To make red, mix your wax with alkanet (a herb from the borage family with a dark red root). Do your brush-work quickly before the wax starts to harden. Heated and dyed wax

---

25 All beekeeping advice above is taken from the following authors. For more details on looking after your bees: Varro, III.16; Pliny, XI.4–23; Virgil, *Georgics* IV; Columella, IX.

could be used for *similitudines* – portraits – and for painting emblems and colour onto ships. Hot wax laid on with a brush withstood the challenges of saltwater, wind and sun very well.

- Talking of ships, wax was used to weatherproof vessels and make them watertight. Wax mixed with pitch was just what you needed between the seams of your ship to help keep the wooden planks watertight. Fabric such as wool mixed with wax could also be used between planking for the same reason.
- In a signature. Wax was used along with a signet ring to stamp a mark of identity. If you had your own signet ring, you could imprint it in warm wax to leave your 'signature'.
- Wax models, called *imagines*, of ancestors were kept in the *atrium* of the home, especially if your family member had achieved the status of an *aedile*, *praetor* or *consul*.[26] These wax sculptures would be carried in funeral processions.

For those who wanted only the best, the Romans thought the following types of wax were the bee's knees:

- Pontus. Wax produced from the region of Pontus (in modern-day Turkey) was known for its incredibly yellow colour.
- Cretan. Remember the *propolis* that came in so handy for the Romans? Cretan wax was believed to have the highest concentration of this gummy medicinal substance.
- Punic from Carthage (modern Tunisia) in North Africa. Punic wax was considered the highest quality wax and especially good for medical preparations.
- Corsican. This wax was produced from the box tree and, again, the Romans believed it to be a top wax for medicinal purposes.

---

26 While the details of their roles changed over the centuries, an *aedile* was a Roman junior magistrate. From this position an ambitious Roman could hopefully move up to the office of *praetor*. The *consul* was the highest elected political office and had military authority; even the year was named after the *consul*.

Horrendous Honey

In the first century BC, at Trebizond on the shores of the Black Sea (in modern north-eastern Turkey), Rome's Mithridatic War with the kingdom of Pontus is still marching on. As the Roman army pass over the mountains, they don't realise that archenemy King Mithridates VI has a poisonous plan to escape his pursuer. He has the help of two allies and only one of them is human: the Heptakometes. The Heptakometes are going to stage a trick for Mithridates and their bees are going to help them. They begin to gather as many honeycombs as they can, but this honey has been made from the area's rhododendron flower. It came to be known as *maenomenon mel*, or 'mad honey', which should give you a clue about how this turns out.

The Heptakometes leave the honeycombs along the path of the Romans and, sure enough, the soldiers take the bait. Filling up on the dripping honeycombs, they have no reason to believe that the honey is naturally poisonous, but soon begin to feel its devastating effects. The Romans are vomiting and delirious, they suffer diarrhoea attacks, can't stand or hold a sword and are left lying helpless and ripe for slaughter.

Around 1,000 Roman soldiers are killed with ease, all thanks to the bees and their honey. One hundred years later, the people of eastern Pontus pay a tax of wax to the Romans for their honey, even though the honeycombs make them no money – because who wants to eat poisoned honey?

You can read modern medical articles on this very honey today, with doctors reporting how treatment with electrocardiographic monitoring, saline drips and even a pacemaker might be needed to treat people who have eaten toxic honey. The Romans had no chance.[27]

Bees weren't just about honey and wax, though. These tiny insects became symbols for some pretty philosophical ideas:

- When his father, Saturn, had plans to eat him, the infant god Jupiter was hidden away and nourished by a goat and the honey from bees.

27 Strabo, *Geography* XII.3.18, and Pliny, XXI.45, both refer to this poisonous incident.

In return, the king of the gods put the goat into the sky as a constellation, *Capricornus*, and gave the gift of wisdom to the bees.
- Considering the way bees live in their hives, with a certain 'hierarchy' where every bee has a role – queen, worker, drone – we can understand why some Roman writers used the life of bees as a metaphor for political shenanigans and Roman society.
- Bees and honey were linked to death, and the bee (like the dog) was seen as a gatekeeper between life and the underworld.

LOCUST LAWS

In the second century BC, a huge plague of locusts was seen heading in from the sea into Apulia (on the heel of Italy's 'boot'). They swarmed over the fields and began their destruction. Officials were immediately sent with full powers to organise as many men as possible to kill the locusts.

Plagues like these, flying over from Africa, sometimes infested Italy, and the Romans brought in laws to literally crush the locusts. The Roman military in Syria commandeered civilians to kill locusts, and in the Roman district of Cyrene (in Libya) there was legislation to make war on the locusts three times a year. First stage: crush the eggs. Second stage: crush the grubs. Third stage: crush the pesky locusts themselves. Any man who didn't take part in this three-pronged locust crushing would be duly punished.

If you lived on the Roman island of Lemnos (Greece) you would have had to get your locust-killing skills honed as there was a law prescribing how many dead insects each man was charged with bringing to the magistrates of the island. Luckily, there was some help from nature itself: jays were kept on the island to swoop in and catch the insects.

GNATTY FACTS ABOUT INSECTS

- Ants were thought to be the only living creature besides humans that buried their dead.
- *Pulex*, or Flea, was a Roman surname.
- Moths were thought to avoid any clothes that had been worn to a funeral.

- A particular species of hornet was said to be able to kill a human being with twenty-seven stings. (Precisely.)
- Mosquitoes were a dangerous pest. Attempts were occasionally made to drain the marshes that surrounded Rome and advice was given not to build houses near marshes. Several Roman authors describe foreign armies who camped near the mosquito-infested areas near the River Tiber as overcome and weak with disease. Modern scholars believe it was the effects of malaria that were draining the unfortunate soldiers of their energy. Mosquitoes surrounding the outskirts of your city? Not good if you were a Roman living in an infested area, but very good if you were a Roman who could depend on the pestilential talents of an insect to ravage an enemy with the debilitating effects of its bite.
- *Melanthion*, or nigella seeds, were used as a repellent against gnats and flies. Burn the seeds and the pesky midges buzz right off.
- This is going to make you scratch. Archaeologists have found head lice on Roman-era combs, body lice on cloth and, if you want to get right down to the grubby details, a Roman pubic louse was found at an excavation in Carlisle in north-west England. Digs at York uncovered huge layers of Roman-era human fleas. Archaeologists have even found Roman head-lice combs that resemble the ones you can buy today: two-sided combs (the Roman ones were made of wood, ivory or bone) with big teeth on one side for combing the actual hair and much narrower teeth on the other for combing out the bothersome head lice.

THE DOG

Canis

I shall speak of the dumb watchdogs; although it is a mistake to speak of the dog as a dumb guardian. For what man more clearly or with such noise alerts us to wild beasts or a thief, as the barking of this animal does? What servant is more affectionate to his master? What friend more faithful? What guardian more genuine? Who can find a more vigilant watchman? Lastly, who is a more steadfast avenger or protector?

(Columella, *On Rural Affairs* VII.12)

Swift dogs for the hunt, fierce dogs for guarding property or your animals, clever dogs for performances and pampered dogs for sitting on laps. Engravings of dogs on funeral reliefs, dogs on mosaics, dog bones, dog gravestones, ceremonies with dogs in. Dogs in books, in working manuals, in poetry and in spoken stories. Dogs were everywhere in Roman life.

In 2010, hundreds of Roman tiles were excavated at the site of a second-century AD Roman bathhouse in Jerusalem. The Roman legion *Fretensis* had been stationed nearby and used the baths, which, in fact, they had built. We know this because the legion's symbol was found stamped on the clay tiles and mud bricks, which were uncovered in the excavation. Imprinted on one roof tile, right on top of the symbol of the Tenth Legion – LEG X FR – was the paw print of a dog.[28] If you want physical proof that dogs took up a lot of space in the Roman world, you need only look for ancient paw prints, because Roman-era dogs have left their

---

28 Shira Medding, 'Ancient Roman Soldiers' Bathhouse Found in Jerusalem', CNN, 22 November 2010, edition.cnn.com/2010/WORLD/meast/11/22/israel.discovery/index.html.

footmarks all over the place. To name only a few, if you were to visit British Roman sites such as Richborough Roman Fort near Sandwich, Lullingstone Roman Villa in Lullingstone or the Roman Baths at Bath, you would find the same evidence of Roman dogs as they found at the baths in Jerusalem: paw prints in *tegula* – clay tiles left out to dry by the potter and trotted over by pesky dogs.

The Romans noticed the same quirks of a dog's personality as we do today. Two millennia ago, Curtius Rufus wrote how '*canis timidus vehementius latrat quam mordet*', which means, 'a timid dog barks worse than it bites' and, when it came to fidelity, the Romans had exactly the same view of dogs as we do. Along with the horse, they were called *fidelissimum animal homini* – 'the most faithful animal to man'.

Nothing can beat a good old faithful dog story and the Romans recorded a few from different times and places in history. There are the loyal war dogs of Colophon in ancient Turkey, who fought bravely on the front line of battle. Then there was a dog called Hyrcanus, who threw itself onto the funeral pyre of its master, King Lysimachus. There was one dog story though, which would have been passed down for hundreds and hundreds of years before the Roman Empire even began. It's still read today and when we hear it we can imagine Roman ears listening to the tale of a loyal dog and the story passed on to settle in the hearts of ancient story lovers. Here it is, a Greek tale, which wound its way to the Romans, the story of the most loyal dog of all from Homer's *Odyssey*.

Argos, the Original Old Faithful

After twenty years away, Odysseus is returning from his Trojan adventures on the long and arduous journey home to Ithaca. On finally reaching his destination, he sees his home is filled with suitors, all vying for the hand of his wife, Penelope. He disguises himself as a beggar in order to secretly enter his home and dispatch these suitors from his house.

Nobody, apart from Odysseus's son Telemachus, knows who this beggar really is. But a dog hears Odysseus's voice. Its ears prick up.

The dog is lying over on a dirty dung pile, its fur covered in fleas. It's old and weak, a shadow of the beautiful, swift hunting dog who used to run by Odysseus's side. But it is Argos. Despite his great age and the twenty years that have passed, he recognises Odysseus. Argos (whose name means 'swift-footed' in Greek) drops his ears and gently wags his tail, too weak to get up and walk to his master.

Odysseus sees him and, realising the dog is Argos, knows he cannot go to him: the dog would surely give away his true identity. He turns away and wipes a tear from his face. Asking if the old noble dog on the dirt pile is a hunting dog or just a dog who begs for scraps at the table, Odysseus is told that this is the dog of someone long gone, a man who died in a distant land. 'If the hound you see before you now looked as he did when Odysseus left him for his journey to Troy, you couldn't help but gaze in wonder at his speed and at his power.'

Hearing these words, Odysseus turns and heads into his house as faithful Argos passes into the darkness of death, finally able to leave the earth and sleep in everlasting peace now that he has seen his master safely return home. (Homer, *Odyssey* XVII)

THE LOYALTY OF A FAMOUS ROMAN DOG

But what about records of Roman loyal dogs? The Romans noted a few of their own, with stories of dogs defending their masters from attack by thieves. For example, Vulcatius, a tutor in civil law, whose dog fought off an attacker when he was coming home at night, or the tale of how the senator Caecilius's dog was killed trying to defend him from armed men. Here's a faithful Roman dog who had his story written down by several Roman authors,[29] and actually attested to in the National Records of Rome in AD 28 …

Under the consulship of Appius Julius and Publius Silius, a punishment was meted out to one Titius Sabinus. Unfortunately, his slaves were also included in his punishment and were duly thrown into prison alongside Sabinus. One of the slaves had a dog, a faithful hound who refused to be driven from the site of the prison that held his master captive.

---

29   See: Pliny, VIII.61.

There is a set of steps in Rome known as the *Scalae Gemoniae*, or the 'Steps of Mourning'. If you think the name sounds a bit sinister, you're right, because this is where your body was flung, bound up, after you'd been executed. The dog-loving slave was duly killed and his body thrown down the steps. Bodies of the executed were usually left on these steps for some time, but the dead slave's faithful dog refused to leave the body and stayed by its side, howling over and over.

The watching crowds listened to the dog's cries; there it stayed howling and refusing to move. When someone threw it a scrap of food, the dog picked it up and carried it to its master. The custom was to throw these bodies into the River Tiber and eventually the slave's corpse was thrown into the waters. Still, the dog would not leave its master's side, as into the river it went swimming alongside the dead body and trying to keep it afloat, as a crowd of people streamed out to watch the sight.

THE WATCHDOG

If you had the money, a scary-looking dog baring its teeth on a mosaic right at the entrance of your house was a good way of letting people know that you had a fierce guard dog inside (even if you didn't). A mosaic like this was uncovered at Pompeii and warns intruders off with exactly the same warning that's hung on gates and fences today: *CAVE CANEM* – 'Beware of the Dog'.

How did you know if your guard dog was a good guard dog? Roman advice was, if you were after a watchdog for your home or your farm, a black-furred dog looked more intimidating. Plus, darker fur meant the dog could not be seen by intruders in the night, which gave the animal a better chance of dealing with thieves. The Laconian dog from Sparta and Sallentines from southern Italy were both considered good watchdogs, and the fierce Molossian dog (a breed of mastiff imported into Italy from Epirus, north-western Greece) could be used as a guard dog for the home, for protecting sheep and for hunting.

Remember the first-century writer Varro, the one who didn't put his feet up when he reached 80 but wrote an entire work on agriculture instead? In one section, he tells anyone who has a farm that it's an absolute no-brainer to keep dogs, since no farm is safe without them: 'You're better off keeping just a few good active dogs rather than a lot of them, and you should get them used to keeping watch at night and sleeping indoors during the day.'[30]

Here's some of Varro's advice on dogs to Roman farmers:

- Get your dog at the right age. If they're too old, they'll be no good at even guarding themselves, let alone sheep, and they could end up as doggy wolf prey.
- Whatever you do, don't buy your watchdogs from huntsmen or butchers. Butchers' dogs are too lazy to follow the flock and huntsmen's dogs run off and desert the sheep the first time they clap eyes on a hare or a stag.
- The best place to get your watchdog is from an actual shepherd. A dog that has had no training at all is preferable, because dogs form attachments to people and sometimes a trained dog can be too close to the shepherd and not the sheep. The last thing you want is to take delivery of a load of sheep with their dogs and the dogs leave you and run off back to their old shepherds. To prevent this happening, do the obvious and throw it a boiled frog. (Mind you, don't forget there are stories of dogs leaving their new masters and running for days back to their old shepherds who haven't even done the boiled frog trick, so who knows?)
- Remember: if you don't feed your sheepdog properly, you risk it going off hunting for itself and that will leave your flock in danger. Dogs like food the same as human food – they need bits of meat and bones, not leaves and grass. They also like barley bread soaked in milk, bone soup and bits of bone, which is good for their teeth. Never, ever, let them taste sheep flesh or they may not do their job properly.
- Protect your dogs from wolves with a *melium*, a leather collar with nails poking out (make sure you have some soft leather under the nail heads to stop them from making the dog's neck sore). A dog wearing one of these will help protect even your dogs who aren't wearing a collar: a wolf who has come up against a *melium* before won't want to risk getting wounded again.

(Varro, II.9.3–15)

---

30   *On Agriculture* I.21.

From the first century AD, one of the famous Pompeii watchdogs reading 'Cave Canem', or 'Beware of the Dog'! (Azoor Travel Photo/Alamy Stock Photo)

THE HUNTING DOG

> Life reveals to us every day the very many other qualities in these animals, but it is in hunting that their expertise and sagacity is at its absolute best.
>
> (Pliny, *Natural History* VIII.61)

The Romans loved a good hunt. Wealthy Romans sometimes had their own hunting parks where their guests could take part in the chase. For those who couldn't go hunting themselves, the amphitheatres gave a taste of the pastime by putting on hunting shows, *venationes*, where you could watch the hunt played out for entertainment. For those Romans who took part in hunting themselves, once they'd sorted out their nets, a three-pronged spear, some cords (not the trousers but twine twisted from broom), a lance, a hare stick, a foot trap and some stakes, amongst other things, they could turn their attention to their dogs.

According to second-century poet Oppian in book I of his *Cynegetica* on hunting, even the colour of your dog's fur was important: you didn't want either a white dog or a black dog because these colours don't deal well with the sun or the snow. (Tell that to a polar bear.) A hunting dog should be the colour of wild animals, of foxes or leopards or wolves; but the fastest hunting dogs of all are tawny dogs, with fur the colour of golden corn.

If you were looking for courage, then the huge mastiff Molossian dogs were perfect, and this was the fierce breed which turned up in the Roman amphitheatres too. Here's Oppian describing the Molossian:

> Impetuous and of steadfast valour, who attack even bearded bulls and rush upon monstrous boars and destroy them, and tremble not even at their lords the lions. They are not swift, but they have abundant spirit and genuine strength, unspeakable and dauntless courage. Array, then, for the hunt such breeds of war-like dogs, which put to flight all manner of beasts. (Oppian, *Cynegetica* I.414 ff.)

Dog breeds used by Romans for the hunt included:

- *Vertagus* or *Vertragus* – greyhounds – from Gaul. Great for hare coursing. These dogs were so fast that hunters could follow them on horseback instead of on foot.
- Laconians from Sparta. Good scent trackers for hunting deer and hares.
- Cretan Hounds from Greece. One of the oldest European breeds of hunting dogs, they are known to pick up scents from tasting the earth or pebbles.
- Acarnanians and Locrians from Greece. The short-faced Locrian dogs were best for hunting wild boar. There was no loud barking from the Acarnanians who were said to stalk prey silently.
- Etruscans from Italy. Not so fast but good scenting dogs. This dog has been compared to the Pomeranian in appearance.
- Umbrians from Italy. Good scent dogs again, but not brave when facing wild animals.
- Agassians. One of the breeds imported from Britain. The size of a domestic dog, it was the Agassians' nose that marked it out as a great

hunter. An excellent tracker, the Agassian was skilled at following scent trails on the ground and sniffing out airborne scents too.

Here's Pliny again, explaining how even an old dog who doesn't have the energy anymore can still be useful in the hunt:

> Even when they are exhausted with old age and blind and weak, the hunters carry them in their arms catching the scent on the wind and pointing their noses towards the lairs and dens. (Pliny, *Natural History* VIII.61)

ROMAN DOG NAMES

> Dogs alone know their master, and they sense straight away if a stranger arrives: they alone recognise their own names and the voice of their household.
>
> (Pliny, *Natural History* VIII.61)

One hundred years after Varro, Columella added his own advice on watchdogs, even telling farmers to give their dogs two-syllabled names – exactly the same advice dog owners are given today to help with successful recall. (My dog is called Barnabus – one syllable over. Terrible.)

Here are some of the Latin names on Columella's list:

- Ferox – 'Savage'
- Celer – 'Speedy'
- Lupa – 'Wolf'
- Cerva – 'Doe'
- Tigris – 'Tiger'

And a few Greek names:

- Skylas – 'Pup'
- Lakon – 'Spartan'
- Alke – 'Valour'
- Rome – 'Strength'

One dog's name isn't from a book, but from an epitaph for a real dog: Myia, meaning Fly, just like the sheepdog in *Babe*.

If you prefer something more poetic, the poet Ovid included a long list of dog names in his description of the goddess Diana's punishment for Acteon, meted out after he'd seen her naked and bathing in a pool. In her fury, Diana turned Acteon into every hunter's quarry: a stag, whereupon he was chased and ripped apart by his own pack of fifty hounds. Here are just a few of the dog names Ovid listed:

- Aello – 'Tempest'
- Dorceus – 'Gazelle'
- Melanchaetes – 'Blackhair'
- Nebrophonos – 'Fawn Killer'
- Theron – 'Hunter'
- Oribasos – 'Mountain Climber'
- Laelaps – 'Hurricane'

And the two most vicious names of all for a dog that is going to tear you apart:

- Sticte – 'Spot'
- Asbolus – 'Sooty'

ANCIENT DOG BONES AND THE FAMOUS DOGS OF POMPEII

An archaeological dig in France uncovered not just the small bones of a Roman baby, but the bones of a Roman dog too. Dated to the early first century AD, the baby was thought to be about a year old and was buried with objects that included a toy hoop and rod. Certain food offerings – two headless chickens, some pork, three hams and half a pig – were left buried around the coffin. Resting on top of a piece of broken shell was a child's tooth left for the baby – perhaps by an older brother or sister as a little piece of themselves, a token of love to accompany their younger sibling in the afterlife. Along with miniature vases and glass bottles, something else lay buried with the child. At the foot of the baby's feet were the remains of a puppy, the rod from the child's hoop toy lying between its legs. Around the dog's small neck was a collar decorated with bronze and connected to the collar was a small bell, leading experts to believe the puppy was a pet.

If we're looking for physical evidence of Roman-era dogs, we need only turn our eyes towards Pompeii, near Naples in southern Italy. When Mount Vesuvius erupted in AD 79, the towns of Pompeii and Herculaneum were hit by a surge of deathly hot gases and ash from the volcano's pyroclastic flow. You probably know the plaster casts of some of the humans who died there, the bodies twisted in terrible death throes.

In 1874, a body cavity was discovered at the House of Marcus Vesonius Primus, a successful Roman fuller.[31] When plaster was poured into the cavity, out came the shape of a dog in its own twisted death pose, similar to that of many of the humans. The dog had a large studded collar around its neck and measured over half a metre to his shoulder.

The animal was probably a guard dog as it was found chained up in the *fauce* – the passageway leading to the atrium of the house – left there to do its job and protect the property when Primus and his household fled as the volcano began to erupt. Trapped by its chain, this poor old Pompeii pooch had no chance of escape, but it has become one of the most famous dogs in history thanks to Primus legging it and leaving his trusty watchdog behind.

Dog skeletons have also been excavated at Pompeii along with dog kennels – one made of plaster and tiles, and the other of a big old urn or pot split in two lengthways. Evidence of dogs has turned up all over the place at Pompeii, including the bones of a hunting dog and the partial skeletons of more watchdogs, one of them with damaged joints (perhaps signifying old age). Nearly all the bigger gardens had dog bones in them – and I don't mean bones buried by dogs.

One large dog skeleton from the date of the eruption was found lying on its side on the top layer of ash in the House of the Menander. Why

---

31 The fuller worked in the business of laundering clothes – which, if they were made of wool, would have taken skill to maintain the shape and size of the garments – and the process of preparing wool for cloth making.

Cast of a dog killed in the Mount Vesuvius eruption, AD 79. (The Print Collector/Alamy Stock Photo)

didn't the dog get away? It's Primus's watchdog all over again, only this time the dog wasn't tied up but trapped in a part of the house which had been shut up. There was no escape, but it looks like the dog kept trying as its skeleton was found not under, but on top of the layers of ash. Eventually, the gases did their job and, despite all its efforts, the dog was suffocated.

The bones of only one small dog have been found at Pompeii, this time in the fruit orchard. As lap dogs were kept as pets rather than as guard dogs, maybe we can assume that these smaller dogs were swept up and taken with their owners when they fled from the disaster. Or, maybe, unlike the dogs who were left to do their jobs as guardians, they simply pegged it out of there themselves.[32]

32 Excavation details from the wonderful *The Natural History of Pompeii*, edited by Wilhelmina Feemster Jashemski and Frederick G. Meyer.

We don't have this watchdog's bones to give us clues to the part he played in Roman life, but we do have his epitaph, which proves that a good guard dog can become a faithful friend and even get his own cremation:

> Guardian of the carriages, he never barked out of place, now he is silent and his ghost protects his own ashes. (*Corpus of Latin Inscriptions* IX.5785)

TAKING CARE OF THE ROMAN DOG

Here's some canine care advice from the Roman authors Pliny and Columella:

- Dog is in a rage? Get down to the dog's level and sit on the ground with it.
- Dogs were believed to be more prone to going mad with rabies when the Dog Star, Sirius, was rising. To protect yourself over this thirty-day period, collect some chicken dung to mix in with your dog's food. If your dog already has rabies, there's nothing for it but to mix hellebore into the food. Forty days after your dog's birth, you could try preventing rabies in the first place by getting your teeth stuck in and docking your dog's tail with a quick bite to cut off the end joint of the tail. The spinal marrow will have been removed, the tail won't grow again and there won't be a chance of the dog catching rabies.[33]
- If your dog has fleas, crush some cumin, add an equal weight of helle-bore, mix them in some water and smear the paste onto your dog. (Even today, some people recommend cumin as a natural deterrent against fleas or even as a topical flea treatment for pets, but with the added twenty-first-century advice: always speak to your vet first!) If you can't get hold of cumin or hellebore, smear the dog with cucumber juice or pour olive oil dregs over the dog's entire body.[34]

---

33 Rabies is transmitted by animal bite and docking a dog's tail does not, of course, prevent rabies. Nor does biting off the end of your dog's tail remove the spinal marrow. In fact, leave those tails alone!

34 Pliny, VIII.61, 63, and for flea treatment: Columella, VII.13.

HOW TO USE HALF A DOG
TO SUBDUE YOUR ENEMY

During Rome's Second Punic War with Carthage in the second century BC, the Carthaginians had annexed a good deal of Spain. Mago, Carthaginian brother of the famous Hannibal, had hold of the citadel of Carthago Nova, but the Romans had eyes on securing this centre of Punic power.

After seizing possession of the city walls, the Romans poured into the town and got ready to carry out their usual orders. The aim was to strike terror into the hearts of the town's inhabitants. The writer and historian Polybius describes how it was the Roman military custom that when cities were captured by Roman armies, they left corpses of humans, animals with limbs severed, and dogs' bodies cut in half. The message was clear: don't resist.

As the Roman general Scipio marched 1,000 men onwards to the citadel, the streets littered with dead citizens and the mutilated bodies of animals, Mago knew the city was lost. He sent a message to the Romans that resistance was over, and the citadel and Carthago Nova fell into the hands of Rome, who became the masters of Carthage in Iberia.

There's nothing that says 'defeated' like streets piled with the dead, but leaving the half bodies of dogs lying amongst the human corpses was a ruthless Roman tactic for adding to the terror and chaos of an attack. (Polybius, *Histories* X.15)

DOGS, DEATH AND HEALING

Talking of dead dogs, the dog was also a symbol of death. After all, it was the three-headed dog Cerberus who sat by the side of the god Pluto and guarded the gates of the Underworld. The image of the dog was used in a few deathly objects:

- Archaeologists have found small figures of dogs in ancient graves – what better animal to guard and protect the dead?
- Dogs also appeared on Roman grave reliefs. Not only were they a symbol of death itself, but they were a sign of fidelity – and what good Roman doesn't want to be associated with a symbol of loyalty and fidelity on their gravestone?

In ancient Epidaurus in Greece, there is a famous temple to the Greek god of medicine and healing, Asklepios (Asclepius to the Romans). Asklepios had his own cult, which the Romans added to their own religious system, eventually building a few temples of their own to the god. Two animals were associated with Asklepios: the snake and the trusty dog. Dogs roamed freely about at Epidaurus and were kept in the temples of Asclepius at Rome. If anyone had a wound, a good lick from a dog was believed to heal it.

Finally, the following inscription on a gravestone for a dog is proof that the Romans could love their dogs as much as we love ours. From the second century AD, the epitaph, now found at the British Museum in London, was engraved for a hunting dog, Margarita – Pearl – who crossed the line from sporting hound into beloved house dog:

> Gaul bore me, the shell of the rich ocean gave me my name: the honour of that name is suited to my beauty. Trained to run with spirit through the shady woods and to chase the shaggy beasts upon the hills, I was never held fast by heavy chains, nor did I suffer savage whips upon my snow-white body. For I used to lie on the soft lap of my master and mistress, and learned the habit of sleeping upon a blanket-covered couch when I was tired. I could speak more than a dumb animal should and no one ever feared my barks. But my destiny was ill-omened, and I died giving birth. Now the earth covers me under this little marble slab. Margarita. (*Corpus of Latin Inscriptions* VI.29896)

THE CAT:
BIG AND SMALL

Feles: a cat, a mouser, but also a thief.

The eyes of nocturnal animals like cats gleam and shine in the dark.
(Pliny, *Natural History* IX.55)

Excavated cat bones and cat images on vases and coins are proof that cats were padding about southern Italy at the end of the fifth century BC. By the time we get to the Roman Empire, there must have been cats galore. So let's start with these small cats and some evidence of their place in the Roman world.

FACTS ABOUT FELINES

- Roman provinces might have lost a few cats to Egypt. The Egyptians worshipped their cats and exporting the animal was illegal. There are records of soldiers being dispatched to 'repatriate' captive cats smuggled out of Egypt.
- Modern archaeological research into the DNA of cat remains has proven that cats travelled on ships on ancient trade routes, spreading the animal across the Roman world. They would have acted as pest control on board Egyptian ships, and Asian wildcats would have kept rodent numbers down on ships travelling the trade route from India.
- Cats didn't feature much in Roman literature, but they *did* leave the tiniest of paw prints in Roman books on farming. They could be a problem (smooth your duck enclosure walls with plaster inside and out to make sure cats can't get in) and a help: cats won't eat your grain, they bury their waste and they get rid of vermin.

- Talking of vermin, the Romans used ferrets to get rid of pests, but ferrets are burrowers and everyone knows that climbers are more useful than burrowers. Cats were especially good at getting rid of mice and rats as they could climb a thatched roof in the countryside or stalk across the tiles of city roofs, cleaning up the area while they stuffed themselves with rodents and helped contribute to the state of the city's public health.

- When we think about a cat's reaction to fireworks and then imagine the noise from the earth tremors at Pompeii before Vesuvius actually erupted, as well as falling pumice and debris, it is clear that any cats would have scarpered at the first noisy rumbles. It is no wonder, then, that only a few cat bones from the time of the eruption have been found at Pompeii: cat bones in two vineyards and a partial cat skeleton in the Temple of Venus.

- If you want to find a bigger cache of cat remains, you should look to Roman military sites, where archaeologists have found plenty of evidence of feline camp visitors – no doubt keeping the soldiers' food stores free of mice and rats. As if Roman cats wanted to leave us proof of their hunting abilities, excavations at the site of the Roman sea port of Myos Hormos at Quseir al-Qadim on the Red Sea coast discovered a first- to second-century AD cat buried inside a Roman administrative building. The cat's body was wrapped in woollen and linen cloths and was well preserved. The animal was a big one and experts believe it was a domesticated cat rather than a feral one. Apart from the skeleton, there were remains of quite a bit of fur, the stomach and a preserved lower intestinal tract, which showed that the cat had just eaten six rats before its death. (No wonder it was big.)[35]

- *Felicula* was a Roman cognomen – an additional name similar to a modern-day nickname – for girls and women, meaning 'Kitty' or 'Little Cat'. This name turns up in Roman inscriptions on funerary reliefs, so while the cat didn't take up anywhere near as much room

---

35 If you want to read more about this Roman cat and other excavated ancient felines, see: Sheila Hamilton-Dyer, 'Pampered Puss? Cats from the Roman port of Myos Hormos at Quseir, Egypt', in *Archaeozoology of the Near East X. Proceedings of the Tenth International Symposium on the Archaeozoology of South-Western Asia and Adjacent Areas*, eds. Bea De Cupere, Sheila Hamilton-Dyer and Veerle Linseele (Leuven, Belgium: Peeters, 2014), 357–71.

in Roman literature as the dog did, it appeared here, in the world of inscriptions for real people, across the cities and towns of the Roman Empire. Donald Engels, in his book *Classical Cats*, tells us there are over 250 cat nicknames surviving on inscriptions in Rome alone.

- Talking of funerals, images of cats appeared on funerary steles and tombstones, often with engravings of children holding cats or a cat sitting at the child's feet.
- Just as pesky as the dog, cat paw prints have been found imprinted on Roman tiles.
- The Latin for cat, *feles*, was used for ferrets and polecats too. In certain Roman plays, the word *feles* was slang for someone who predates on young women: *feles virginaria* and *feles virginalis* – translating to 'virgin cats'. The 'cat' part of the phrase had the unpleasant meaning of 'virgin predators' or 'virgin mousers'.

A CAUTIONARY TALE FOR ANCIENT CAT KILLERS

In 59 BC, when Julius Caesar was a consul, King Ptolemy XII of Egypt was trying to work out an alliance with Rome. Roman envoys arrived in Egypt and amongst the soldiers who accompanied them was one unlucky legionary. Watching events unfold was historian and author Diodorus Siculus. The Egyptians revered cats and the last thing you wanted to do was harm one. But sometimes accidents happen. Diodorus gives us all the details: if a cat dies in Egypt, there is wailing and crying and the cat is wrapped in linen and taken off to be embalmed; if a cat is killed, the perpetrator is put to death. Even if it's an accident, Diodorus writes that the locals will gather together and kill the cat killer before there's even been time for a trial. If anyone sees a dead cat, they back off and shout that they had nothing to do with it, but just found the cat in this condition.

So what happened to the unlucky Roman soldier? Diodorus says he witnessed the whole event with his own eyes. The legionary had killed a cat completely by accident. Crowds rushed to his house determined to punish him. Never mind trying to keep on Rome's good side, never mind trying to keep the envoys sweet. Despite King Ptolemy sending officials to beg for the Roman's life, neither they, nor any fear of Rome, could save the soldier, who was killed for harming this sacred animal. (Diodorus, *Siculus* I.83)

BIG CATS ~ STARRING THE LION

It is believed that a dying lion bites the earth and surrenders a tear upon its death.

(Pliny, *Natural History* VIII.19)

If something interesting or unusual was brought to Rome, the emperor Augustus was always keen to show it to the people. In 11 BC, he did just that with a tiger. This was the first time the animal was seen at Rome, displayed on stage in a cage. Where did Rome get its tigers from? India, Armenia and Hyrcania.[36] Lions and leopards were far easier to get hold of – reaching Rome decades before the first tiger ever did – meaning tigers were nowhere near as common a sight as lions at Rome and academics believe they may not even have been displayed at all outside of amphitheatres in the capital.

There's certainly evidence that lions had some up-close and personal experience of the Romans. Here's our old friend Pliny again with some Roman knowledge on lions that suggests the animals would have preferred to be left alone:

- The only malady a lion is prone to is not wanting to eat. This can be cured by treating it in an insulting manner, for example tying a monkey to it. This drives lions crazy and the only thing that will cure that is tasting the monkey's blood.
- If a lion is cornered by a large pack of hounds and horses, it retreats slowly and with a look of contempt. As soon as the lion reaches the brushwood it takes off at top speed.
- A wounded lion will recognise his attacker and mark him out, even in a crowd.
- If a mother lion is fighting for her cubs, she fixes her eyes on the ground so as not to flinch from the hunting spears.
- Even though the lion is such a fierce animal, it is frightened by chariot wheels.
- What frightens the lion the most is fire.
- When an African shepherd threw his cloak over a lion as it charged him, his instinctual defence against the animal made its way into the

---

36   Hyrcania was an ancient region located in modern-day Iran and Turkmenistan. It's from Hyrcania and Armenia the Romans sourced the now extinct Caspian tiger.

Roman arenas where the trick of throwing a cover over the lion's head was shown as a method of making an easier kill.

- Pliny recorded how the writer and historian Polybius said that, when lions get too old to hunt wild animals, they kill humans and start encroaching on African towns to find this easier game. Apparently Polybius witnessed actual hung and crucified lions, left as a deterrent to any other aged lions with an eye on eating human flesh.

(Pliny, VIII.18–21)

CAPTURING BIG CATS

Need a cache of cats? Get hold of some experienced African hunters who are skilled in the following methods, or get the Roman military up to speed in these hunting techniques from Oppian:

Pits

For capturing lions in a pit, make sure you've got your plaited, tightly woven cages at the ready and some roasted meat to hand. Good hunters will look out for lion tracks, and the perfect place to spot them is the path to an animal drinking source. If you've tracked a lion's paw prints to a water hole, dig a large circular pit in this area. In the middle of the pit, build a tall pillar and tie a lamb to the pillar. Next, put rocks and boulders around the edge of the pit so the lion can't see your trench. When the lamb starts bleating, its cry will attract the lion, who will leap over the wall and plunge into the pit. While the lion is pacing about, put your roasted meat into the cage and lower it down on straps into the pit. The lion will go for the meat inside the cage, at which point drop the cage door shut and you have him.

This same method can be used to trap leopards, but with the pillar made of oak and not stone. Use a puppy for the bait, not a lamb. Tie the puppy's private parts tightly so that it howls and yelps, which will attract the leopard.

Nets

Lions will catch your scent as well as the scent of your nets and net stakes. Pay as much attention to wind direction as a sailor would. Drive prey into the nets against the wind. How do you get your big cats into your nets? Place a hunter on each far corner of your plaited net and one hunter in the middle. The net should curve round as if in the shape of a great pair of horns. The hunters on the wings of the net should be able to hear the middleman. Other hunters holding flaming pine torches in one hand – remember, lions are terrified of fire – and a shield in the other should make as much noise as possible with their shields. Men on horseback should rush the lion, while the hunters clash their shields and wave their torches, closing in on the lion and driving it towards the great nets.

Leopards can be captured this way too, and, if you're lucky, you can even drive a big cat pick 'n' mix into the nets.

Wine

Use alcohol, like the hunters in Libya do, where they trap their leopards with wine. Find a still spring and, as night falls, pour jars of sweet wine into the water. Camp nearby, with the hunters camouflaged in goat skins or by your nets. At dawn, the leopards will come. They will be thirsty and attracted to the smell of the wine. After they have drunk their fill, they will lie about, heavy and stupefied, then your hunters with their nets can capture an easy prey. (Oppian, *Cynegetica* IV.77–211)

LIONS AND A CIVIL ROAR (SORRY, WAR)

During the civil war, in 48 BC, Julius Caesar and Mark Antony defeated their enemy Pompey at the Battle of Pharsalus. How could Mark Antony show the people of Rome that he had subdued such a mighty foe? By using lions in a grand parade, of course. He became the first person to harness lions to a chariot as he showboated to the crowd, the actress Cytheris at his side and the lions, duly broken by the yoke, pulling his chariot.

In the middle of the first century BC, during the same civil war, Gaius Cassius (one of Julius Caesar's future assassins) had procured some lions to show at Rome. Civil wars interfere with all sorts of things and lion transportation was one of them. The lions were delayed in Megara and were still there when the town was taken by one of Caesar's right-hand men, Calenus. Just as their city was captured, the Megarans decided to resist the oncoming enemy with an unusual weapon: Cassius's lions. As they were let loose, the lions did not play their part, forgot which side they were supporting and turned on the unarmed people of Megara. Taking the city, Caesar also appropriated Cassius's lions, a fact which apparently fuelled Cassius's hate for Julius Caesar even more. (Plutarch, *Parallel Lives: Life of Brutus* 8)

BIG CATS ON THE BILL

In the Venus mosaic from Rudston in Yorkshire,[37] there's an image of men and wild animals in combat. The lion has the name *Leo Flammefer* – 'the Fiery Lion'. We know the names of some ancient leopards because the Romans understood a show is all the better if you know who the stars are. In the Magerius mosaic and the Lepcis Magna frieze (both from Roman North Africa), the huntsmen are named but so are the leopards, whose names are as follows:

- Victor
- Crispinus
- Luxurius
- Romanus
- Rapidus
- Fulgentius
- Gabatius[38]

The hunters in the Magerius mosaic are enjoying a leopard bloodbath. The hunter called Spittara is killing the leopard Victor with a stab to the animal's throat – and all while Spittara is wearing a pair of stilts. The hunters Bullarius and Hilarinus – the latter of whom prefers to hunt with a

---

37 Imagine the Yorkshire farmer who was ploughing his field in 1933 and discovered this wonderful mosaic from the late third century AD, originally measuring 4.67m x 3.2m. If you want to see this example of Roman life and art, it is part of the collections at Hull Museum.

38 Victor, Crispinus, Luxurius and Romanus are from the Magerius mosaic and Rapidus, Fulgentius and Gabatius are from the Lepcis Magna frieze.

A section of the third-century AD Magerius mosaic in Roman Tunisia. The bare-cheeked Hilarinus still manages to spear the leopard Crispinus to death. (The Print Collector/Alamy Stock Photo)

bare bottom – are killing Crispinus; the leopard Luxurius is gushing with blood and lying slaughtered on the ground, and the hunter Mamertinus has pierced Romanus with a spear.

Let's leave the speared and dying big cats and end with a live one who has become immortalised and lives on 2,000 years later.

The Greek-Egyptian writer and teacher of rhetoric Apion told the story of an incident with a lion in the arena at Rome. Androcles had been slave to a Roman master in Africa. After running away, he had taken refuge in the desert where he realised he was sheltering in the lair of a lion. After helping the lion with a wound to its foot, man and lion lived together for three years until both were captured. Androcles was condemned to death, and both he and the lion ended up in the animal spectacles at Rome. The encounter between Androcles and his lion was recorded as an eyewitness account:

> When that lion saw him from a distance, he suddenly stood stock still as if in astonishment, and then slowly and calmly walked towards the man as if he recognised him. Then, wagging his tail in the manner and fashion of fawning dogs, softly and carefully he came right up next to the man, who was just about out of his mind with fright, and gently licked his feet and hands. The man, Androclus, letting himself be petted by such a fierce beast, pulled himself together and gradually turned his eyes to look at the lion. Then, you could see man and lion, happy and full of joy, as if they had recognised one another.
> (Apion's account, retold in Gellius, *Attic Nights* V.14)

A fanciful story? If any Roman was going to give the unembroidered, rational facts about an animal encounter, it would be the famous Stoic philosopher, and tutor to Nero, Seneca, who recorded his own eyewitness account of an incident between a man and a lion in a show at Rome. Seneca and Apion were in Rome during the same years and academics believe both men saw the same incident with the same lion. Seneca tells of a *bestiarius* – a wild beast fighter – who came face to face with a lion in the arena. The *bestiarius* had been the lion's keeper and the animal recognised him. It refused to attack him and actually protected him from attack by other wild animals.[39] Whichever story you prefer, there is no doubt that a first-century Roman lion caused a stir and a name for itself by proving that wild animals could recognise and feel affection for humans.[40]

---

39 Seneca, *De Beneficiis* (*On Benefits*) II.19.1.

40 We've got proof of the lion's memory for faces and capacity for affection for humans now. You need only watch Christian the lion on YouTube to see a lion who recognised his human keepers a year after they returned him back to the wild. His actions when he recognises his two human friends are exactly the movements that Apion described. 'Christian the Lion – Full Ending', uploaded 28 July 2008, Born Free Foundation, YouTube video, 6:05, www.youtube.com/watch?v=cvCjyWp3rEk.

THE SNAKE

Serpens

How things change. We see the snake as something to be scared of, a symbol of all things evil, but the Romans associated snakes with good things. They not only aligned snakes with healing and prophecy but saw them as the slithery guardians of the household who brought luck to the family. Roman houses had *lararia* – shrines to the household gods – which would protect the family. Your *lararium* might be in a little nook with a statue standing inside, or it could be a painting depicting your household gods, or a mosaic. The snake was the *genius* – guardian spirit – of the house, and this special role meant it often decorated Roman *lararia*.

THE HEALING SNAKE

Remember how dogs were connected to Asclepius, the god of medicine and healing? The other animal to entwine itself around this religious cult was the snake. Images of the god show the snake wrapped around the staff Asclepius holds (look out for snake symbols in modern-day pharmacy logos. Asclepius's staff entwined with a snake stands proud on the London monument to Dame Louisa Brandreth Aldrich-Blake, one of the first women to enter British medicine).[41]

In 293 BC, the Romans were suffering a terrible plague in the capital. On consulting the Sibylline books (books of oracles), they believed that

---

41   For more, see: 'The Origins and Meanings of Pharmacy Symbols', Wellcome Collection, 9 November 2017, wellcomecollection.org/articles/ We9Wqx4AAA5amD91.

transporting Asclepius's snake from the original temple in Epidaurus to Rome would end the pestilence, and so a shrine to Asclepius was eventually built on an island in the River Tiber. Snakes, like dogs, were part of Asclepian temple life. If you needed healing and visited an Asclepian shrine, as you lay in repose and focused on restoring your body, a priest carrying a sacred snake would bring the animal to you where its tongue would flicker out and lick your wounds to bring you back to health.

The snake appeared in a few Roman religious cults. A huge serpent was kept at the Temple of Juno Sospita in Lanuvium (south of Rome). Once a year, a ritual took place when the snake was fed by a young virgin from the town who had the worst snake-feeding job in history. The unfortunate girl would enter the snake's cave, a basket of food trembling in her hands. If the snake took the food and didn't kill the girl, it meant she was chaste and that the harvest would be good that year.

SNAKES, EMPERORS AND GENERALS

The snake helped create propaganda myths that certain figures were more than just ordinary men. A serpent was said to have given birth to the Roman general Scipio Africanus, and the story was that a great snake watched over his ghost after he died. Alexander the Great was said to be descended from a serpent and it was only right that the emperor Augustus should have a birth story of his own aligning him with this hero of the past. So, of course, the story came about that Augustus too had been sired by a snake. His mother, Atia, was said to have attended a religious ceremony at the Temple of Apollo. As she fell asleep, a serpent slid up her body. After it had left, Atia woke up and purified herself but couldn't remove a serpent-shaped mark from her thigh. Nine months later, Augustus was born. A story like this was the perfect way of setting Augustus above mere mortal men and placing him in the realm of heroes such as Alexander. (Suetonius, *Augustus* 94.4)

Just as Queen Elizabeth II was given jaguars from Brazil and Princess Anne a Syrian brown bear, Roman emperors were similarly gifted. The geographer Strabo tells us that ambassadors from India visited the emperor Augustus and presented him with several large vipers, a huge river tortoise, a massive partridge and a snake 10 cubits long – that's about 15 feet. (Strabo XV.1.73)

There was a bit of gossip that Messalina, wife of Claudius, sent men into Nero's bedchamber to strangle him while he took his afternoon nap. A snake darted out from under his pillow and frightened them away. The root of this story wasn't a live snake but a piece of shed snake skin found near Nero's pillow. After this snake scaring incident, and at the advice of his mother, Nero had the skin enclosed in a golden bracelet, which he wore on his right arm. (Suetonius, Nero 6)

THE DEADLY SNAKE

The Romans knew, of course, that snakes could be deadly. (Plutarch tells us that a certain Gaius Villius certainly did as he was executed by being shut up in a cage with a load of vipers and serpents.) What if a snake wasn't licking your wounds to make them better, but biting you to make you die? Here's some Roman advice on snake bites:

- Constrict the limb above the wound. First, cut around the bite with a scalpel to make sure you can get as much poison out as possible. Next, use suction cups to draw out the poison. If there's no cup, use any vessel you can find. Failing this, get someone to suck the poison from the wound, but make sure they have no wounds or sores in any part of their mouth. Put the patient in a warm room with the bitten body part inclined downwards. What if there's no one to suck out the poison or no vessel to cup it? Give the patient veal, mutton or goose broth and induce them to vomit, then kill a chicken or a lamb and put the warm part of the cut animal flesh on the wound. (Celsus, On Medicine V.27)
- Find an expert. The Marsi people (from central Italy) were thought to be skilled snake charmers, but the African Psylli were the snake experts the Romans have written about the most. They had a certain resistance to snake venom, were experienced in sucking out the poison from snake bites and in how to use incantations

to mesmerise a snake if you needed to distract one from causing mischief. Psylli saliva was even believed to cure a snake bite. When Cleopatra killed herself, Augustus so wanted her to live to parade her at his triumph in Rome that he had Psylli people brought to her to treat her snake bite and suck out the poison from her wound. (Suetonius, *Augustus* 17)

- Try some of these remedies for your snake bite: eat salted fish, then follow up with a drink of undiluted wine until the concoction induces vomiting. Drink your own urine or mix urine with ashes and apply to the wound. An application of fresh sheep's dung boiled in wine could also be spread on the snake bite. Drink vinegar; hopefully it will dissipate the poison inside your body.[42]
- Got any weasels handy? Gut your weasel, salt it, burn it over flames, leave it to dry out for a while, then drink two spoonfuls of weasel in wine as a remedy for snake bites. (Dioscorides, *On Medicinal Substances* II.27)
- Use the milky juice of the euphorbia plant. This was recommended by King Juba of Mauretania as a treatment not only for snake bites but for all kinds of poison.
- Catch the snake that's done the damage. Hold it on a stick over the steam of boiling water and it will cure the person who's been poisoned. If you burn the snake, you can apply its ashes as a liniment for the wound.
- Surround yourself with storks and don't get near snakes in the first place. In Thessaly, it was a crime to kill a stork because storks were great at keeping the snake population down. If you don't live near any storks, get some garlic. Snakes and scorpions don't like its scent at all, and garlic is still used as a natural snake repellent today. (Pliny, X.31 & XX.23)
- Since deer were considered to be an enemy of the snake, any part of a deer was thought to be a remedy against snake bites. You could sleep on a deer skin or keep a stag's tooth in your pocket to make sure no snake came near you. Just the smoke and smell alone of burning stag horns deterred snakes according to Pliny, and Varro advised just this to poultry keepers for keeping the slithery pests from the hen house. (Pliny, VIII.50 and Varro III.13)

---

42 Should you have the misfortune to get bitten by a snake, please get some medical help and don't just neck a load of undiluted wine, vinegar, urine or preserved fish.

SNEAKY SNAKES

You recall the fierce serpent in Africa, more dreadful to the Roman legions than the war itself.

(Seneca, *Letters to Lucilius* 82.24)

Snakes even played their part in the art of battle. Here are some stories of snakes who slithered into the theatres of war to scupper the Romans or administer an agonising death.

During his war against Mithridates, Roman general Pompey had to pause his plans and sort out a revolt from the Albanians. With gritted teeth, he turned back to deal with them but knew his army were going to have to march through difficult and waterless land. Ordering 10,000 animal skin flasks to be filled with river water, Pompey and his men met the Albanian army. Numbering 6,000 foot soldiers and 12,000 horses, the Albanian enemy was poorly armed, and dressed, for the most part, only in animal skins. But it wasn't just the thousands of Albanian soldiers who thwarted Pompey's plans. After subduing the unwelcome revolt, he got back to business and headed for the Caspian Sea. Just three days' march from its shores, he had to turn his army around as the land he was crossing was crawling with too many deadly snakes. (Plutarch, *Pompey* 35–6)

In the second century BC, the Carthaginian Hannibal was drumming up allies against his big enemy, Rome. King Eumenes of Pergamus was getting in the way of this, and in three days' time Hannibal would face him in a naval battle. Hannibal's ships were outnumbered; what he needed was a cunning strategy. For three days, he ordered his men to collect as many venomous snakes as they could and had the serpents put into clay pots. As the battle began, Hannibal's men were instructed to hurl the pots onto the enemy ships. The Pergamenian soldiers laughed at first: what kind of weapon is a clay jar? But as the snakes began to slither about the decks, panic and terror ensued. What to do first? Fight the enemy ships or deal with the snakes? The ships retreated and Hannibal won the day. (Nepos, *Hannibal* XXIII.10–11)[43]

Snakes were used in another military trick, this time in 356 BC. The Faliscians and Tarquinians, who were fighting the Romans, disguised some of their men as priests. The 'priests' held torches in their hands and snakes in front of them to appear like the Furies, the goddesses of vengeance who have snakes for hair:

> The Romans were beside themselves with fear and rushed in a panic-stricken mob to their entrenchments. The consul, staff officers and military tribunes laughed at them and bawled them out for running in panic and falling for such a trick like a bunch of little boys. (Livy, *The History of Rome* VII.17)

How could you make your arrows even deadlier? Adding barbs to the arrow will make them hook into flesh, but dipping them in snake venom will make them even more lethal. The Roman writer Aelian tells us that the Scythians pimped their particular snake venom with human bodily fluids, forming a festering and fatal poison that made their arrows feared by any enemy. The geographer Strabo wrote about the *Elephantophagi* – the 'elephant eaters' – who used snake venom on their hunting arrows to take down elephants. We know that when Rome's old enemy Hannibal attacked Sagantum in the Second Punic War, the arrows which rained down on his men were 'doubly fatal', since they had been dipped in 'serpents' poison'.[44]

---

43   Hannibal's biography comes from Nepos's surviving book *On Great Generals*, taken from his larger work, *On Famous Men*.

44   Aelian, IX.15; Strabo, XVI.4.10; Silius Italicus, *Punica* I.322.

FINALLY ...

The poet Lucan wrote the epic poem *Pharsalia* about the civil war between Julius Caesar and Pompey. In book IX, we find ourselves with Caesar's enemy Cato and his army in Libya. The legionaries are having a tortuous time crossing the desert; they've faced starvation and sandstorms, but now there's a new enemy and it's all over the place. Lucan gives a catalogue of Libya's deadly snakes. He describes the 'swollen-necked sleep-inducing asps', snakes that cause victims to bleed to death, snakes that leave a trail of smoke (pardon?), snakes that poison wells, snakes that foam at the mouth, and then there is the *dipsas* – the 'thirst snake'. Even though Cato had planned ahead and taken the Psylli snake experts with him, he still lost soldiers in the most gruesome way: the standard bearer, Aulus, suffers a bite from a *dipsas* and develops a fatal and unquenchable thirst; another soldier is bitten and dies an agonising death from necrosis; one snake sinks its fangs into Tullus, who bleeds to death from every part of the body that can bleed; and another's body swells with venom...

> Upon his face there burns
> A redness as of flame: swollen the skin,
> His features hidden, swollen all his limbs
> Till more than human: and his definite frame
> One tumour huge conceals. A ghastly gore
> Is puffed from inwards as the virulent juice
> Courses through all his body; which, thus grown,
> His corselet holds not.
> (Lucan, *Pharsalia* IX.791ff.)

PART TWO

ANIMALS IN THE ROMAN WORLD

Hold tight, we're going to the races …

THE WORLD OF
THE CHARIOT HORSE

The horses burst through the sky and with swift-hooved feet cut a dash through the clouds, which blocked their way as borne on wings they passed the east wind.

(Ovid, Metamorphoses II.157–60)

The Formula One of the Roman world was the high-adrenalin sport of chariot racing, where rival teams of superstar charioteers and horses destroyed the opposition in front of thousands of roaring fans. It may seem strange to skip forward to twentieth-century Hollywood now, but bear with me because it's here that we can get some idea of just how risky chariot racing was. The closest we can get to the reality of this Roman sport is by taking a look at what was perhaps the most dangerous shoot in film history: the chariot race in the 1925 silent movie *Ben-Hur*.

The fact that the film industry had established no animal rights laws yet means the experience of the horses in *Ben-Hur* might be comparable to those on ancient circus tracks. During filming, a cash prize was offered to the stuntman who rode his chariot into first place, and second unit director B. Reeves Eason didn't worry himself about the welfare of the horses on set: 'If it limped, they shot it.'

This attitude, and the carrot of the cash reward, ramped up the risk-taking and resulted in a violent, crash-bang chariot race, which, by the end of shooting, saw the deaths of over 100 horses. The final scene of the race featured a spectacular choreographed crash with five horses killed in this wreck alone. On one of the dangerous turns in the track – this time, totally *un*choreographed – chariots and horses piled into the wreck and a photographic still of the accident – dead horses, smashed chariots and stuntmen sprawled and injured – was used in publicity shots for the film. It certainly reconstructs the dangers of this ancient sport and gives us an idea of just how perilous chariot racing was, particularly on those hazardous turns.

THE CIRCUS MAXIMUS

With over sixty racecourses spread throughout its empire, from Carthage in modern-day Tunisia to tracks in Spain, Portugal and Egyptian Alexandria, charioteers and horses thrilled crowds across the Roman world. But if you were a top chariot horse breeder or a first-rate charioteer, the Circus Maximus in Rome was the place to aim for. This was the biggest and most impressive stadium and it was here that the premier horses raced.

With galleries three storeys high, the Circus Maximus could hold more spectators than the capacity of both Manchester United's and Manchester City's football stadiums combined. A crowd of 150,000 watched from stands surrounding the great horseshoe-shaped course. As the air filled with the sounds of trumpet calls, cheering, shouting, cracked whips and horses' hooves trampling the sun-baked track, and the sights of flying manes, swirling dust, jostling horses and dramatic crashes, the atmosphere at a chariot race would have been a thrilling experience. In the same way as football clubs have teams of workers behind the scenes, a crowd of professionals kept the chariot wheels turning: stable managers, stable assistants, grooms, vets, blacksmiths, senior charioteers, juniors, cartwrights and apprentices, as well as talent scouts on the lookout for potential chariot stars of the future.

THE MOST DANGEROUS PART OF A RACE

Chariot racetracks were constructed in a horseshoe circuit with a straight wall known as the *spina* – meaning backbone – running down its middle. Charioteers and horses raced down this central barrier hurtling towards three large cones protruding from the *metae* – turning posts – at the end of the *spina*. This was the crucial race point where the horses would take the sharp 180 degree turn to gallop back along the other side of the course. If you wanted to see a crash close-up, the seats at the turning posts were the ones you wanted.

Those charioteers who dared to drive their horses as close as possible to the inner barrier on these turns would have less ground to cover than those who drove their chariots further away from the *spina*. But getting so close on the turns was a risky move, as horses and chariot only needed to touch the barrier to crash with explosive results.

Crashes were referred to as *naufragia* – shipwrecks – and when these inevitably occurred, horses, chariots and men would litter the track, turning it into a treacherous obstacle course for those charioteers still in the race.

CHARIOT RACE FACTIONS

The Circus grabs the whole of Rome today, and an ear-splitting din tells me that the Greens have won. For if they'd lost, this city would look as mournful and dazed as it did when the Consuls were conquered in the dust of Cannae.

(Juvenal, *Satires* XI.197–201)

The ancient equivalent of footballers playing for teams, charioteers rode for *factiones* – factions. There were four *factiones* and the superfans lived for them.

- *Veneti*: the Blues
- *Prasini*: the Greens
- *Russati*: the Reds
- *Albati*: the Whites

In the days of Empire, the Blues and the Greens became the premier league players in the world of chariot racing.

Chariot race fans were like football fans today, following their team with a passion, wearing their colours and sometimes placing bets on their faction. In the same way a seething rivalry can exist between different football teams today, the Blues hated the Greens and the Reds couldn't stand the Whites. A riot at Constantinople in AD 532 amongst rival circus faction supporters resulted in the deaths of thousands of fans.

The emperor Nero wore the Greens colours. Other Greens fans included the emperors Caligula, Domitian, Verus, Commodus and the third-century Roman emperor Elagabalus. High-status fans of the Blues included the emperors Vitellius, Caracalla and Justinian I.

A charioteer could be sold to another team and might switch factions in his career, but it was unlikely someone would switch their colours along with the charioteer, just as a football fan today wouldn't dream of changing teams if their best player was sold to a rival club.

One wealthy Roman kept swallows and would take some of these birds to the Circus Maximus at Rome. After the race, he would smear the winning faction's colour onto the birds and send them flying back to their nests so his friends at home would know who had won the chariot racing.

Not everyone was a fan though. Here's what the first-century AD writer Pliny the Younger thought about chariot-racing enthusiasts and their teams.

> I am amazed that so many thousands of men are desperate, like a bunch of children, to see horses running over and over and men driving on their chariots. If it was the speed of the horses or the skill of the charioteers that captivated them, I might understand it, but it's the racing colours they cheer on, the racing colours they love and if, on the track, right in the middle of a race, their colour was changed from this one to that one, their support and enthusiasm would switch, and as quick as a flash they would abandon the drivers and horses whom they recognise from far off and whose names they yell aloud. Such is the regard, such is the power of one paltry cheap tunic. (Pliny the Younger, *Letters* IX.6)

THE HORSES

Horses yoked up to chariots in the circus absolutely understand the shouts of encouragement and applause.

(Pliny, *Natural History* VIII.65)

Chariot racing wasn't just thrilling entertainment; a lot of money was at stake and those horses were big business. Where did the Romans get the best racers from and what made a good chariot horse? Here are some horsey facts from the world of the circus:

- The average speed of a Roman chariot horse in a race was 35kph (22mph), with each race taking about eight-nine minutes.
- Horses would complete seven laps of the circus in a race. At the Circus Maximus, this would mean a horse running about 4.5km (3 miles) a race. If a charioteer was not so skilled and found himself jostled to the outside of the course, his horses would run further and covered about 6.5km (4 miles).
- Horses might be broken at 2 years old for other services, like the cavalry for example, but for chariot racing they tended to be at least 5 years old before racing. Most of the horses that raced were stallions.
- Buyers looked for horses with strength, stamina and speed; they had to be able to take those turns at the *metae* and keep up the momentum until the end of the race. A good chariot horse had to be able to cope with a harness, have a strong heart, a strong neck and fit in physically with the sizes of the other horses on his team.
- Premier chariot horses came from Spain and Africa – particularly the North African province of Numidia. Carthage, in modern Tunisia, was the place to trade horses. Horse trading was big business and breeders used ships called *hippagogi* to transport the animals between countries. By the late Roman Empire, the best racing horses came from the imperial stud farms.
- Between 700 and 800 horses were needed on a game day at the chariot races in Rome during the Empire.
- During Augustus's reign, so many horses were in demand for the chariot races that there weren't enough for the cavalry.
- At the end of a race, when palms, wreaths and money were handed out to the winning charioteer, the horses were not forgotten as palms were

threaded into the horses' harness as a mark of their achievement. The winning team would do a lap of honour and soak up the applause.

- Horses were stabled about a mile from the Circus Maximus at the Campus Martius in Rome where they trained at the training ground called the Trigarium. If you're ever lucky enough to be in Rome in the Via Giulia, imagine this: in 2009, construction workers building an underground car park there found something unexpected when they began to dig. There, below the city, were the stables built during the reign of emperor Augustus for horses racing at the Circus Maximus. The walls bore the marks of ancient graffiti cheering on the colours of the four racing teams that generated such passion and enthusiasm amongst chariot racing fans. (Pliny the Younger, who wrote the letter you just read at the end of 'Circus Factions', would have hated it.) The plans were to preserve the site and open it to the public, but due to a lack of funds, it was not to be. The site has been covered in damp cloths and reburied, safeguarded from erosion or thieves and waiting for the day when the stable can be uncovered for good.

CELEBRITY HORSES

Roman chariot horses could become celebrities in themselves, with some even having their achievements inscribed on tombstones.

In a *quadriga* – four-horse chariot – two centre horses known as the *iugales* – yoke horses – were yoked to the chariot. These horses took the strain of the chariot and charioteer's weight. Harnessed to the two yoke horses by a set of reins or straps called the 'traces' were two trace horses. These trace horses took the outer positions, the left trace horse running on the outer side of one yoke horse and the right trace horse running on the outer side of the other yoke horse. The reins were the only thing that attached the trace horses, so the charioteer would have to use all his skill and experience to control them along the track and turns and keep them in line with the other horses.

It was the inside (left-hand) horse of these two trace horses that a race depended on. This was the horse whose name the crowd chanted and was the boss of the horse racing team – the *funalis*. The star of the show, the *funalis* needed a lot of spirit and a lot of muscle to take charge of the other animals, and it was this horse who took the brunt of bodily damage.

Charioteer Polydus, with raised whip, holds the palms of victory, showing just what a superstar winner he was. He wears his cap and leather protective strips wrapped around his tunic. Compressor was his lead horse – the big boss with the muscle and spirit to control the horses he raced alongside. (The Print Collector/Alamy Stock Photo)

Being on the inside, the *funalis* was closest to the barrier on the dangerous turns and so took them at a sharper angle, meaning the horse was more prone to stresses on the joints, tendons and back. If there was a crash at the turn, the *funalis* took the full impact, crushed between the *spina* and the other horses. It's no wonder, then, that this is the horse that is named on inscriptions. This is the celebrity horse, the horse that made the race and the one that could go down in history, just as in this epitaph for an African circus horse called Speudusa – 'Quickie' – who died young and is now running in the Underworld:

> Born from the sands of Gaetulia, sired in a Gaetulian stud, equal to the winds in speed, torn away from your unsullied youth, you live in Lethe, Quickie.[45]

One team of chariot horses even made it into Roman literature. Our favourite Roman encyclopedist, Pliny, recorded how in AD 47 at the

---

45   From the *Corpus of Latin Inscriptions* VI.10082.

Secular Games, during a chariot race at the Circus Maximus, a charioteer for the Whites called Raven was thrown from his chariot. His horses raced on alone, taking the lead and keeping it, jostling other teams out of the way, blocking them and doing everything a skilled charioteer would have guided them to do. When the horses had won the race and completed the course they stopped just before the chalk finishing line, as if they were embarrassed for horses to win on their own without the know-how of men. (Pliny, VIII.65)

The illustration on the previous page shows just how famous a chariot horse could become. The third-century horse Compressor – 'Crusher' – went down in history, commemorated alongside the superstar chari-oteer Polydus, who raced for the Reds, on a huge mosaic at the imperial baths of Trier in Germany. Compressor is pulling a *quadriga*, a four-horse chariot.

CHARIOT HORSE NAMES

Important enough to remember, important enough to show off, the names of hundreds of Roman chariot horses have been found on inscriptions. Here's just a small selection.

- Adamatus – 'Much Beloved'
- Gemmula – 'Little Jewel'
- Lues – 'Boundless'
- Celer – 'Swift'
- Ballista – 'Missile'
- Passerinus – 'Sparrow'
- Hilaris – 'Merry'
- Arator – 'Ploughman'
- Sagitta – 'Arrow'
- Catta – 'Puss'
- Hiberus – 'The Spaniard'
- Spumosus – 'Foam'
- Polyneices – 'Ever Victorious'
- Patronus – 'Defender'

- Crinitus – 'Long Locks'
- Percussor – 'Striker'
- Frunitus – 'Jolly'
- Amandus – 'Darling'
- Regnator – 'The Ruler'
- Romanus – 'Roman'
- Garrulus – 'Chatterbox'

RACE EQUIPMENT

Chariot racing was such a dangerous and unpredictable sport that charioteers needed to have the right equipment to protect themselves while also giving them the physical tools to get those horses into a winning position. Each charioteer needed the following items during a chariot race and, when we look at the ones designed for protection, we can't help but wonder how much defence they actually gave against the very serious dangers of this risky and life-threatening sport:

- A leather or felt helmet – *pilleus* – was intended to give some protection to the head.
- Leather or linen strips – *fasciae* – were used to protect the legs and torso. *Fasciae* were bound around the legs and around the thick tunic that charioteers wore for added protection.
- Reins were used to drive the horses. The charioteer wrapped the reins around his waist, which allowed him to lean back into his chariot and have more control over the horses when he negotiated the dangerous turns. This was a uniquely Roman technique; the Greeks drove their chariots with reins in their hands.
- A knife – *falx* – was kept inside the leather straps wrapped about the charioteer's tunic. In the event of a crash, he may have needed to cut himself free of the reins to prevent being dragged round the course; this knife could save his life – if he could get to it.
- A whip – *flagellum* – was held in the right hand and used throughout the race to urge the horses on.

THE CHARIOTS

The chariots in the 1959 Hollywood film *Ben-Hur* aren't the best examples of those used by the Romans. The last thing a charioteer at the circus wanted was a big-wheeled heavy chariot made of thick wood and deadweight.

- In reality, the wheels were small and chariots were constructed from lightweight material, such as wicker, leather or canvas. The less weight the horses had to pull the better, and smaller wheels and a lightweight chariot gave the charioteer more speed and more manoeuvrability for getting into a good position and taking those dangerous turns. Historians calculate that a chariot weighed between 25 and 30kg.
- The front of the chariot was curved, like a rounded windscreen, while the back was open. This was where the charioteer would lean his weight, with his foot or knee on the curved front. He used his body weight to steer the chariot and control the horses, slowing them down at the bends, and releasing his weight on the back to drive them forward along the straights.
- Two-horse chariots – called *bigae* – were common, but the four-horse chariots – *quadrigae* – were the big deal of Roman chariot racing. The more horses pulling a chariot, the more dangerous the race, as more horses meant less control for the charioteer. Now and again, charioteers might use six-, eight- or even ten-horse teams, but this would have been incredibly dangerous and hard to control, especially manoeuvring the animals around the turning posts at high speed. Racing with this many horses would have been a treat for the crowds, a real display of showmanship and spectacle.
- The emperor Nero tried driving a ten-horse chariot at the Olympian Games in Greece. This would have taken a lot of skill and a lot of guts. On his own on the chariot board, and stooping over the reins, it was not something that could be faked: the outcome was down to Nero and his ten horses. It must have been a sight for the crowds to see their emperor attempting such a dangerous race. Thrown from the chariot, Nero took up the reins again, but still wasn't able to make it to the end of the race without being hurled from the chariot once more. Seeing as he was emperor, he was still crowned the winner. These particular Olympic games weren't recorded, perhaps because it was just too big an insult to record the failed attempt of Nero as a sporting 'win'.

- Most often, three chariots would race from each of the four teams, meaning there would be twelve chariots with twenty-four horses per race in a *bigae* contest; in a *quadrigae* race, there would be twelve charioteers, twelve chariots and forty-eight horses. (Keep up.)

THE CHARIOTEERS: *AURIGAE*

Oh! What a crime! That you, Scorpus, in the prime of your youth, were snatched so quickly to harness the shadowy horses of death. The chariot races were always over in a flash with your speedy driving but why did your own life race to its end so soon?

(Martial, *Epigrams* X.50)

The premier league charioteer was a showman in the biggest spectator sport of the Roman Empire, a sport which lasted 1,000 years. What made a good charioteer? Control the horses. Keep your animals parallel with one another: they have to race together. Know when to accelerate and when to position yourself close to that inner barrier. The best charioteers could really show their skill in a race called the *diversium*, when the winner of a race swapped horses with the charioteer who had come second and they raced against one another again. Running a race with horses a charioteer had never trained with and winning really showcased tremendous skill and horsemanship.

Aurigae – charioteers – were usually slaves, often foreign, particularly Greek. Just like a gladiator, their origin as slaves or freedmen meant they were of low status, but the rags-to-riches life could become reality for a highly skilled sportsman. Talent scouts travelled the provinces of the Roman Empire looking for the next circus star. Just as football scouts today source talented children for training, charioteers would start as boy apprentices, taking part in races (and risking their lives) from as young as 13 years old.

Aurigae may have been born slaves and carried the low status that came with such a birth, but if successful, charioteers could become superstars, and might even buy their own freedom. Once a charioteer had bought his freedom, his cut of the winnings meant the best of the best could amass huge wealth. Historians have averaged a Roman legionary's annual pay at around 900 sestertii (in the first century BC) to 1,200 sestertii (in the first century AD), but the prize money for one chariot race could be anything from 15,000 to 60,000 sestertii.

The sarcastic poet Juvenal compared the pay of a popular charioteer called Lacerta – 'The Lizard' – who rode for the Reds to that of a lawyer, saying it took the combined wages of 100 lawyers to equal the amount of money Lacerta made.

Mind you, being a lawyer was a much safer bet. There may have been big money in chariot racing but life was short. Charioteers thrown onto the hard surface of the heat-baked track, or dragged around by the reins wrapped about their waist, risked their lives during every race. We know of famous charioteers who did survive their careers, but it was such a dangerous sport that the average age of death for a charioteer was around 25.

The charioteer Fuscus – 'tawny'– who raced for the Greens, set a record in AD 35 for being the first driver to win in his first ever race, but he died at 24. Crescens, who raced for the Blues and started as a 13-year-old apprentice, died on the emperor Claudius's birthday, at only 22.

How do we know all this? Inscriptions often give us detailed information: how many races a charioteer won, the names of the horses who raced to victory with him, the horse's lineage and the age the charioteer was when he died.

Superstar charioteers included the first-century Greens sportsman Scorpus. He started life as a slave with nothing and ended it as a spectacularly famous and wealthy celebrity who had bought his freedom and won 2,048 chariot races over ten years before his death at age 26. He became so famous that the Roman poet Martial wrote this epitaph for him:

I am Scorpus, the glory of the roaring circus, you cheered me on, Rome, and I was your darling for a little while. Totting up my victories and believing I was an old man, jealous Lachesis[46] snatched me away in my twenty-seventh year. (Martial, *Epigrams* X.53)

The charioteer Diocles, from the mid-second century AD, made the equivalent of not millions but *billions* of pounds during his career. Perhaps his greatest success was actually surviving because, unlike Scorpus, Diocles did not die on the circus racetrack. Here are just a few of the details from the inscription that memorialises his racing life:

- Diocles was from Lusitania in Spain, one of the top countries for Roman racehorse stud farms.
- In AD 122, aged 18, Diocles drove his first race for the Whites and raced for this team for two years. He then switched factions and raced for the Greens for eight years until finally transferring to the Reds, where his career hit the heights of fame.
- Diocles came in first 1,462 times, mostly racing for the Reds. Of these wins, 815 were when he was first off at the starting gate and kept his lead to the end, 36 of them were when he had been passed by other charioteers and 502 of them were dramatic last-second wins over the finishing line.
- Diocles raced in four-horse teams for twenty-four years, and was skilled and lucky enough to survive and retire from chariot racing at the age of 42.
- If you're interested in numbers, here is just a sample of some of the figures on Diocles's inscription. Nine of Diocles's horses won with him 100 times, and one particular horse won 200 times with him. The charioteer even won twice racing a six-horse team and once with a seven-horse team, which would have been a tremendous show of skill and showmanship as handling a team this big was incredibly difficult. Diocles's horses Cotynus and Pompeianus just

---

46   Lachesis was one of the Fates. She spun the thread of life and decided how long a person would live for.

missed winning a century, coming first ninety-nine times.
- Diocles is called, on his inscription, 'the greatest charioteer ever'.[47]

EMPERORS AND CHARIOT RACING

Thanks to the records of Roman historians, we know that certain emperors were huge fans of the races. There were emperors who liked to get stuck into a bit of chariot racing themselves, emperors with favourite horses and at least one emperor who couldn't be bothered with the sport at all. An enthusiasm for chariot racing even got one emperor into trouble at school.

During the reign of the emperor Augustus, there were about ten or twelve races a day, but Caligula's passion for chariot racing saw this number go up to twenty-four. This emperor was such a huge fan of the Greens that he would eat and sleep in the stables where the Greens' horses were kept, and, according to historian Cassius Dio, he was even said to have poisoned the horses and charioteers of rival teams.

We know from the historian Suetonius that Caligula's favourite chariot horse was Incitatus – 'Swift' or 'In Full Flight'. The night before the races, he would send his soldiers to the neighbourhood where Incitatus was stabled with instructions to make sure the area was quiet and peaceful so that the horse would get a good rest before racing. Caligula loved this horse so much, Incitatus's stable was made of marble, he ate from an ivory manger and Caligula is said to have appointed the horse with a house, furniture and a retinue of slaves. The famous story goes that he planned to make the chariot horse a consul; whether this is true or not, or more likely a sarcastic joke, we may never know. It was certainly a good bit of negative branding for an unpopular emperor.[48]

Claudius put on live animal fights for the crowds after every five races at

47   All of Diocles's statistics can be found on his inscription in the *Corpus of Latin Inscriptions* XIV.2884.

48   Cassius Dio, LIX.14; Suetonius, *Caligula* 55.

the Vatican Circus. He also built marble barriers at the Circus Maximus, rebuilt its turning posts and made sure the senators had proper seats at the races there.

Nero was obsessed with chariot racing from childhood – he even got into trouble at school for talking about the circus too much. At the start of his reign as emperor (when he was still a teenager), he would amuse himself with model chariots drawn by four ivory horses on top of a table. He increased the number of real races so that they didn't stop until nightfall and was so enthusiastic about the sport that he took up driving chariots himself; first in private with his slaves watching, and eventually – as you already know if you gave Nero the attention he deserved above – in front of the crowds at the Circus Maximus. (Suetonius, *Nero* 22)

Nero wasn't the only imperial racing fanatic to drive chariots himself; the emperors Domitian, Commodus, Caracalla and Elagabalus also used to practise the sport.

The philosopher emperor Marcus Aurelius (AD 121–180) was not a big fan of chariot racing. In his list of gratitudes in book I of his *Meditations*, he writes how grateful he is to his boyhood tutor for teaching him not to become a supporter of the Greens or the Blues, or to be a fan of gladiators at the amphitheatre.

The emperor Domitian added two new factions to chariot racing, Purple and Gold, but the Roman public didn't take these to their hearts in the same way as they did the original teams. He once had 100 chariot races staged in a single day. To fit in such a huge number of races, the course was reduced to five laps instead of seven.[49] A massive fan of the sport, Domitian had his palace built on the Palatine Hill, giving him the ultimate grandstand view of the Circus in the valley below.

The emperor Commodus had a favourite chariot horse called Pertinax – 'Constant' or 'Steadfast'. Pertinax raced for the Greens, and after a splendid career the horse retired and left the racetrack for the country. Commodus had Pertinax brought back to the Circus where the horse was displayed with gilded hoofs and a gilded skin cover for its back. This emperor was so enthusiastic about chariot racing that he once put on thirty races in just two hours.[50]

The elderly retired charioteer Euprepes, who had won 782 races, was killed by the emperor Caracalla purely because he supported the rival faction to the one Caracalla supported.

The chariot horse Volucer – 'Flyer' – was a favourite of the emperor Lucius Verus. Verus carried a golden statuette of Volucer about with him, fed the horse treats of grapes and nuts instead of plain old barley and made sure the horse had a supply of expensive purple-dyed blankets. At the end of Volucer's life, the emperor gave him a tomb on the Vatican Hill in Rome. (*Augustan History: Verus* VI.3)

49 Filming the 1959 movie *Ben-Hur* in the heat of a Roman summer, horses could only complete eight laps in a day.

50 Dio, LXXIII.16 and LXXIIII.4. For the murdered Eprepes, see Dio, LXXVIII.1.

INJURIES TO HORSES

They take off, they crowd together, they pull, fight on, inflamed, they leap, they fear and are dreaded, they don't hold back, but with restless hooves they lash the hardened ground … A mass of crushed legs caught in the wheels and the twelve spokes were crammed, the spaces between them jammed until a cracking sound erupted and the revolving edge broke the horses' feet.

(Sidonius Apollinaris, *Carmina* XXIII)

Constant racing and training would have taken its toll, and racing in a sport with no rules meant the horses would have been at risk of injury during every race. The speeds they were driven at, the distances they covered race after race and the inherent dangers of the circus track would certainly have resulted in health problems for these sporty equines:

- Hooves took a hammering on the heat-baked track. Even though sand was scattered on the racetrack, it was still a hard surface and the Romans didn't use horseshoes – at least, not as we know them today.
- Tendons and muscles suffered from stress and ruptures due to constant racing.
- Tongues were cut and injured from the horses' bit. Sometimes the horse's tongue was cut so badly that it needed stitching.
- Joints suffered concussions – where the hooves hit the ground and send a force up through the legs which, if too strong, can lead to lameness. The risk of concussion increases with speed, and racing on harder ground makes horses more susceptible to concussion too. Joints could also suffer a specific injury called a *stremma*, which was a dislocation.
- Eye injuries caused by blows to the horses' heads from rival charioteers and lashes from oppponents' whips. *Sparsori* were employed to sprinkle the sandy track with water to try and reduce the dust, which rose in clouds during a race, but horses' eyes still suffered inflammation from dust irritation.
- Shoulder and back injuries from the great strain on horses' bodies during the dangerous turns at the end of the *spina*.
- Blows inflicted by wheels of opponent chariots.

- A flying tail could become tangled in the traces, the wooden pole of the harness or the chariot itself. Horses' tails were tied up, sometimes with ribbons, to prevent this from happening.

Expensive horses would have been well cared for. If it were possible, swimming sessions were used for treatment of injuries, just as racehorses are given this treatment today. The sulphuric waters west of Tivoli in central Italy were even recommended for warming and healing the injuries of damaged circus horses. Warmed manure wrapped in vine leaves could be applied to reduce inflammation, and salves for the injuries to eyes were made from wool fat (lanolin) and henbane. The seeds from this nightshade family plant were used as a painkiller and mild anaesthetic for both horses and men.

Historians have noticed an object on images of chariot racing, which looks a lot like an axe or a mattock. The speculation is that, in the event of a crash, axes would have been to hand to cut charioteers free from reins, free chariots from their teams of horses and get them off the track as quickly as possible. This tool may also have been used to kill injured horses. Racehorse injuries can end in euthanasia even today, and considering the custom at Roman amphitheatres of making sure gladiators who seemed dead really were dead by hitting them with a mallet at the end of a show, it seems likely that seriously injured horses would have been killed and removed from the racetrack with this axe or mattock.

CHARIOTS AWAY

At last the trumpeter with a blare of his resounding horn calls the restless four-horse teams and propels the swift chariots into the field.

(Sidonius Apollinaris, *Carmina* XXIII)

At the start of a race, the circus procession entered through the *porta
pompae* with the horses in their stalls either side of this gate. If you won
the race, you left through the *porta triumphalis*. The gate you didn't want
to exit through was the *porta libitinensis*, which is the gate through which
the wounded and the dead were carried.

At the start of the race, each team of horses was held in its own starting
box, the *carcer* (prison), behind the starting gates. The horses and charioteers
had no idea what was going on outside, held as they were inside these cells.
It mattered which starting box your team was in because whoever was in
the boxes next to you could affect the outcome of your own race. Which
team would your chariot and horses be racing alongside? Were they going
to block you? Were they riding with the same colours as you, meaning they
would help you, shielding you from a rival faction? In races where more than
one chariot team from the same faction were racing, charioteers could help
the top team from their own faction to win, blocking opponents and using
defence techniques to protect their team members from rivals.

The important decision of who raced in what position was decided
fairly in front of the whole crowd. Rather like the balls that are drawn
from a revolving barrel for teams in the World Cup, balls for each racehorse team would be drawn from a revolving urn. As soon as your team's
ball was chosen, you could choose which starting box you would race
from and, hooves crossed, it was a good choice.

A white cloth – the *mappa* – was dropped to signal the start of a race. At
the same time, a trumpet would sound and, since the charioteers could
see nothing behind the *carceres,* this was their signal to go. The fanfare

would alert the horses too, who, depending on their temperaments, could become very excited and agitated to burst out of their stall.

As soon as the *mappa* was dropped, the spring-loaded mechanism of the starting gate would be set in motion by the men who unbolted the gate. This was so well designed that all the gates opened simultaneously – no false starts – and all the horses burst from the gates at once.

In the first straight stretch of the race, each team of horses kept to its own lane, minimising the chances of a crash at the off. A white line – the *alba ligna* – on the track marked the point where the rules changed. Once they'd crossed the line, it was a hell for leather, anything goes race for first place.[51] Here are some tips on how to eliminate a rival chariot horse team:

- Remember: there are no rules.
- Break the axle of your opponent's chariot.
- Whip the horses in the rival team.
- Rein blows down on your opponent's horses; blows to the head are good.
- Jostle your rival charioteer's chariot.
- Steer your horses into competitors.

These tactics should help force your rival towards a crash into the *spina* wall – an excellent result.

CURSED HORSES

Curse Tablet Found at Hadrumentum in North Africa
I adjure you, demon, whoever you are, and I demand of you from this hour, from this day, from this moment that you torture and kill

---

51   Is this where we get the idiom 'to cross the line' from? Once you cross the line, good behaviour is thrown out the window and it's a 'no rules, do as you wish' game.

the horses of the Greens and Whites, and that you kill in a collision their charioteers Clarus, Felix, Primulus and Romanus, and leave not one breath in their bodies. I adjure you, in the name of him who has set you free in these times, the god of the sea and of the air.

(*Inscriptiones Latinae Selectae*, No. 8753)[52]

While racehorses often wore amulets to protect them from harm, curse tablets were used to invoke the gods or the ghosts of the dead to bring down trouble and death on the heads of rival horses and the men who drove their chariots. These tablets were vicious in their content, perhaps wishing that a rival team might be dragged, broken and destroyed, or cursing them to have a bad start to the race; that right there at the starting gate, the horses would see the ghosts of those who had died a violent, gruesome death and rear up in terror, their race over before it had begun.

To give the curse added power, it was written on lead, if possible. Lead was thought to be the best material to empower the black magic to full force due to its harmful properties, which, it was hoped, would transfer to the tablet's victims. It was no good just cursing the charioteers; you really had to stick the knife into those horses too. So, alongside the names of the *aurigae* – the charioteers – the names of horses were written into the lead, so that they might suffer the same violent misfortune as their charioteer.

The curse needed to be as powerful as possible, and adding some herbal magic to the lead tablet was one way to bring further harm to the horses. Archaeologists have found traces of the herb sage in Roman circus horse curse tablets, as it was thought to cause seizures in horses. The hope was that adding sage to the tablet might cause those damned rival horses to suffer a fit of epilepsy at the starting gate or during the race itself.

---

52   Volumes of Latin inscriptions edited by Hermann Dessau.

Images were sometimes included with the words: bindings drawn around a horse or man, or nails sticking into the charioteer. To 'fix' the curse, actual nails might be driven into the tablet itself.

The location of the curse tablet was another way to give added potency to the magic. If you could manage it, good places to bury the tablets were at the starting gate, the turning posts or in the drains alongside the *spina*. Burying the tablet in a grave, preferably of someone who had died prematurely or violently, also added an extra layer of dark magic to the curse laid upon the heads of horses and men.[53]

Reading some of these curses aloud, it's hard not to feel the absolute intensity and malice of the words. Here are just a few examples of real curses. The fact that the horses are named shows how the destruction of the animals was as important as destroying the charioteer himself.

This first example was found on a lead tablet unburied near Carthage in North Africa and is most likely from the third century AD. What you read here is only part of a quite lengthy curse, the target of which is the Red faction who were due to race on 8 November:

> I invoke you ... that you serve me in the circus on the eighth of November and bind every limb, every sinew, the shoulders, the wrists and the ankles of the charioteers of the Red team ... Torture their thoughts, their minds, their senses so that they do not know what they are doing. Pluck out their eyes so that they cannot see, neither they nor their horses, which they are about to drive: Aegyptus, Callidromus and any other horses yoked with them, Valentinus and Lampadius ... and Lampadius's offspring, Maurus, and Chrysaspis, Iuba and Indus, Palmatus and Superbus ... Bubalus, the offspring of

---

53 Archaeologists have found curse tablets buried at all these locations.

Censorapus, Ereis and any other horse of theirs that might run … may none of them gain victory.

This next curse tablet from Hadrumentum (in Roman Africa) is once more firmly aimed at the horses. It was buried in the grave of someone who had suffered a violent death.

… infernal demones, bind the feet of those horses so that they are unable to run, those horses whose names you have here inscribed and submitted: Incletus, Nitidus, Patricius, Nauta … Bind them so that they cannot run tomorrow or the day after tomorrow in the circuses: … Domina, Canpana, Lambteras … so that at every hour they collapse in the circus.

Found buried in the grave of a Roman official, here's a fragment from a curse tablet, again from Carthage in North Africa, first to third century AD. Five other curse tablets were found with this one, which is aimed at two Blues charioteers: Victoricus and second-team charioteer Secundinus. All the other names on the curse tablet belong to horses and you can see that each and every one of them is soundly cursed:

I invoke you by the mighty names so that you will bind every limb and every sinew of Victoricus – the charioteer of the Blues, to whom the earth, mother of every living thing, gave birth – and of his horses, which he will race: belonging to Secundinus are Iuvenis and Advocatus and Bubalus; under Victoricus are Pompeianus and Baianus and Eximius and Dominator who belongs to Messala. Also bind any others who may be yoked with them. Bind their legs, their speed, their bounding and their running; blind their eyes so they cannot see, and twist their soul and heart so that they cannot breathe. As this rooster has been bound by its feet, hands and head, so bind the legs and head and the heart of Victoricus the charioteer of the Blues tomorrow; and also bind the horses which he will race.[54]

---

54   Translations of these curses reproduced with the kind permission of John G. Gager, author of the fascinating and detailed book *Curse Tablets and Binding Spells from the Ancient World*.

Before we leave the races, and to clear your mind of all that cursing and eye plucking, here are some lines from the Roman poet Virgil's description of chariot horses and racing:

See above all their courage and their years
Their other merits and their lineage
The pain they feel in defeat, the honour of a victory.
Behold the chariots in headlong race!
Bursting from the barrier they seize upon the plain.
The hopes of young charioteers rise up
And shaking fear drains the leaping heart.
How they urge the whirling whip
And bending forward let loose the reins.
With burning force the wheel flies
Now bending low, now reaching high
They seem carried through the empty air
And soar uplifted to the sky.
No delay, no rest, a cloud of yellow sand is borne aloft
Wet from pursuer's foam and snorting breaths
So great the love of fame, so dear the victor's palm.

(*Georgics* III.103–12)

ANIMALS IN THE WORLD OF FASHION AND BEAUTY

'Cilician Socks'
These aren't made of wool but the beard of the stenchy goat. Your
foot can hide in this hairy pocket.
(Martial, *Epigrams* XIV.140)

FURS, FLEECES AND FEATHERS

Nothing says glamour more than a pair of goaty socks. The Roman province
of Cilicia in south-eastern Anatolia (modern-day Turkey) was famous for its
production of this popular goat-hair cloth. Cilicia was where the goats with
the longest hair were bred and the province gave its name to the Latin for
'hair-cloth' or *cilicium*.

The goat was just one animal that provided the Romans with a useful
product. Even the mole contributed to Roman comfort, according to writer
of all things animal, Pliny, who noted seeing coverlets made from the skins
of these tiny animals. Exotic animal furs and skins were imported from the
east, along with the ivory and turtleshell used for expensive hair pins and
combs. Whether it was a bird, a sheep or a spiny hedgehog, the following
shows how the Romans could put an animal to good use.

What a luxury to lie back on bedding stuffed with the inner layer of
swans' feathers. Can't get your hands on a swan? Not only could you eat
geese, including their pickled feet, but selling their feathers by the weight

to those who could afford a bit of goose feather bedding could generate an extra income. Some geese could even be plucked twice a year as they grew new feathers. Feathers that grow closest to the goose's body were best, and German geese had a good reputation as their feathers were the most brilliant white. We do know, however, that some goose feathers caused a bit of a flap in the Roman military. When Pliny was writing in the first century, he recorded how Roman officers were getting into trouble because they were sending whole cohorts of soldiers out on literal wild goose chases – instead of guarding their outposts, legionaries were sent off to capture geese. (Pliny, X.27)

Apulia, Parma and Altinum in Italy could all provide first-rate fleeces, with Apulian fleeces having a good reputation for cloak making in particular. If a breed of sheep was considered to provide excellent wool, they could even be given their own jackets (the best were made from the wool of Arabian sheep) to prevent their own fleece from getting too dirty so that washing, dyeing and bleaching was easier. The wool from Narbonne (modern-day France) and Egypt was a bit too coarse and hairy for garment making but was excellent for extending the life of old clothes that needed darning. This kind of shaggy wool was great for carpet making too. If you couldn't stuff your mattress with the wonderful wool from Leuconia (in modern-day Turkey) or were too poor to use any wool at all, you'd have to swap animal for plant and use 'circus stuffing': cut-up marsh reeds – a rough substitute for the soft wool of a sheep.

If you were a slave or a gladiator, you would have been very happy to put a *pilleus* on your head because it meant your days of slavery were over. This tight-fitting conical hat was made of felted wool[55] and was given to a slave when they were granted their freedom, or to a victorious gladiator when he was finally discharged. According to Roman military writer

---

55 Wool was felted before it was spun. The method is to press and flatten the wool. My daughter, Alice, felted a model of our dog by brushing out his loose fur then bashing a clump of the loosened fur (not the dog) with a felting needle. It takes a lot of hard work and time to get the wool/fur flattened and shaped. The Romans used felted wool and fur for both hats and shoes. It's a comfortable, compact and relatively waterproof material.

Vegetius, Roman soldiers also wore the same little hat (this time made of leather) when they were off duty, the idea being that, always having something on their head, the helmet would feel less burdensome.

It's no surprise to read that animal hides and fur were used to make Roman clothes (if they needed brushing down, why not use an ox-tail brush to do the job?), but who would have thought the spiny skin of the following tiny animal would have been used in Roman clothes manufacture to clean, smooth out and 'card'[56] wool before it was spun?

How to Kill a Hedgehog

1. Since the hedgehog rolls up into a ball when it's afraid, your first job is to get it to unroll.
2. Sprinkle the hedgehog with hot water.
3. Now that it's unrolled, take one of the hind legs and hang the hedgehog up.
4. The animal will die of starvation. There's no other way of killing it without damaging the skin.
5. Collect the spiny skin and get to work on that wool.

(Pliny, VIII.56)

THE PRICE OF SKIN

In AD 301, the Roman emperor Diocletian issued a list of price caps on everything from the cost of an egg to the wage of a sewer cleaner. Here are the maximum prices allowed for a range of animal skins:

- Wolf, untanned: 25 denarii
- Goat, untanned: 40 denarii
- Hyena, untanned: 40 denarii
- Deer, first class, tanned: 100 denarii

---

56 Carding is the process of brushing the wool to separate and clean all the fibres to get them ready for spinning.

- Bear, untanned: 100 denarii
- Bear, tanned: 150 denarii
- Lion, tanned: 1,000 denarii
- Leopard, tanned: 1,250 denarii

According to average wages at the time, at 2 denarii per customer, a barber would have to serve 500 people to earn the cost of a tanned lion skin. No wonder such an animal as this was a status symbol for the wealthy.

THE COLOUR PURPLE

'Murices, The Purple Fish'
You dress, ungrateful man, in cloaks dyed in our blood, and as if
that weren't enough, we are eaten too.
(Martial, *Epigrams* XIII.87)

Wool and leather were dyed with all sorts of things: seaweed, used for green dye; the madder plant, to make red dye; and kermes, an insect that lives on oak trees, used as a scarlet dye. But there was no higher-status colour for the Romans than purple; the tiny marine snails and shellfish that provided the dye were big business as there was an absolute *insania* – madness – for this hugely expensive colour.

Here are some purple facts.

- The murex marine snail was also called *purpura* – the 'purple fish' or simply 'purples'. Not just the term for a marine animal, *purpura* was the word for 'purple' and also for 'high status', and even eventually meant 'emperor' – the 'Purple One'.
- Different species of marine molluscs were used for creating different shades of dye; for example, *Murex trunculus* produced a blue-purple colour. The 'reef-purple' was so named as it was caught on sea reefs, while the 'pebble-purple' was named after a pebble in the sea. The 'seaweed-purple' was, you've guessed it, fed on seaweed, and the 'mud-purple' was believed to feed on slimy mud.
- Shellfish came from all over, including from Meninx in Africa and Sparta in Europe, but the most expensive and sought-after purple dye came from the shellfish of Tyre (in modern-day Lebanon).

- Which piece of the murex caught the attention of humans? Unfortunately for certain species of sea snail, a hypobranchial gland right next to their rectums produced a mucus that could be processed into dye. Even worse luck for the sea snail, each gland only produced a tiny bit of mucus, so it took *a lot* of snails to make this dye. Researchers have come up with the figure of about 8,000 to 10,000 marine molluscs to 1 gram of the dye. Even when enough molluscs had been collected, it was a long process to produce the sought-after purple. That's why the trade in shellfish for dye manufacturing was such big business, why purple was the most expensive colour and why purple was the colour of wealth.
- But there are different shades of wealth, which had to be reflected in the shades of purple. (Dyed twice, not just once, Tyrian purple was the most expensive and famous purple.) Sometimes, emperors would forbid the use of particular tones of purple dye for clothing, so that only they could wear it. According to the historian Suetonius, Nero was said to have hauled a woman out of one of his recitals for wearing a restricted purple. Who did she think she was?! After the woman had been stripped of her clothing, she was stripped of her property too. (Suetonius, *Nero* 32)
- This really wasn't the colour to get wrong. Those little sea snails were even the cause of an execution. During the reign of Roman emperor Caligula, King Ptolemy of Mauretania came in to take his seat at a gladiatorial show, dressed in a purple cloak. His purple attire attracted a lot of attention and this didn't go unnoticed by Caligula. Surely choosing to wear this colour meant Ptolemy had ambitious plans? According to the historian Suetonius, Ptolemy's clothing was a red flag (or rather, a purple one) and Caligula had Ptolemy put to death. (Suetonius, *Caligula* 35)

DYING FOR DYE

How did the Romans catch their shellfish? First, they would chuck a few cockles into a small woven vessel, a bit like a little lobster pot, and throw it into deep water. The pot would have had a rope attached for hauling it out of the water. The 'purples' would go for the cockles, which would shut up fast when they were nipped at. The pot was then lifted out and all the shellfish would be hanging from the bait.

The juice from the gland was discharged only at the moment of death, so fishermen would deliver live molluscs to the dying factories where the sea snails could survive for up to seven weeks. Manufacturers would keep the snails alive until it was time to start the process of putting that mucus to work, and then the larger snails would have their shells stripped off, leaking out their expensive slime as they died. Smaller molluscs were crushed alive and the mucus collected.

The Romans really didn't like things to go to waste, so those broken shells were not just thrown away. They were used for decoration (how about making a grotto look magical?) and as ingredients in beauty products. Larger shells were used as beautiful containers. Shells were also dug into layers of soil to give good drainage and great quantities of broken shells were used in construction work as aggregate.

What To Do With Your Mucus

Once all that mucus had been collected, it needed to be turned into dye:

1. Put all the mucus discharge into a leaden vat and add loads of salt. The salt will help avoid decay. Leave the vats in the open air for three days.
2. Put your salty concoction into a stone or metal container, add water and begin to heat. Keep on a moderate heat for about nine days, then strain the mixture.
3. Test the colour by dipping in a clean fleece. Heat for longer if the colour isn't right.
4. Different blends in your mixture can give you a scarlet dye if preferred. To create this luxury blood-red hue (the famous 'Tyrian purple'), you will need to add whelk mucus to your shellfish concoction. Don't use whelk mucus on its own as it doesn't create a colour-fast dye.[57]
5. Fleeces should be soaked for five hours then carded. (*Cardus* is Latin for thistle – at least this is what to tell any nervous hedgehogs.)
6. Dip your fleece again until it has soaked up all the liquid.

(Pliny, IX.62–3)

---

57 Other factors that affect the shade of the dye are sunlight intensity, the amount of salt used, and types and amounts of molluscs used.

THE PONG OF PURPLE

The first-century poet Martial counts purple dye in a list of things that stink: sulphurous waters, the putrid smell of a fishpond, a goat, a soldier's pair of old shoes, a fox or a fleece dyed twice in Tyrian purple. (*Epigrams* IV.4)

Was Martial right? What with the fishy smell of the sea and the long process of heating a salty discharge from a gland near a sea snail's bum, this whole dying process was incredibly whiffy. If it just wasn't foul enough, there was a little extra ingredient to up the stench: human urine was added in equal quantities to the water to give a more delicate purple tone. This meant that although you might absolutely reek, you could rest easy in the knowledge that your outfit was a high-status colour in a stylish shade.

ANIMAL BEAUTY PRODUCTS

It seems a trifle but to keep the women happy I won't omit it: the knuckle bone of a white bullock boiled for forty days and nights until it melts into a liquid and applied on a small linen cloth does an excellent job at giving the skin a radiance and smoothing out wrinkles.

(Pliny, *Natural History* XXVIII.50)

The Romans were just as bothered by wrinkles, body hair, eyebrows and complexions as we are today. Hadrian (r. AD 117 to 138) was the first Roman emperor to sport a full beard, triggering the beard as a trend for the emperors who followed him. Although only fragments of it survive, one famous Roman author even wrote an entire work on women's beauty tips (Ovid's *Medicamina Faciei Femineae*, known as 'On Cosmetics' or 'The Art of Beauty'). Archaeologists might have found beauty product containers made of costly ivory, but they've also found examples made of inexpensive material, such as cheap glass and wood, so we know that cosmetics were not just used by the rich. Animal products formed a good deal of these products, with all sorts of animal body parts contributing to the business of beauty.

Just like a celebrity today can start a trend for a beauty product, it was the emperor Nero's wife, Poppaea, who started the fashion for using ass's milk for the skin. Wrinkles? Ass's milk. Want soft skin? Ass's milk.

Poppaea would apparently bathe in bathtubs of the stuff and was never without herds of she-asses. She also came up with a doughy facemask made of flour and ass's milk, which was named after her – *Poppaeana* – and copied by other elite Roman women who used Poppaea's beauty treatment and bathed their faces in ass's milk up to seven times a day. (Juvenal VI.461–3)

Deer antlers seem to turn up in a few Roman beauty treatments. Hair falling out? Burn some deer antlers down to ash, mix it with some wine and use it as a hair mask to prevent hair loss. This concoction will also help get rid of head lice if you have any.[58]

If you were an ancient Roman ass, the last person you wanted around you was someone with thin and greying hair since it was the ass's very own genitals that were looked on as a treatment. The genitals were burnt to ash, then ground with oil in a leaden mortar. This ashy mixture was then applied to the shaved head of the grey- and thin-haired person, whose hair would supposedly grow back thicker. Urine from a young ass, collected and applied to the scalp, was also believed to be a good hair thickener. Mix some nard – a very expensive perfume – with it to get rid of the smell. If you can't get hold of an ass, hare's flesh reduced to ash and mixed with myrtle oil will do the job. (Pliny, XXVIII.46–9)

Want to dye your hair the colour of a raven? Collect some leeches and leave them to rot for forty days in a vat of red wine. Alternatively, mix your leeches with about a litre of vinegar, then apply the mixture in the full sun. When you're dyeing your hair, make sure you have some oil in

58   Deer antler and hooves, known as 'hartshorn', has a chemical reaction when it's burnt and produces a type of baking soda substance. Perhaps it was this chemical ingredient the Romans were working with.

your mouth as a slick protective layer, as the dye is so strong that if it gets near your teeth you'll end up with raven black teeth too. (Pliny, XXXII.23)

In the Roman Gallic provinces a soap was used that dyed the hair red. It was made from animal fat and ash, the best combination being a paste or liquid made from beech tree ash and goat's fat, a particular favourite of the German men of Roman Gaul. (Pliny, XXVIII.51)

If it was your eyebrows you wanted to darken, apply a mixture of goat's flesh burnt to ash and mixed with oil. (Pliny, XXVIII.46)

Unwanted hair? Body hair was a no-no for the Romans; women's legs had to be smooth and under-arm hair plucked and dealt with. There's even a recipe for removing hair that was used on slaves who were being sold at market, because the last thing a Roman wanted was a hairy slave. The blood, gall and liver of a tunny fish (fresh or preserved) was mixed with cedar oil and then stored in a lead box for a handy hair removal paste. Here are a few other Roman depilatories for rubbing onto your hairy body:

- Dried and ground frog boiled down in oil.
- Beaver oil and honey.
- Roasted leeches applied with vinegar – an added bonus is that the smell of the burning leeches is a good insect repellent. (Pliny, XXXII.47)

The Romans recommended eggs and honey as face masks for nourishing the skin, goose grease for dry and cracked lips, and egg as a sunscreen. I think that all sounds pretty reasonable, but how about these animal ingredients for a beautiful complexion:

- Lion fat mixed with rose oil to feed the skin and keep the complexion clear. (The Romans liked to make use of everything and we have to wonder if all those lions killed in the amphitheatres came in handy after their death.) (Pliny, XXVIII.25)
- All those shellfish, so integral to dye manufacturing, were useful for the skin too. Reduce the crushed shells to ash, mix this into a paste with honey and apply to the face for seven days in a row. On the eighth day, paste the face with egg white (known to tighten the skin) and your face will be plumped and wrinkle free. Interestingly, 2,000 years after the Romans were selling it, there are beauty companies today that advertise products made from crushed shellfish. Full of calcium carbonate, apparently it detoxifies the skin. (Pliny, XXXII.27)
- For a rosy-coloured complexion, rub some bull's dung on your cheeks. Or get your hands on some crocodile dung. Crocodile dung

A first-century AD Roman pyxis – a cylindrical container used to store beauty products, whether it was cosmetics, jewellery or perfume bottles. This one, decorated with several Cupids, is made of ivory. (The Metropolitan Museum of Art, New York)

is mentioned by a few Roman writers as a beauty product for the skin. Perfect for a Roman who wanted a paler complexion, this dried reptilian dung could be patted onto the skin. Mixed with cypress oil, the same poop was used to get rid of spots and blotches on the face. (Pliny, XXVIII.28)

- The Romans really didn't seem to appreciate the beauty of freckles. If you wanted to give someone freckles, you had to drown a gecko in wine, whip it out and then whoever drank the lizardy wine would be freckle-faced. If you didn't want freckles, you needed to mix up some egg yolk with honey and soda, then use the mixture to remove the freckles. Alternatively, the old crocodile dung treatment has the same effect. (Pliny, XXIX.22)
- You could always cover up a spot with a *splenium* – a soft leather patch that you stuck onto the skin. It might even be cut into a pretty shape, like a crescent moon.
- *Oesypum* – the grease and dirt from unwashed wool, equivalent to our lanolin and used in skin products today – made a softening face cream. The greasy sweat was gathered from any part of the sheep's wool, then warmed and cooled in a bronze pot. The fats that floated to the top were collected, strained through linen and then heated in the sun. The result was a white cream that you stored away in a box. (Pliny, XXIX.10)
- The best-made *oesypum* creams were the ones that did not melt in the hand when rubbed in water and those that still smelled strongly of the grease, which is probably why when the Roman poet Ovid talked about this beauty treatment he also mentioned how much it stank. (Ovid, *The Art of Love* III.213)
- Ovid also gives a recipe for getting rid of spots which involves getting your hands on some *alcyoneum*. This ingredient, he tells us, is extracted from birds' nests. Mix it up with some Attic honey 'from yellow cones' to make your concoction into a spreadable paste, and apply to the spot-troubled skin. (Ovid, *The Art of Beauty* III.77–82)

Finally, a Roman recipe for keeping breasts in tip-top shape. Reduce partridge eggshells to ash, then mix in a bit of beeswax and cadmia.[59] Apply

---

59 Cadmia is a zinc oxide produced when zinc is burnt and is an ingredient still used today in all sorts of skin preparations.

to the breasts to keep them firm. You can also perk up drooping breasts by tracing a circle around them three times with a partridge egg. If you can't find a partridge, a quail egg does the same job. Good luck with that. (Pliny, XXX.45)

Now that you've been soothed with moisturisers and have put your feet up in some goat-hair socks, forgive me for breaking the mood of the spa with the roar of the Roman arena.

ANIMALS IN THE AMPHITHEATRE

He thrust his spear into a charging bear
once king beneath the Arctic heaven's vault,
he laid low a lion, of extraordinary size, wondrous to behold,
a lion worthy of Herculean hands,
and he stretched dead a swift-footed leopard with a far-dealt wound.

(Martial, *On the Spectacles* 17(15))

There's no doubt that animals suffered for the sake of Roman entertainment, not just in the arena itself but in their training too. What did the Romans see at an animal display in the Roman games? Not every animal had to be a dead animal to make a show spectacular.

Harnessed bears and tigers kissed by trainers; lions trained to chase after hares, catch them and then give them up from their jaws; bulls ridden by stunt riders; seals trained to salute the audience and come when their names were called; a lion decorated with gold leaf in his mane – and don't forget the tightrope-walking elephants who swayed and danced their way through our earlier chapter on elephants.

The beastly bottom line, however, was that animals ended up in amphitheatres to die for human entertainment, and you had to get there early to see it happen. Here's the timetable for the day:

- Morning: Beast hunts. Starting the day off were the *venationes*, which were displays where animals were hunted by *bestiarii* – human 'beast fighters' – or pitted against one another in wild beast fights. You might have a favourite *bestiarius*, like Carcophorus, killer of the 'Arctic' bear and 'swift-footed leopard', who starred in the poem at the opening of this chapter.

- Lunchtime: Human executions. The emperor Claudius was said to arrive at dawn and loved to stay and watch the lunch-break executions.
- Afternoon: Gladiatorial combats began. As the fighters took to the arena and battled it out with one another, the crowd joined in, shouting out *Habet!* ('He is hit!'), when a gladiator was wounded; *Missos!* ('Spare them!'); or *Iugula!* ('Cut his throat!'). At the end of a fight, an attendant dressed as the god Mercury walked round and tested any prostrate bodies with a red-hot iron to make sure they were really dead.

From the first to second century AD, part of a Roman relief, which shows animals in a venatio *– a 'beast hunt'. The inscription tells us that this was a scene from the third day of the games. (The Metropolitan Museum of Art, New York)*

READING BONES

In 2004–05, excavations were carried out at two properties in Driffield Terrace in York, north-east England. What did they find deep down in the layers of earth? Eighty-two Roman-era skeletons. At least forty-six of the bodies had been decapitated by a blow coming from behind, right at the moment of death.

Most of the skeletons were young males and they had a long list of injuries. When experts examined the bones, they found evidence of teeth knocked out by blows coming from the right; healed injuries to the skull; a healed sword cut to the thigh; sword wounds to the backs of the hands; blade cuts to the neck; broken wrists; twisted ankles; blows to the chin; and fractured vertebrae. What's this got to do with animals? One of the skeletons showed large bite wounds to the pelvis. Experts believe the bite marks were made by a large carnivore, probably a lion but possibly a tiger or bear.

For a few years in the third century AD, York was home to a Roman emperor, Septimius Severus. About 100 years later, the Roman emperor Constantius Chlorus lived and ruled for a short while in York. If the centre of the Roman world is based in York – or *Eboracum*, as the Romans called it – then it's going to get some important visitors. High-status people required top-quality entertainment. Some experts believe that these young male skeletons, with their sword wounds and decapitated skulls, belonged to gladiators – a hammer blow to the skull or decapitation were quick ways of finishing off a dying gladiator – and that the Driffield excavations are the site of a gladiators' graveyard.

With York being so important and attracting high-status politicians and officials – after all, a Roman emperor was ruling from there – the grizzly wound to the pelvis suggests that York wasn't just putting on small shows on a tight budget in which deer and rabbits were hunted for entertainment. It seems Roman *Eboracum* was where you could see the big carnivores in action. This great carnivore who roared in an amphi-theatre in the north-east of England clearly got his teeth stuck into his human opponent.

HANDLING YOUR ANIMALS

Huge logistics were involved in supplying animals to the Roman arenas. If the weather was bad at sea, maybe all those African panthers you'd bought just weren't going to make it on time to the games or your expensive menagerie might have been wrecked on the ocean waves and not arrive at all. The animals that arrived in Rome would have travelled over land and across waters from Africa, Europe or the far-off lands of the East. Leopards were caught in nets and delivered from Syria; bears were bundled into cages and transported from Armenia, Germany, Greece, Persia, Spain and even Scotland. Kalliena – known today as Kalyan – in western India exported exotic animals including tigers, leopards, monkeys and hyenas, which were shipped on long, stress-filled journeys around the Indian Ocean to the Egyptian port of Alexandria, and then on to the Roman port of Ostia. No wonder animals could sometimes arrive bedraggled, unhealthy or even dead.

It wasn't always the big predators who stalked and roared across the sands of Roman arenas either, especially if you were in the audience at one of the smaller amphitheatres when locally sourced animals were on display. Even at the biggest arenas, huge numbers of domestic game animals, such as hares, rabbits, boars, goats and deer, filled up the entertainment menu as audiences got to watch a real-life hunt play out in front of them, complete with hunting dogs and hunters on horseback chasing the panicked prey on display.

How do you get hippos, lions, panthers, deer, bulls, bears, crocodiles and a rhinoceros onto the stage floor of an amphitheatre such as the Colosseum? And how do you get the animals to perform once they're there? Follow these handy tips to ensure they put on a good show.

- First of all, make sure you've paid any taxes on imported exotic animals. If you live in the fourth century AD, this will include bears too.
- Keep your animals in *vivaria* – enclosures – as far away from built-up areas as possible. Remember: there are laws about animals escaping and harming or killing anyone. No animals should be kept on a

public way. If your animals damage any property – slaves included – you'll have to pay a hefty fine.

- Transport your animals to the arena the night before a show. You've got to have them ready for action first thing in the morning.
- If the show is at a big amphitheatre like the Colosseum, underground tunnels will channel your animals to holding cells underneath the arena.
- When it's time for the show, haul your animals up in cages using the pulleys and chains provided and then release them onto the arena floor via trapdoors. If you're putting on a show in Rome's Colosseum, you'll need about 200 staff to hoist up the twenty-four animal elevators around the amphitheatre. Each of these lifts can take the weight of two lions. You will really wow your audience when the animals suddenly appear from underground and run out of the trapdoors.
- Animals at less spectacular amphitheatres can be kept in cages at ground level around the arena and their cage doors raised up when it's time to perform.
- The thunderous roar of thousands of spectators, the unfamiliar surroundings, the physical condition of the animal after the stresses of transportation and confinement, as well as basic fear, could mean your wild beasts might not do what the crowd expects. Have whips and fire handy to goad reluctant animals into performing. If they won't move out of their cages, smoke them out. Starve them before a show if you have to. Work them up into a rage in any way you can – throw straw dummies at the bulls – hopefully this will result in the display of ferocity that's expected. After all, no one wants to see a docile animal. Don't forget what happened at the emperor Probus's games in the third century AD. When 100 maned lions were let loose from their enclosures, they were so listless they didn't rush from their cages in the way that excites a crowd. Some of them were reluctant even to exit into the arena at all. This is *not* what a crowd wants to see! In the end, the animals that didn't have the spirit to charge were simply killed by an onslaught of arrows. Not much of a show.
- It's so annoying when a bear or lion just won't attack the person tied to a stake in front of them. You don't want the crowd to get bored, so force the victims to wave their hands about. Animals react to this type of movement and will hopefully go in for the kill.

- Keep alert. Remember these stories to remind you of the dangers of working with wild animals: the lion that attacked and killed two boys who were raking the sand-covered arena between shows; the trained lion who bit its trainer in the arena and was then speared to death on the orders of the emperor.

The docks at Ostia can be a perilous place – after all, it's where the exotic animals are shipped in for the shows. It might not be the safest environment to lose yourself in an artistic reverie. The famous sculptor Pasiteles was sitting here working on a caged lion for his next piece of art when a leopard escaped from its own cage and caused the artist some serious danger. (Pliny, XXXVI.4)

EMPERORS AND WILD BEASTS

It was important for a Roman emperor to be seen, and what better place than on a high podium seat at the Roman games? Attending these *spectacula*, or shows, was a good political move and a way of interacting with the people. Ancient historians help give us a view into just what these powerful men brought to the Roman spectacles:

Caligula is said to have saved some money by finding a replacement for the costly cattle needed to feed the wild animals he was providing for his games. Why buy cattle for them when you can get free meat from elsewhere? Free meat being a few of the criminals condemned to die in the arena. (Suetonius, *Caligula* 27)

Claudius put on a wild beast show, which included 300 bears and the same number of African animals, every one of them slaughtered, and made all the more entertaining by races where the chariots were not pulled by horses but by camels. (Cassius Dio, LX.7)

It was the emperor Titus who finished the building of the Colosseum, which was known originally as The Flavian Amphitheatre. In AD 80, he put on the first big shows to celebrate its opening, giving the crowds a display of cranes fighting with one another, as well as four elephants in combat. These inaugural games went on for an incredible 100 days and up to 9,000 animals were said to have been slaughtered in total. (Cassius Dio, LXVI.25)

Domitian built a school for wild animals and *bestiarii* – the beast fighters. Just like the human fighters, animals would be put through their paces to get them 'arena ready'. If an animal showed a lot of ferocity it would be marked out as suitable for human executions.

The same emperor, Domitian, was an excellent bowman and loved to show off his skills. One of his trademark tricks was shooting two arrows into an animal's head so that it looked as if it had horns. (Suetonius, *Domitian* 19)

Marcus Aurelius was not a fan of gladiatorial fights or wild beast shows. His son, however, was entirely different. The complete opposite of his father, the emperor Commodus had a huge enthusiasm for gladiatorial combats and animal hunts. (Commodus was played by Joaquin Phoenix in the film *Gladiator*, and if you remember the character you already know we're in for trouble.) He collected any exotic animals he could get his hands on and either used them in arena spectacles or enjoyed killing them himself on his own private estates.

Commodus seems to have been a top-notch marksman, perfecting his skills with lessons from Parthian bowmen and Moroccan javelin throwers. His skills became so honed that he couldn't keep these talents to himself and loved to show off his animal hunting expertise to the public during arena shows.

On one occasion, he is said to have killed five hippos and two elephants over two days, as well as slaughtering rhinoceroses and a giraffe, all by his own hands. The historian Cassius Dio gives us the details, writing that he was actually there himself at some of these shows and witnessed Commodus's actions first-hand. In AD 192, over 100 years after the games held to celebrate the opening of the Colosseum, Commodus is said to have killed 100 lions in one show, and at another he walked along raised platforms firing javelins at animals from these high terraces. From his advantageous position, he was entirely safe from attack but could get pretty up close to his prey. On the first day alone he slaughtered 100 bears.

Another historian, Herodian, also alive at the time, adds deer, lions and leopards to the animals Commodus killed as he ran around on his platforms. His aim was apparently so good that he only needed one javelin shot per animal, as after one death wound to the forehead or heart the animal died. (Cassius Dio, LXXII.10 & 18 and Herodian, I.15.3)

The emperor Caracalla (AD 188–217) was just 10 years old when he became emperor. He was known to look away and weep when criminals were killed by wild animals. (*Augustan History: Caracalla* I.5)

HOW TO SECURE ANIMALS FOR THE ROMAN ARENA

If you want to make it in the political world or raise your profile, you need to give the public a good spectacle. So how do you get the animals you need for the games?

- Use your contacts. Do you know a Roman governor in the provinces who can help you with a supply of animals? Or are you friends with a king? During the Republic, Roman general Sulla had an ally in King Bochus of Mauretania, which meant Sulla got a supply of 100 lions for his games.
- Hire professional animal hunters from Africa or India.

- Can you accept exotic animals instead of money when collecting tax from any Roman provinces?
- Use the army. *Venatores immunes* (literally translating as 'exempt hunters') were soldiers who were released from regular duties and assigned to collect animals native to the provinces in which they were stationed. Written by a Roman soldier called Antonius Proculus, a letter found in Egypt from the late first century records how soldiers had carried out their orders and hunted every species of Egyptian wild animal and bird that they could find for a year. Proculus added that all the animals, cages, nets and hunting equipment were sent on to his superior. Soldiers might specialise in hunting a particular animal depending on which province they were stationed in. *Ursarii* – from the Latin word *ursus*, meaning bear – were specialist military bear hunters. We know from military inscriptions that, unfortunately for German bears, these soldier-hunters were active in that particular part of the world. One centurion, Tarquitius Restutus Pisauro, caught fifty bears in six months when he was stationed in Cologne

How a Lack of Leopards Can Ruin Your Political Career

If you were a Roman official, then getting hold of animals and putting on games was a major way of promoting your career (and gobbling up your cash). In 51 BC, when the great Roman statesman, writer, orator, philosopher and lawyer (what have I been doing with my time?) Cicero was governor of Cilicia in modern-day Turkey, a certain Marcus Caelius Rufus wrote to him repeatedly, badgering Cicero for help with some leopards. Could Cicero organise the capture of the animals? It would be such a help to Caelius's career, as he really did need to put on some games and everyone loves a leopard. Other governors had sent animals to that other politician, Curio, so why couldn't Cicero do the same for him? More letters arrived. Hello? Remember the leopards? Caelius wouldn't give up, but it was good news for the big cats – Cicero had no plans to send out any animal hunters. Here's Caelius getting desperate:

I have raised the question of leopards in almost all of my letters to you! It will be a stain on your character that Patiscus has sent ten panthers to Curio and you are not sending many more than that to me.

Curio has given me these ten <u>and</u> ten others from Africa. If you will only remember and fetch some from Cybria and write to Pamphylia – they say they are captured mostly from there. What you want you'll get. (Cicero, *Letters to Friends* VIII.9.3)

And here's Cicero's sarcastic reply:

As regards the leopards – on my orders the normal hunting parties are performing their work assiduously but there's a mysterious shortage! They're saying what leopards there are, are complaining non-stop on account of the traps and ambushes made for them and no one else here in my province. Consequently, the leopards have decided to hightail it out of the province and into Caria. (Cicero, *Letters to Friends* II.11.2)

If you want any more proof that securing those animals for the arena wasn't always easy, we can travel forward several hundred years from Cicero's dealings with Caelius and read the letters of a fourth-century AD Roman statesman called Symmachus. In order to promote his son's political career, Symmachus decided to put on games in his son's name. Letter after letter details all the paperwork and hoops he had to jump through to organise his beast shows and chariot races. We know that he arranged for sixteen horses to be delivered, all collected from Spain. Did sixteen horses race? Five died during their transportation to Rome. Others died at Rome before bursting through the starting gates and making it onto the racetrack. Some of his animals for the games died at sea in a shipwreck during transportation. His twenty-nine German prisoners, who were to fight as gladiators in the arena, took charge of their destinies by taking their own lives. The night before these games opened, the only bears that had actually been delivered were a few cubs, and these were exhausted and wasting away from hunger. Dead gladiators, dead horses and cute bear cubs who looked close to death instead of fierce-looking man-eaters: not the results Symmachus was looking for.

HOW TO OUTDO A RIVAL
AND PROMOTE YOURSELF

Animals could really affect reputations. Here's how to use them to advertise yourself to the masses. Just think of it as an ancient game of Top Trumps where upping numbers, wowing with a particular animal or being inventive could elevate one man's games above another's.

Take lions, for example. In 93 BC, Lucius Sulla showed a combat of adult maned lions, the first unchained lions to be put on display at Rome. Then, at his games at the Circus Maximus in 55 BC, Pompey (the Roman general whose chariot harnessed with elephants wouldn't fit through Rome's gate) outdid Sulla with 600 lions, 315 of which had glorious manes. Nine years later, Julius Caesar held a series of four triumphs[60] where he showed off 400 lions. Male lions were especially prized (probably the hairstyle), so if Caesar's were maned, they would have outdone Pompey's 315 males.

So much for lions. How about impressing the crowd with a new species? Be the first person to show a hippopotamus at Rome and you'll get your name in the history books like a certain Marcus Scaurus did in 58 BC. Three years later, Pompey gave the Roman public their first sight of a rhinoceros and a Gallic lynx at Rome, and Julius Caesar topped it with the first giraffe. In fact, Caesar spent huge sums of money promoting his career through spectacular shows, going into debt with an innovative display of Thessalian bull-fighting (where bulls were killed by men riding horses beside them and breaking the animals' necks by twisting them back by the horns) and wowing the crowd with men fighting on castles on the backs of elephants. (Pliny, VIII.70)

Once you'd impressed your public by showing them a strange new species, what else could you do to make your games memorable? You could be inventive and have the animals used in new and exciting ways. Here are some examples from the Roman arenas:

---

60   The *triumphus* was a huge processional display put on to celebrate military success.

- Animals pitted against one another that would never have confronted each other in the wild. In AD 80, tigers were made to fight against lions in the emperor Titus's games at the Colosseum. These two big cats had never been seen in combat with one another before. Other fighting animal pairings included a bull chained to a bear; a leopard against a bull; and a combat staged between an elephant and a bull.
- A pregnant sow, slaughtered as it was giving birth. (Perhaps actually giving birth *because* of the danger it found itself in?) When this actually happened in the arena at Rome, the piglets were seen tottering from the body of their dead mother. 'What genius from unexpected events!' wrote the poet Martial when he witnessed this (*On the Spectacles* 16(14)).
- Flood the arena with water and have trained horses and bulls swim around pulling carriages while a naval battle is fought between men. (Cassius Dio, LXVI.25)
- At the games of the emperor Septimius Severus in AD 204, sixty wild boar fought together, and a host of animals were killed, including an elephant. How could the show be a spectacle to remember? The whole amphitheatre was constructed to look like a giant ship. As it broke apart, hundreds of animals poured from the ship into the arena. Bears, lions and lionesses, panthers, bison, asses, tigers and ostriches all ran through the arena and were slaughtered in front of the crowd. The ship full of animals ended up on a coin with the words *Laetitia Temporum* stamped on it. Loosely translating as 'Happy Times', it was a great way to advertise the emperor who gave the show and the spread of Rome across the world. (Cassius Dio, LXXVII.1)

How about impressing the crowd with numbers? The greater the number of animals on display, the greater the status of the powerful man who was giving the public such a spectacular show. Here are some figures, which give you an idea of the numbers killed from roughly the last years of the first century BC to the very early years of the second century AD:

- 3,500 animals killed over 26 shows in the reign of emperor Augustus (63 BC–AD 14).

- 9,000 animals killed over 100 days at the games of Titus in AD 80. (Women are recorded as killing some of these animals.)
- 11,000 animals killed to celebrate and commemorate emperor Trajan's AD 107 conquest over the Dacians.

All this killing and hunting must have had an impact ecologically …

Animal Wipeouts

Humans seem to be really good at wiping out animal numbers and the Romans were no different. All the hunting of animals for the games, along with a love of ivory, eventually had impacts like these:

- Hippos disappeared from the lower Nile. The Roman historian Ammianus Marcellinus wrote that hippos were often brought to Rome for the games but were hunted so much that they were no longer seen in this part of Egypt.
- The extinction of the North African elephant, *Loxodonta africana pharaohensis*. Also known as the Atlas elephant, this species was up against it in ancient times. It was captured and trained by the Egyptians as well as being the Punic battle elephant that Hannibal used in his war against the Romans.
- The disappearance of the Asian elephant, *Elephas maximus asurus*, from western Asia.
- The removal of lions from Thessaly and western Asia.
- The disappearance of tigers from Armenia and northern Iran.[61]

ANIMAL EXECUTIONERS

When animals weren't being hunted in the arena or pitted against one another in combat, they were also put to good use as an entertaining way of providing a gruesome end for people who had been condemned to

---

61   If you want to read more on this, take a look at: J. Donald Hughes, 'Hunting in the Ancient Mediterranean World', in *A Cultural History of Animals in Antiquity*, ed. Linda Kalof (Oxford: Berg, 2007), 47–70.

death. Top tip: better to get killed by a big cat, which might give you a swifter death. Worst death? A bear – not such a quick kill. Popular animal used in executions? Bears.

What kind of punishment could be better for a lowly criminal than to be ripped to pieces by a lowly animal? Either offer the victim as outright prey or force them to fight a wild beast. This type of execution was first used by a Roman general called Aemilius Paullus in the second century BC as a punishment for foreign soldiers who deserted from the Roman army. About 200 years later, as the Roman Empire drew back its shoulders and marched across the known world, it had become more common to be executed by wild animals – known to the Romans as *damnatio ad bestias* – than it was to be killed by crucifixion or fire.

Death by wild beast was considered the most degrading punishment of all and was reserved for low-status criminals guilty of crimes such as murder or arson. When the Christian 'cult' began to surface, animal executioners were used for those Christians who refused to denounce their new religion. The Roman historian Tacitus recorded that during the reign of Nero, a sect of Christians in Rome were arrested. They were obstensibly detained for arson, but Tacitus describes their conviction as being for *odio humani generis* – 'a hatred of mankind'. While some were dressed in animal skins and thrown to dogs for execution, others were said to have been fastened to crosses and when it became dark, set on fire like lamps lighting up the dark. Several decades later, the emperor Trajan replied to a letter from one of his governors on what to do with Christians:

> They should not be hunted out; if they are reported, accused and found guilty, they should be punished, in such a way, however, that whoever denies that they are a Christian, and proves it by direct evidence, i.e. by worshipping our gods, although they've been suspected in the past, he shall receive a pardon from his repentance. (Pliny the Younger, *Letters* X.97)

But why not use punishment as a form of entertainment and put on a show? After all, who wouldn't be deterred from crime after seeing some of the spectacularly inventive deaths on display? Sometimes executions were staged as scenes from well-known mythological stories and the animals played their part. Here are a couple of creative deaths to make your toes curl:

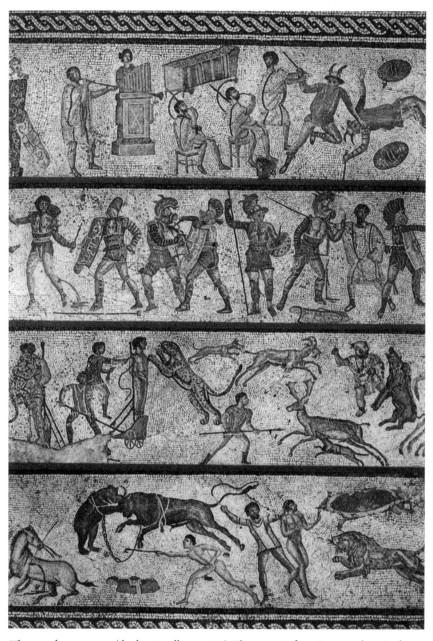

The second-century AD (the date is still uncertain) Zliten mosaic from Roman Libya. In the lower part of the mosaic a bull is chained to a bear and a man suffers damnatio ad bestias *– 'condemnation to beasts' – as he is pushed towards a lion for execution. (The Picture Art Collection / Alamy Stock Photo)*

- In the first century BC, a rebel called Selurus, whose nickname was 'Son of Etna' (after the volcano in Sicily), had been captured after carrying out raids around the Etna region. He was taken to the Roman forum and put on top of a stage prop: a high scaffold, which played the part of Mount Etna's volcano. As the volcano 'erupted', the scaffolding collapsed and Selurus fell headlong onto a heap of wild animals trapped in fragile cages designed to break apart, leaving Selurus to be ripped apart by the teeth and claws that surrounded him. (Strabo, VI.2.6)
- Heard of Prometheus? He had made the gods' blood boil by stealing fire and giving it to humans. His punishment was being tied to a rock while an eagle pecked out his liver. During the night, his liver would grow back so it could be pecked out again, meaning he was tortured for eternity. In the opening games of the Colosseum in AD 80, an unfortunate criminal called Laureolus and a Caledonian bear (the eagle was busy) acted out Prometheus's fate. The criminal was hung on a cross and the bear ripped his body to pieces until there was no body left. As Martial wrote, 'What had been a story, became a punishment.'[62]

BEASTS ON THE BILL

Let's take our seats in the arena and have a look at some of the animals on display close-up.

The Crocodile

Unfortunately for the crocodile, when Rome grabbed Egypt as another Roman province in the late first century BC, this was the animal used to advertise and celebrate the expansion of Rome and its victory over Cleopatra's land. Putting the reptile on a coin with the words *Aegypta Capta* – 'Egypt Captured' – was a great way of broadcasting the message of Rome's victory. But bringing the crocodile to the arenas of Rome had the added bonus of displaying a dash of entertainment in the story

---

62   Martial, *On the Spectacles* 9(7).

of Rome's conquest of Egypt. What a coup to be able to exhibit such an exotic animal from such an exotic place! In 2 BC, the emperor Augustus put on special games to celebrate the opening of the Forum of Augustus in Rome. During these games, 260 lions were killed, a mock naval battle was fought with gladiators and a special area of the Circus Flaminius was flooded. In went thirty-six crocodiles and the specialist crocodile hunters did their job and slaughtered every one of them. Just like Egypt itself, not even these fierce carnivores could survive Roman power. (Cassius Dio, LV.10)

Who gets your crocodiles for you? People who have lived their lives around the reptiles and developed expert crocodile-catching skills. The Egyptian crocodile – *quadripes malum*, or 'a curse on four legs', as one Roman writer called them – was hunted by the Tentyritae, natives of a town on the west bank of the River Nile. These expert hunters would enter the waters, mount the back of the crocodile as if riding a horse, and as the animal opened its mouth they would ram a staff inside and force the crocodile to shore. (Pliny, VII.38)

It was people like the Tentyritae who handled crocodiles in the Roman arenas. During the shows, the reptiles would be kept in a type of reservoir. The hunters would get into the water with nets and drag the animals out onto a raised platform at one side for the audience to get a good look at them, and then drag them back into the water. (Strabo, XVII.1.44)

Remember Symmachus and his starving bear cubs? He didn't have much luck with his crocodiles either. He had collected the animals from Egypt and they'd taken part in an exhibition. Some of Symmachus's relations hadn't been able to make it to Rome in time and he really wanted them to see these crocodiles. It's here that the crocodiles provide us an example of how arena animals didn't just suffer when they were on display and slaughtered for entertainment. Symmachus kept his crocodiles captive and they became listless. No matter what was offered to them, they refused to eat, and after fifty days they were in a wasted and pitiful condition. All but two of the crocodiles were finished off at the next games, before they died behind the scenes. It can't have taken much to slaughter the wasted animals. The two that were held back were for Symmachus's relations to see. Their condition was so bad that who knows if they survived long enough to give even the weakest crocodile smile to their visitors.

The Ostrich

Even ostriches couldn't outrun the arena. Captured alive with great nets and transported to Roman amphitheatres, these birds were referred to by the Romans as *struthiocamelus* – 'little sparrow camel'. While they might stand stock still in terror as deer ran frantically around them pursued by the great hunting dogs set loose for attack, they also gave the emperor Commodus an opportunity to show off his hunting skills (again) to the crowds. Aiming his unique crescent-shaped arrowheads at the unfortunate ostriches, he sliced off their heads leaving their bodies to run headless for a moment, as the giant birds provided a bloody display for a gripped audience.

The Bear

The poor old bear was hunted and sourced from all over, but it's hard to imagine a polar bear making an entrance in the amphitheatre. Remember the epigraph that opened this chapter? Academics are still arguing whether or not the 'Arctic' bear described in this verse (written by an eyewitness to the show) and killed at the games in the Colosseum was a polar bear.

What did the Roman audience see when they watched a bear fight for its life? When animals were forced into combat with one another, the crowd was entertained by the the sight of bears hanging with all four paws from the heads and horns of bulls in order to tire them out with their weight. If a beast fighter was faced with a bear? Bears were said to be killed by a single blow to the head, as this was thought to be the weakest part of their body. At arenas in Rome's Spanish provinces, however, the thinking was that a bear's head was full of poison, so when a bear was killed in the arena, its head was burnt in the presence of a witness, 'since drinking the poison drives a man bear-mad'. (Pliny, VIII.54)

How were bears captured in the first place? If you lived in Roman Armenia, here's how you bagged yourself a bear:

Employ a hunting trick called 'a scare'. First use skilled huntsmen and hunting dogs to track down a bear's lair. Form a run from the lair, stick stakes in the ground at the end of the run and fix a net to them. Pairs of hunters should hide under forest foliage on both sides of this net.

On one side of your run, hide groups of hunters between rocks or under 'hides' made of branches. On the opposite side of the run hang out your 'scare'. This is a flaxen rope with feathers and coloured ribbons hanging from it. Now make a lot of noise, blow trumpets and, as the bear appears, the men on one side of the run should make a great din, clap, shout and rush the bear. The rope should flap the feathers and ribbons, driving the terrified bear in the direction of the open nets.

When the panicked animal gets to the end of the run, hunters should jump into action, pulling the ties on the nets to trap the bear. Quickly pile on more nets because one net isn't enough to stop her fighting her way out. A strong hunter should lasso one of the bear's paws and bind the end of the lasso rope to heavy planks of wood. Now get the bear into a strong wooden crate of oak and pine. She's ready for transport to the amphitheatres. (Oppian, *Cynegetica* IV.354–424)

Elephants and an Unlikely Protest

At the dedication of the temple of Venus Victrix, twenty, or as some record, seventeen elephants fought in the Circus against Gaetulians armed with javelins. One elephant put up an extraordinary fight; when its feet had been seriously wounded, it crawled on its knees towards the band of hunters and seizing their shields it threw them up high and as they fell they made circles in the air to the delight of the audience. It was as if they were being thrown by a skilled performer and not an enraged beast. (Pliny, *Natural History* VIII.7.20)

The first time an elephant was forced to fight in a show at Rome was in 99 BC at the Circus. Twenty years later, there's a record of elephants fighting bulls, but when elephants appeared on the last day of a series of five animal hunts and combats put on by the great general Pompey (around 55 BC), something surprising happened. The last thing an audience wanted was to be attacked themselves by any escaping animals. Various devices were used to prevent this. For example, net barriers were hung between posts on walls surrounding the arenas and archers were often stationed in strategic spots between the arena and the netting. Sometimes, horizontal rollers with a coating of ivory were secured on top of arena walls; the smooth rollers would prevent any escaping animal from getting a good grip with its claws.

At Pompey's show in 55 BC, it was the elephants who gave the audience cause for concern. The poor shield-throwing elephant, which Pliny described earlier, was part of a troop who ended up going down in Roman history – in fact, these elephants made it into the books of no fewer than four Roman writers. When another elephant in its herd had been killed with a single javelin throw just under its eye, the whole band of elephants ran at the iron barriers that enclosed them and tried to break through to the public. To the audience's relief, the barriers stood firm and this desperate escape attempt failed.

But the elephants hadn't finished. Herding themselves together in a protective group, they began to trumpet loudly in what was seen as a sort of entreaty to the crowd: a collective and almost human cry for help or mercy. The brave elephant crawling on its knees, the pitiable escape attempt of the entire troop, the cries and trumpeting trunks raised as if to heaven; if all this sounds quite upsetting, unusually the Roman audience thought so too. The crowd rose in protest and began to curse and boo Pompey, as the air filled not with cheers or applause but with angry shouts and jeers. What a failure Pompey's elephant display had turned out to be! You go to a show to get excited and entertained, and end up full of tears and compassion instead! (Pliny, VIII.7)

The writer and statesman Cicero was an eyewitness that day and wrote about the incident in a letter to a friend. He told his companion the crowd were astonished at what they saw but got no pleasure from it. What did they get instead? A feeling of pity for the elephants, 'a sort of feeling that that wild animal has a certain fellowship with the human race'. For just a moment, the arena crowd saw the elephants as living creatures not so separate from themselves after all. (Cicero, *Letters to Friends* VII.1)

That little moment, when an elephant was seen as sharing something with humankind, didn't last. Elephants still played a role in the animal shows and the only change from the protest at Pompey's games was that when Julius Caesar put elephants on the programme at his games nine years later, he had a canal dug round the Circus Maximus arena to give better protection to the crowd. (Suetonius, *Julius Caesar* 39.2)

SHOPPING FOR ANIMALS

Centuries after Pompey's elephants – more than three centuries to be precise – this was the cap on various animal prices according to emperor Diocletian's edict:

- Lion, first class: 150,000 denarii
- Lion, second class: 125,000 denarii
- Lioness, first class: 125,000 denarii
- Leopard, first class: 100,000 denarii
- Leopard, second class: 75,000 denarii
- Bear: 20,000–25,000 denarii
- Wild boar, first class: 6,000 denarii
- Ostrich: 5,000 denarii
- Stag, first class: 3,000 denarii

Along with purple-dyed silk, the male lion was the most expensive item on Diocletian's price list.

CELEBRITY ANIMALS

The Rampaging Rhino

Back at those first-century AD games when the spectacular Colosseum was opened to the public, a certain two-horned rhinoceros ended up becoming one of the most famous arena animals that Rome displayed. According to Roman records, it had been over seventy years since a rhino was last put on show at Rome.[63] It would have been the first time most of the crowd had seen such a strange-looking animal. Not only was he a rare beast, but he showed the audience exactly what an angry rhino could do. This animal gladiator thrilled the crowds, charging round the amphitheatre and tossing even a mighty bull into the air.

The Colosseum's celebrity rhino is an example of how animals weren't always killed but were used over again if they had more to offer. When the animal's combats were over, the rhinoceros left the stage and was

63   At the games of Germanicus in AD 8.

Domitian's copper coin, struck around AD 83–85. Small change for the people, memorialising the spectacular rhino from the inaugural games at the Colosseum. (Classical Numismatic Group)

driven back into his holding cell. Hauled back out again later for more entertainment, he was not keen to repeat his performance or even enter the arena. Nowadays, we can imagine a rhino in its natural habitat: it's a herbivore not a meat eater; it doesn't need to stalk prey and go in for a bloody kill and is quite content to roam about munching on vegetation and keeping itself to itself. Unless it feels threatened. Once going into aggressive mode, a rhino can charge at speeds of up to 40mph. Seeing the power and brute force of this incredible animal, watching it charge, turn at speed and change direction – the rhino must surely have taken the audience's breath away.

The animal handlers at the Colosseum knew they had to provoke their rhino in order to give the Roman audience a repeat of the explosive show they wanted. Trainers goaded him out onto the sand again, working him up, no doubt, with the usual fire and whips, until the rhino was full of the rage he'd shown before. Threatened now, the rhino would have made his distinctive vocal sounds: the loud snorts the animal makes when angered, the growls and bellows, or the high-pitched screams and shrieks the rhino emits when it feels fear. Rampaging across the arena, this time he tossed two steers into the air – up flew a bison and a buffalo – he lifted a bear into the air, and finally the rhino charged a lion, who panicked so much it ran straight into a stream of spears. The rhino gave the audience a show to remember and was forever immortalised on a Roman coin issued in the reign of emperor Domitian in the years AD 83–85. The fact that the coin was a low-value one meant that you didn't have to be well-off to see it, so this rhino became probably the most well-known animal star of arena shows. (Martial, *On the Spectacles* 11(9); 26(22))

The Kneeling Deer

It wasn't just the powerful rhino whose arena story is still remembered. In AD 80, at the same games in the Colosseum, a doe that had been chased around by the huge and fierce Molossian hounds used in animal shows somehow ended up in front of the emperor's seat. The deer fell on its forelegs, looking to the crowd as if it was on its knees and begging for mercy. The hunting dogs kept their distance and the doe was unharmed. Its turn in the amphitheatre ended up in the Roman book of poems *On the Spectacles*, still read 2,000 years later. (Martial, 33(29))

The Tamed Lion

Certain Roman animals from the arenas are immortalised by the Roman poet Statius, but one animal in particular was singled out for a poetic description of its heroic death in front of the emperor Domitian. The lion ends up carried from the amphitheatre like a leonine Russell Crowe when his body is carried from the arena in *Gladiator*.

This lion was not on show to fight to the death or execute any criminals but had been carefully trained to catch prey in its jaws and release the catch to its trainer without tearing off any arms. Nor did the animal die in any of the usual ways (trapped in a pit, caught in a net or pierced with a spear); it lost its life accidentally, killed in the Colosseum by a blow to a fatal part of its body when another animal was fleeing.

But why listen to me relating this story 2,000 years after it happened? Let's hear a real Roman voice commemorating a real Roman lion, and leave the bloodied arenas with Statius's poem to this trained animal: *Leo Mansuetus* – 'The Tamed Lion'. Here is the king of the beasts fighting to live, but ultimately succumbing to death like a heroic soldier:

BATTLE ELEPHANTS AND FLAMING FOXES

What good did it do you to be tamed and smother your rage?
What good to unlearn vicious nature and the slaughter of men?
Or put up with commands and suffer orders from a master less mighty than yourself?
What good? To be wont to leave your den and return to a barred cage
and to willingly let go the prey you capture
to free the hand thrust into your wide jaw?
You are dead, expert killer of great beasts.
You were not hemmed in by a Numidian band in a curved net,
nor provoked over spears in a terrified leap
or tricked into the gloomy depths of a trap
but overcome by a beast as it fled.
Unlucky lion, your cage hangs open on its hinges
and surrounding you on all sides from their locked pens
lions fill with rage that this crime is allowed.
Their manes fell, they dipped their foreheads and turned their eyes
when you were borne away.
But that shame from your recent blow didn't crush you as you lay there dying:
for in the midst of death your spirit endured
and your courage fought back as your life slipped away.
As a dying soldier, conscious of his fatal wound,
still charges the enemy, and raising his hand
threatens them with falling sword,
so you lion in faltering step and stripped of magnificence,
stand firm with jaws agape
searching out the enemy with your eyes.
Yet there is solace in your sudden death mighty beast,
since the grieving people and the city fathers have mourned your passing
as if a famous gladiator had fallen on the sad arena sand.
Amongst so many beasts from Scythia or Libya or the shores of the Rhine
or Pharia, animals whose deaths are of little worth,
Caesar was moved by the loss of a single lion.

(Statius, *Silvae* II.5)

ANIMALS ON
A PLATTER: FOOD

You would think that you weren't eating a cooked sow's udder,
so plentifully does it flow and swell with living milk.

(Martial, Epigrams XIII.44)

Pliny the Younger, nephew of Pliny the Elder who died at Vesuvius's
eruption, once wrote a letter to a certain Gaius Septicius Clarus who quite
rudely didn't turn up to a dinner at Pliny's, despite accepting his invita-
tion. What a waste of Pliny's money! Septicius could damn well pay him
back for the no-show. Every guest had enjoyed some lettuce, three snails,
two eggs and some spelt in honey and snow (and snow wasn't cheap).
There were cucumbers and onions and thousands of other delicacies.
What had Septicius done instead? He went off to another dinner and had
oysters, sow's womb and sea urchins. (Pliny the Younger, *Letters* I.15)

A MEAL OF TWO HALVES

There was a huge difference between what a poor Roman chewed on and
what a rich Roman enjoyed. If you were a poor Roman, the fancy animal
products Pliny referred to in his letter didn't apply to you, as meat was not
much on your menu. If you did get some meat, it was the pig who was
most likely to provide it. The great writer and statesman Cicero wrote
about free distributions of meat to the public, and it looks like there was
one place you might get a bit of a fleshy treat: the amphitheatres.

How did you get your public to like you? Put on a good show and give
away free stuff. Tokens were given out at arena shows and if you got one

you could pick up your prize on the way home. Some academics believe that amongst these free gifts was a prize of meat; after all, why just throw away the dead animals from the *spectacula*? What a waste – and the Romans really didn't like wasting anything.

Sometimes the animals were alive and kicking. The emperor Elagabalus handed out lots at the games he gave, which included prizes of ten bears, ten dormice or ten lettuces. The historian Cassius Dio wrote about little wooden balls thrown into the crowd at Titus's games in AD 80, each inscribed with the offer of a free gift: pack animals, cattle, horses. (Dio, LXVI.25)

Here's the poet Martial talking about the public getting tickets for prizes in his book of epigrams written to celebrate the opening of the Colosseum at those same games of Titus in AD 80:

Sometimes playful coins come down in sudden showers; sometimes a liberal ticket bestows on them the animals which they have beheld in the arena. Sometimes a bird delights to fill your bosom unexpectedly, or, without having been exhibited, obtains a master by lot, that it may not be torn to pieces. (Martial, *Epigrams* VIII.78)

BIRDS OF A FEATHER BOIL TOGETHER

If we want to see which animals ended up in Roman stomachs, we have to visit the homes of the wealthy. Meat was a great way of showing just how elite and rich a Roman you were. Duck, fowl, deer, eel, hare (the emperor Alexander Severus was said to eat a hare a day) – these were all fine. But want to really impress your guests? Give a dinner party and serve up something weird and wonderful that shows you are richer than the next person.

For elite Romans, this might be thrushes and songbirds from your own aviary, ostrich, flamingo tongues, crane, parrot or peacock. Alexander the Great was said to have admired peacocks so much that when he saw peacocks in India, he threatened severe penalties for anyone who killed the bird.

Several hundred years later, however, the first-century BC Roman orator Quintus Hortensius looked at a peacock and saw something completely different: dinner. Hortensius is recorded as the first Roman who had a peacock slaughtered and served up on a plate. The business of fattening up peacocks was started around 67 BC by Marcus Aufidius Lurco, who made a fat profit from his fat birds. The Latin word for 'glutton', by the way, is *lurco*. Just saying. (Pliny, X.23)

How to Boil a Crane

No one likes to chew on a hard sinew, so here's how to get rid of the sinews in your crane, according to the Roman gourmet Apicius:

1. Boil the crane in water but make sure its head is hanging out of the pot.
2. When it's cooked, take it out of the pot and wrap it in a towel.
3. Twist the head until it comes off and pull the sinews out with it.
4. You'll just be left with bones and flesh.

What if your game birds start to whiff a bit? Apicius has the answer for that too: crush some fresh olives, stuff them inside the bird, sew it up, cook the bird, then remove the olives. (Apicius, *On Cooking* VI.5.7)

The Cooked Goose

Saving the Capitol did not save the goose from offering up its liver on dinner platters. (Ovid, *Fasti* I)

Never mind being a bird sacred to queen of the Roman gods Juno. Unfortunately for the goose, the Romans discovered that stuffing these birds with food makes their livers grow. Once the liver is nice and fat, kill the goose, remove the liver, soak it in milk sweetened with honey before cooking, and then you had a culinary treat. (For pigs' liver, overfeed your pig with figs, then give it as much *mulsum* – wine mixed with honey – as it can drink. The liver will swell up nicely and the pig will be so full to bursting that death should follow.)

Forget about the liver, how about the feet? A first-century Roman called Messalinus Cotta invented a recipe for goose feet: first, grill the soles of the feet, and then pickle them with the fleshy combs from the heads of cocks. Tasty. In ancient Britain, by the way, the barnacle goose was the most luxurious feast on offer. (Pliny, X.27)

PIG TALES

While veal was eaten, cows were for sacrifice, and steers were there to haul loads and were more use alive than dead. It was often pork, not beef, which was the main meat for those Romans who could afford a bit of flesh. All sorts of cuts were available in the Roman *ganeae* – eating houses. However, this was the animal whose meat was subject to pages of laws, with certain pieces of pork prohibited and off the menu because they were seen as excessive. Which were the extravagant pork cuts? Pigs' stomachs, testicles, cheeks, udders and wombs. Did this stop people serving up a bit of sow's udder at a banquet? A certain pantomime writer called Publius got the nickname 'Pig Paps' because he served up the dish so often.

There was a Roman story, recorded as 'a well-known fact', that when a herd of pigs was stolen, they recognised the voice of their swineherd and ran over to one side of the boat they had been carried off on, capsizing the boat and swimming back to shore. (Pliny, VIII.77)

Sow's wombs – *vulvae steriles* – were a Roman delicacy for the rich. These weren't just any wombs but sterile ones from spayed sows or from pigs that hadn't had any piglets yet. To spay a sow, you should starve it for two days, hang it up by the front legs, then cut out the womb. A spayed sow apparently gets fatter faster too. If the womb has miscarried it is even tastier. Next best to this is a womb from a sow the day after she has given birth. And if the piglets haven't drunk from her teats yet, this is the best kind of pig's udder you can eat. (Pliny, XI.84; VIII.77)

To fatten up male pigs, castrate them at 6 months, or if you want them to breed first, see to those testicles when your pigs are about 3 years old. Spring and autumn are good times to do this. Simply make two incisions and squeeze a testicle out of each. (Columella, VII.9 and 11)

Roman recipe writer Apicius gave a method for stuffing a suckling pig:

1. Immediately after the pig is killed, pull its entrails out through its throat before rigor mortis sets in.
2. Make your piping bag: put your stuffing into a cow's bladder and then attach a bird keeper's pipe to the neck of the bladder.
3. Next, make a cut under the ears of the pig and start piping the stuffing in from the cow bladder piping bag. Cover the ears with papyrus and fasten tightly to prevent the stuffing falling out.

(Apicius, VIII.7.366)

What a Boar

When it came to the wild boar, its meat was considered a bit of a luxury. In 184 BC, Roman statesman and writer Cato the Elder (who really didn't approve of extravagance) gave speeches denouncing the eating of boar's meat. It wasn't until more than 100 years later that Publius Servilius Rullus became the first Roman to serve a whole boar at one of his banquets instead of just part of the boar (show-off). The boar continued on its culinary journey through Roman history, and by the first century AD boar was, if you were wealthy, all the fashion; two or three boars might be eaten as the first course alone at a big dinner. Mind you, the emperor Tiberius, in a display of how much he could rein in the luxury, sometimes served meat left over from the day before, and is recorded as dishing up half a boar at formal dinner parties. After all, half is plenty – who needs a whole one? (Pliny, VIII.78 and Suetonius, *Tiberius* 34)

Talking of curbing extravagance, the *Sumtuariae Leges* were Roman laws passed from the second century BC designed to cut down on excess. Here are a few examples throughout Roman history.

- Julius Caesar enforced laws against extravagance by dotting watchmen about the markets ready to confiscate anything being sold that was against the law and allowing soldiers entry to dinner parties to whisk away anything designated as excessive.

- Tiberius put restrictions on what the street cookshops – *ganeae* – could sell.
- Claudius banned the selling of boiled meat, and Nero issued laws that no cooked food except vegetables and pulses could be sold in the *popinae* (street taverns).

(Suetonius, *Julius Caesar* 43, *Tiberius* 34 and *Nero* 16)

SNAILS

First-century BC entrepreneur Fulvius Lippinus not only introduced gamekeeping and hunting preserves full of wild boar, but he also had the bright idea of bringing snails to the Roman table. The first ever snail farmer to make it into the history books, Lippinus built different *coclearia* – 'snail pens' – for different breeds of snail and fed them on boiled wine and grain. Here are a few varieties popular with the Romans:

- The tiny whites from Reate (in Italy).
- The huge ones from Illyricum (along the Adriatic coast).
- The medium-sized snails from Africa, although the *solitannae* from Africa were giant.

(Varro, III.14)

You can fatten your snails on meat, but here's how to do it with milk:

1. Use a sponge to clean the snails and take out the membrane so the snails come out their shells.
2. Put them in a vessel full of milk and salt for one day, then just milk for a few days. Clean all the *stercus* (scum) off the snails every hour.
3. When they are too fat to get back into their shells, fry them in oil and serve with a wine sauce.

(Apicius, VII.16)

HOW TO LOOK AFTER YOUR DORMICE

Unfortunately for dormice, Fulvius 'Snail Man' Lippinus had his eye on these tiny rodents too and the enterprising businessman became the first Roman to introduce the dormouse to wealthy menus. Fortunately for budding dormice chefs, Varro has some instructions on how to keep dormice until they're fat enough to eat:

- First, build a *glirarium* (dormice enclosure). Construct a wall and make sure the plaster is smooth on the inside so your dormice can't climb out. Create a few little hollows in the ground for your dormice to nest in.
- Plant nut-bearing trees inside the wall to supply your dormice with food, and throw in some acorns and chestnuts when the trees aren't in fruit.
- If you don't want an outside enclosure, pop to the potter and buy some dormice jars. You can keep these in your villa and fatten your dormice up in them. There are channels along the sides of these pots and a little place for keeping food like acorns, walnuts or chestnuts. Put a cover over the jar and your dormice will eat up in the dark and grow nice and fat.[64]

(Varro, III.15)

Once your dormice are fattened up, you can either sprinkle them with honey and roll them in poppy seeds or stuff them with pork, pepper and nuts then roast them. (Apicius, VIII.9 and Petronius, 31)

---

64 Dormice are still eaten in Croatia and Slovenia today. You can check out travel blogs with writers trying out a dormice dinner, for example secretcroatia.blog/2012/02/05/eating-dormice-on-hvar-island/ or breghouse.com/2016/08/26/a-date-with-the-dormouse-hunter-slovenias-pohl-position/.

IMPERIAL PLATTERS

Emperor Vitellius (AD 69) liked an extravagant feast. According to the historian Suetonius, Vitellius's brother gave a huge banquet for him when he came to Rome, which included serving up 2,000 fish and 7,000 birds. Vitellius topped this with a platter of food, which was so enormous he called it the Shield of Minerva, Defender of the City. Piled on the platter were pike livers, pheasant and peacock brains, flamingo tongues, and – wait for it – the milt (sperm-filled reproductive gland) of lampreys. (Suetonius, *Vitellius* 13)

The young Roman emperor Elagabalus (AD 204–222) seemed to have let his power go to his teenage head and fully embraced the whole idea of high-status food for the elite. He's said to be the first person to serve up ostriches, apparently serving guests with an ostrich head each, and loved a few camel heels and fleshy cockscombs cut from the birds while they were still alive. Also on his list were flamingo brains, thrush brains, the heads of parrots, pheasants and peacocks, and the beards of mullets.

Elagabalus was also said to give out spoons at his dinners with prizes inscribed on the back of the cutlery. What could you win? Ten ostriches or ten eggs. Ten camels or ten flies. Performers, too, were given prizes, but it was a lucky dip as to what they could win: a chunk of good meat or a dead dog, for example. After being told that they would make him immune to the plague, the young emperor was also partial to a few peacock and nightingale tongues, all served to him and his guests on his couches, which were made of solid silver.

In the end, it wasn't the plague he had to worry about, as no amount of peacock tongues could protect him from his own Praetorian Guard who murdered him after just a few years. (*Augustan History: Elagabalus* XX, 4–7 and XXII)

OYSTERS

Oysters from the ancient settlement of Coryphas in Asia Minor (western Asia), oysters from Spain, Turkish oysters, oysters from the *Lucrinus Lacus* or Lucrine Lake in Italy, from the shores of the Black Sea and the Indian Ocean – the Romans loved an oyster. By the first century AD, British oysters such as the 'Rutupian' oysters found their way to Roman tables. These oysters, harvested from the Kent and Essex coast (Colchester oysters were particularly highly regarded), were called 'Rutupian' since they were transported to Italy from the ancient port town of Rutupiae (modern-day Richborough in Kent). Rutupiae was a major gateway to Britain, the source of traffic across the Channel for the Romans who so associated this Kent town with Britain that some Roman poets even used the word *Rutupinus* to mean Britain itself.

Gnaeus Julius Agricola, Roman general and governor of Britain from AD 78 to 85, had oysters transported to Rome from Reculver on the Kent coast, the delicacies packed in snow to keep them fresh. More than 100 years before this Roman passion for British oysters reached the Roman dinner table, Julius Caesar had the breastplate he dedicated to Venus Genetrix (the goddess Venus) decorated with oyster pearls that had been harvested from British shores.

Giant clams imported to Rome from India were so big that they got the nickname *tridacna*, from the Greek words for 'three' and 'to bite', because it took three good bites to eat them.

FISHY FACTS

What type of fish did the Romans enjoy? Fresh fish, preserved fish, fish sauce made from the whole fish, fish sauce made from the innards and the blood. Expensive fresh fish served up on a dish at a posh dinner for the elite or swimming around alive and well in the same elites' high-status fishponds. Preserved and salted fish loaded onto ships to feed the crew or transported with the Roman military to feed the soldiers. Fish swam through Roman life, landing in markets, on dinner tables and even being presented as gifts to the emperor as the following fishy facts show:

- By the first century AD, the mullet fish had become so outrageously expensive that the emperor Tiberius proposed limiting the price of the fish. But when the Roman writer Juvenal was writing years and years after Tiberius's death, he quipped how one red mullet was sold for more money than it would cost to buy the man who'd caught the fish in the first place. (Suetonius, *Tiberius* 34 and Juvenal, IV.15–26)

- How could a rich Roman make sure they were able to get hold of the right expensive fish? By building fancy *piscinae* (fishponds) on their estates and stocking them with something special so they could show off elite fish dishes at posh dinner parties.

- Roman biographer Suetonius tells us how, when the emperor Tiberius was visiting the island of Capri (one of his favourite places), a local fisherman saw him sitting alone, clambered over the rocks and offered him the gift of a mullet he had caught. Not happy about being surprised by the fisherman, Tiberius had the poor man's face scrubbed with the fish. When the fisherman was heard to cry out in thanks that he was glad he hadn't given the emperor the huge crab he'd caught, Tiberius is said to have ordered the man's face rubbed with the crab too. (Suetonius, *Tiberius* 60)

- According to the top gastronomers of the time, the mullet fish changed colours as it died. Marcus Apicius, the Heston Blumenthal of first-century AD Rome, came up with the idea of killing the mullet in a sauce called *garum*, made ingeniously of the mullet fish themselves, or, as Pliny referred to them, the mullets' *sociorum* – companions and allies. (Pliny, IX.31)

- *Garum*, sometimes referred to as *liquamen*,[65] was such a popular sauce that the Romans took it with them to the provinces, like ancient business travellers packing bottles of Heinz Tomato Ketchup in their bags. The expensive version of the sauce was made from fermented fish guts mixed with salt and fish blood. A cheaper version was made from whole pasted fish. I don't want to put you off your dinner, but academics believe the popularity of this fish sauce was the reason for an increase in the fish tapeworm in the Roman era.

---

65   The difference between *garum* and *liquamen* is a matter for discussion among scholars. In general, *liquamen* was the sauce made from the whole fish and *garum* the sauce made from the fish blood and viscera.

- Remember Pliny writing about *garum sociorum* and the image of fish being killed in a sauce made of their allies? By the first century AD, *garum sociorum* was the name of the highly prized and expensive sauce from Carthago Spartaria (Cartagane in Spain). This was the *garum* for the elite. (For those with a more ordinary income, *garum* from tuna fish was the sauce to use.) Pliny tells us that no other liquid except for perfume was as costly as the '*garum* of the allies' fish sauce. Made from the blood of mackerel, it was said to be of a bloodied black colour. (Pliny, XXXI.43)
- If your commercial business was making *garum*, you needed a salt-works and a strong nose, but a *garum* sauce factory would have been big business. Gades (modern-day Cadiz in Spain) was a big player in the fish sauce trade, and closer to home in Italy we know that there were at least ten businesses around the Pompeii area and a saltworks right by the port. Wealthy Romans could have *garum* in everything: a bit of fish sauce with your sausages, a sprinkle of fish sauce with your fish, a dash of fish sauce with your rabbit – or you could even kill your mullet in it, remember?

BUNNIES IN THE OVEN

Talking of rabbits, analysis of a rabbit tibia bone excavated from Fishbourne Roman Palace in the 1960s got academics' noses twitching. It is evidence that it was the Romans, and not the Normans, who introduced rabbits to Britain, meaning Roman rabbits were hopping about Britain 1,000 years earlier than previously thought. We know from Pliny that over off the east coast of Spain, rabbits were so prolific in the Roman Balearics that the people petitioned the emperor Augustus for military assistance to stop the spread. Ferrets were used to hunt the rabbits, thrown into the burrows to flush the bunnies out. Once driven in a panic to the surface, the rabbits could be killed by the rabbit catchers.

Pliny also tells us just what a delicacy the rabbit was. If you're a rabbit lover look away now, because it was the rabbits' kittens or babies that were considered to be the delicacy. Baby bunnies would be cut from the mother's womb or taken from the teat, killed, cooked without being gutted and served. (Pliny, VIII.81)

ONE TEAT OR TWO?

The Romans used milk more for making cheese than drinking. The thinking was that cheese from cow's milk was the most nourishing but terrible for constipation; sheep or goat's milk cheese was thought to be better for you in this respect. Camel's milk got the thumbs up from some Roman writers, but it was best if watered down to three parts water to one of milk. Thick ass's milk could be used as a substitute for rennet (needed for cheese making), but here's the big question: how many nipples should an animal have if you were going to make cheese from their milk? The answer is two: animals with two teats supplied milk for the best cheese, unlike animals with more than four teats, which were not considered good for cheese supply. (Varro, II.11 and Pliny, XI.96)

Here are some more of emperor Diocletian's price caps, from AD 301. It's a long time after Apicius's recipes, nearly 400 years after dormice were first introduced and nearly 300 since Tiberius had the cheek to serve up only half a boar at dinner. Keep in mind the average wage for a mule driver at this time was 25 denarii a day and an advocate could earn 1,000 denarii for pleading a case in court.

- Ten quails: 20 denarii
- One pig's uterus: 24 denarii
- Ten dormice: 40 denarii
- Ten thrushes: 60 denarii
- Oysters, about 100: 100 denarii
- One hare: 150 denarii
- One peacock: 300 denarii

FOOD FASHIONS

Now this is my kind of simple maths: if you worked at the check-in at the Roman baths earning 2 denarii a customer in the third century AD, looking after the clothes of ten customers would be enough to buy you ten quails – if that's how you wanted to blow your hard-earned cash and didn't mind a scuff up the back of the head for not buying something more substantial. Centuries before Diocletian's list, the quail had been an expensive bird fattened-up and afforded only by the wealthy. By the first century AD, Pliny was writing how the birds were 'condemned' from the Roman menu as they were very fond of eating a poisonous seed. Migrating quail can, in fact, feed on plants that are poisonous to humans, causing coturnism (from the Latin word for quail, *coturnix*), an illness which can affect some people after eating quail. So, once again, Pliny was on the ball. Clearly the quail regained its popularity as Diocletian's list is proof that by the third century the birds were solidly perching back on the dinner table.

The Greek philosopher Pythagoras was famous for his vegetarianism and there were some Romans who followed his doctrines. Seneca, tutor to emperor Nero, tried out vegetarianism when he was young, but the philosopher Plutarch (born AD 46) wrote a whole debate on the ethics of meat eating, arguing that animals can't talk or rationalise but they can certainly suffer. Let's leave the dinner table, then, with a section from Plutarch, which says you can eat meat, but let's have less of the cruelty:

> Let us eat flesh; but let it be for hunger and not for wantonness. Let us kill an animal; but let us do it with sorrow and pity, and not abusing and tormenting it, as many nowadays are used to do, while some run red-hot spits through the bodies of swine, that by the tincture of the quenched iron the blood may be to that degree mortified, that it may sweeten and soften the flesh in its circulation; others jump and stamp upon the udders of sows that are ready to pig, that so they may trample into one mass in the very pangs of delivery, blood, milk and the corruption of the crushed and mangled young ones, and so eat the most inflamed part of the animal; others sew up the eyes of cranes and swans, and so shut them up in darkness to be fattened, and then souse up their flesh with certain monstrous mixtures and pickles.
> (Plutarch, *On the Eating of Flesh* II.996–7)

Blimey, I might have to go and cuddle a pig.

THE WORLD
OF SCIENCE
AND HEALTH

Nor is it any wonder that aquatic birds or, in fact, birds as a whole, can sense indications of a change in the atmosphere.

(Pliny, *Natural History* XVIII.88)

THE WEATHER

In about 26 BC, the emperor Augustus was travelling on a night march during the Roman campaign against the Cantabrians of northern Spain. As he sat in his litter, a great storm rained down and a lightning strike hit his carriage, grazing it but killing the slave who was carrying a torch in front of the litter. It was a close shave for Augustus, leaving him shaken and in no doubt of the dangers of thunderstorms. In order to protect himself and lessen his chances of ending up like his unfortunate slave, he dedicated a shrine to Jupiter the Thunderer on the Capitoline Hill in Rome and made use of an animal as part of his anti-lightning strategy.

There were a few things that were believed to be immune to lightning strikes. One of these was laurel – which is the reason the emperor Tiberius would put a wreath of laurel on his head during thunderstorms – and the seal and the eagle were the others. This is why the eagle was represented alongside Jupiter and his thunderbolts, why tents made of seal skin were thought to be a good defence against those deadly bolts from the sky and, of course, the reason Augustus always kept a seal skin on hand in case of a sudden thunderstorm. (Suetonius, *Augustus* XXIX.90 and Pliny, II.56)

Animal Weather Forecasters

Need a bit of rain? Got a lizard handy? Burn the head and throat of a cha-meleon on oak wood or burn its liver on house tiles, and thunderstorms and rain will follow. (Pliny, XXVIII.29)

Chameleons aside, Roman writers have left us lists of animals' behaviour connected to changes in the weather. Birds landing on sailors' rigging at sea and sounding an alarm was the kind of animal sign that would make a sailor take a deep breath and shake his head because it wasn't a predic-tor of calm weather. Several Roman writers made it clear that these sorts of weather warning were nothing to do with superstition but completely natural. Take Cicero, for example – you can't get more sensible than this intelligent Roman statesman and lawyer. He recorded that ship pilots kept their eyes on dolphins to predict the weather from their behaviour, but he didn't believe this was like predicting the future from dreams; it was nature, it was natural and it was rational. (Cicero, *On Divination* II.70)

So, let's look to the land at the animals and up to the sky at the birds to see some Roman weather forecasters at work.[66]

Signs That There Will be a Change in the Weather

- Sheep gambolling around
- Oxen sniffing upwards at the sky and licking their hair
- Pigs ripping up the hay
- Bees not buzzing out and about, but staying in their hives
- Ants running around in an extra busy way and carrying their eggs back and forth
- Earthworms slithering out of the earth

Watch Out: Storms are Coming

- Sea birds flying in towards the land and sea urchins burrowing into the sand
- Frogs croaking much more than usual

---

66   See: Pliny, *Natural History* XVIII.87–88 and II.28 and II.83; Aelian, *On the Characteristics of Animals* VII.7–8.

- Goats lying in a huddle together or sheep digging at the earth with their hooves
- Coots making a loud chatter in the morning or seagulls flocking together
- Geese making a hullabaloo and gabbling at an unusual time
- Pine martens and mice making a lot of squeaking noises
- Cockerels and chickens clucking, flapping their wings and strutting about with their chests out
- Tree-dwelling birds keeping to their nests or robins flying in to shelter in cattle sheds
- Spiders raising their webs higher means rain is going to fall and the rivers are going to rise. Spiders reweave their webs in cloudy weather, so a lot of webs means rain

High Winds are Blowing in

- Ducks cleaning themselves with their bill or cranes making for land
- Dolphins playing in a calm sea means wind is on its way from the direction the dolphins came from
- Ravens croaking continuously and shaking their feathers

Fine Weather is on the Way

- Cranes flying high in silence
- Owlets screeching in a shower
- A lot of hares all gathering in the same place

Ants shifting their eggs and croaking frogs? It's easy to dismiss the Romans and their weather predictions, but modern science might make us think twice before sniggering at the ancients. The vitali organ, found in the inner ear of birds, is super sensitive to air pressure and acts like a barometer giving them an indication of rain and bad weather. Entomologists have stated that ants going on the march and carrying their eggs are reliable predictions of oncoming rain, as some insects have a protein – that us humans don't have – in their antennae, which means they can detect changes of moisture and humidity in the air. Spiders have the same kind of receptor cells and there are research papers on animal behaviour as earthquake predictors, as well as papers on how Brazilian spiders weave their webs higher in the rain.

HEALTH[67]

Animals played a big part in the history of Roman medicine. Their (live) bodies were cut up for dissection to examine such things as how the brain and lungs worked. Parts of their bodies were used to treat illness or in superstitious remedies to keep the body safe. Their products, be they wool, honey, fat or bodily fluids, became part of the Roman medicine cabinet. Even a weasel could come in handy: burn a weasel whole and rub yourself with the ashes to relieve gout, or rub weasel blood on your glandular swellings to remedy the lumps. Easy.[68] Let's take a trip to the doctor's and have a look at how animals contributed to keeping the Romans in good health.

Stars of the Roman Medicine Cabinet

Honey

Honey was a major ingredient in Roman medicine; taken internally, applied externally, on its own or mixed with other ingredients. Even the wax was used, with wax from Punic honey (along the North African coast) said to be the best. Honey was used as an antibacterial, for throat infections, a remedy for ulcers, wound care, getting rid of nits, for preventing outbreaks of scurvy on Roman ships and for treating snake bites, to name but just a few of its medicinal uses.

---

67 Just a caveat: while I'm a great believer in the health benefits of honey, even if you do have access to mouse droppings or the head of a wolf, please don't try any of these Roman cures.

68 Dioscorides, *On Medicinal Substances* II.27.

Fat

Pig fat, goose fat, goat fat, bull fat, bear fat, wolf fat, even squirrel fat; all sorts of animal grease were used as ingredients in ancient remedies. Feeling suspicious of someone? Lion's fat was said to be 'an antidote to those who intend treachery' according to Roman army doctor and author Dioscorides, who lists all sorts of ways of making your animal fats smell lovely. This animal product was used for everything from soothing burns (swine fat), to enemas (goat fat), to rubbing on yourself to repel snakes (elephant or deer fat). (Dioscorides, II.94)

The goose supplied the fat in a famous Roman preparation called 'commagenum' after the area in the Roman province of Syria (now in modern-day Turkey), where the remedy was originally made. Goose grease was mixed with cinnamon, cassia, white pepper and the commagene herb.[69] The whole lot was put in a vessel and buried in the snow. The resulting sweet-smelling ointment was used as a painkiller spread onto sprains and pains. (Pliny, XXIX.13)

Wool

Unwashed wool – favoured as a great material for absorbing liquids – was an ingredient in lots of Roman preparations, with wool from the neck or thigh recommended as the softest. Dip your wool in vinegar, wine or oil, depending on what you're using it for, and apply to aches, pains and dislocations. For dislocations, dip your unwashed wool in vinegar mixed with salt and apply to the body. Mix wool with animal fat and use it on swellings or bruises; mix it with honey or wine to treat wounds and sores; or dip your wool in rose oil and stuff up the nose to staunch a nose bleed.

Unwashed wool was used as a pessary to draw out a dead foetus, and the ash of wool was used for wounds and burns. Lanolin from the grease on unwashed wool was as useful to the Romans as it is for us today. Ancient advice sees it being used on ulcers, mixed with goose grease for sores or burnt in a ceramic jar and turned to ashes to form an ointment for eye infections. (Pliny, XXIX.9–10 and Dioscorides, II.82–4)

---

69   This herb is unknown to us but is thought to be Syrian nard. Nard was used in perfume making so would have added to the sweet-smelling fragrance of the goose fat ointment.

Eggs

Got a problem with your eyes? Egg whites were especially used for eye problems; just add butter to it for treating a baby with eye inflammation. Eggs were used on scalds to prevent blisters and the white of the egg mixed with pig's fat was used on sores from burns. It might be the last thing you want when you've got terrible diarrhoea, but egg yolks swallowed raw were used as a remedy for dysentery. Mix your eggs with goose grease for neck pain and beat up with garlic as a remedy for colic. As Pliny said of the useful egg: 'There is no other food which nourishes in sickness without overloading the stomach and it has the attributes of both food and drink.'[70]

The Beaver

The beaver also gave the Romans something useful. Castoreum is a secretion from the beaver's castor scent glands right next to the animal's anal glands. Sounds stinky? It was. The Romans used it in remedies to help with cramps, vertigo, tremors, stomach troubles, sciatica and scorpion bites. It was also thought to affect menstrual flow, and if taken in water was used to encourage the delivery of the placenta after child birth. Added to Attic honey, it was used for eye troubles and mixed with oil those beaver secretions were used to relieve toothache and earache too.

Can't sleep? Rub your head all over with beaver oil mixed with rose oil; don't forget the rose oil or you'll never drop off because of the terrible stench – beavers spray this whiffy musk mixed with urine to scent mark. The pungent smell meant if a Roman found someone passed out on the floor, a waft of some beaver oil under their nose was just the thing to bring them round again. (Pliny, XXXII.13)

Gory Ingredients

A stone in the bladder? Mouse dung rubbed on the belly cures it. All sorts of animal dung is listed in Roman medicinal preparations: horse dung, goat dung (mixed with honey), dove droppings, stork droppings, fox poo, cat poo – you get the poopy picture. Cow dung could be wrapped in

70   Pliny, XXIX.11.

leaves, warmed in hot ashes and applied as an ancient heat pack to relieve sciatica or horse manure mixed with vinegar used to staunch bleeding.

Spiders' web was recommended for the same thing. A soldier wounded in battle? Clean the wound with a mixture of honey and vinegar and cover it with spider webs to stop blood loss.[71]

How about urine? Boar urine, dog urine, lynx urine and ass urine are just some of the ing*wee*dients (sorry) listed in medical preparations. Another animal bodily fluid also played a part: blood. Examples of its use are blood from stallionsmixed into antiseptic preparations, and the blood of goats, deer or hare fried up in a pan and eaten as a cure for dysentery. (Dioscorides, II.97–8)

At the Doctor's

What kind of animal products were used in medical instruments? Let's take a look at some examples:

- A good hard quill from an old goose was just the right kind of probe for extracting warts. Powdered medicine could be blown through a hollow quill into any hard to reach places.
- Animal bone, ivory or horn were used to make mortars for grinding up medicine.
- Cups were made of horn for 'cupping': make a small incision in the flesh, put your cup over it, seal it with beeswax and the blood will be drawn out of your patient. (Leeches were also used for bloodletting. Sometimes the tip of the leech's tail was snipped off to encourage the flow of blood.)
- Needles made of bone or ivory were used for stitching bandages together.
- Animal bladders were used to make *clysteres* (syringes). The tube of the syringe could be made of bronze, horn or even silver. Attach a

---

71 You might be interested to know that scientists today are researching into spider silk-treated bandages and the use of spider web in healing wounds, thousands of years after the ancients used it. See microbiologysociety.org/blog/ antibiotic-spider-silk-that-can-heal-wounds.html or www.news-medical.net/ life-sciences/Role-of-Spider-Silk-in-Biomedicine.aspx.

sow's bladder to the end of your tube and there's your instrument for enemas and injecting the nose, the ear or any orifices.

- Sutures were often made of flax, but people were also stitched up with woollen threads.
- Sponges were used for just about everything: to stop haemorrhages; dipped in honey and used on eye infections; used as a type of bandage. They were used for painful joints, wounds and ulcers, mixed with everything from rainwater and vinegar to wine and salt. Sponges could also be used in place of wool.

Looking After Your Teeth

This is so simple: pop out, find a wolf's head, burn it, collect the ash, and use it as a mouthwash and pain reliever. You could also remove the bones from wolf excrement and use these in an amulet. If you can't find a wolf, the ash from a burnt hare's head is just as good. Alternatively, frogs boiled in water and vinegar can help with toothache and with keeping your teeth clean.

Gum disease giving you the odd wobbly tooth? Burn some deer antlers until they are reduced to ash, then use as a gargle or rub over the loose tooth. If your tooth is loose because of a blow to the head, ass's milk will help strengthen it.

A special bone shaped like a needle and found in the hare can be used to scrape aching teeth.

Teeth can be brushed clean with powders made from ground shells, ash from burnt dogs' teeth mixed with honey, burnt animal hooves or ground animal bones.

Earache

Here's a remedy to help relieve pain in the ears – unless you're a fox with earache, in which case: run. Apply a mixture of ground-up fox testicles and dried bull's blood to the painful ear. Or, if the testicles are out of stock, pour a few drops of warmed goat urine into the ear and then apply a paste of goat dung and axle grease.

Headache

How lucky are we that we can nip down the road and buy some paracetamol? Here's a Roman remedy for a headache requiring a bit more effort: touch the head with an elephant's trunk. And it works even better if the elephant sneezes.

Leprous Sores

Dissolve some calves' genitals in vinegar, honey and sulphur, stir with a fig branch and apply to your leprous sores twice a day.[72]

Head Lice

Got head lice but run out of honey? Goat's milk is said to get rid of the nits. And if you should have any sores on your head, some cat poo, applied with an equal measure of mustard, should heal them up.[73]

Birth and Babies

It was legal for Roman women to get married at age 12, although you will be relieved to know that most waited until their mid teens or twenties. The poorer someone was, the worse their nutrition, resulting in a delayed pubescence and ability to become pregnant. It was aristocrats, in fact, who were more likely to marry younger; after all, nothing could unite two elite families better than bonding them together with a good marriage. What with the risks from haemorrhage, poor hygiene and infections, childbirth was a risky affair whether you were rich or poor. Julius Caesar's only child from marriage, Julia, had already lost one baby before she died in childbirth a year later at the age of 22 and the great writer and statesman Cicero lost his beloved

---

72 You might scoff at the calves' genitals, but hold fire on the sulphur as it's still used in some modern treatments for skin conditions including acne, scabies and dandruff. For an example of research on sulphur's use in skin problems, see www.espalibrary.eu/search/465/.

73 This list of remedies is a selection from Pliny's *Natural History* books XXVIII–XXX, worth reading for Roman treatments for everything from the teeth to the feet, including haemorrhages, itchy skin and jaundice.

daughter, Tullia, to childbirth too. When we look at some of the health tips below and see the Roman advice on newborns, it's clear babies worried their parents with the same, familiar problems in ancient times as they do today.

- To prevent conception, use wool soaked in olive oil, honey or the juice of the balsam tree. Insert this into the vagina and rub around the neck of the womb. This should slow down the motility of the sperm. Or use a barrier method and block the entrance to the womb with a piece of fine-spun wool. After sex, the woman should squat and sneeze to expel any sperm. Wool dipped in vinegar used as a vaginal douche will help see off sperm too.
- To conceive a boy: eat the testicles of a cock or the uterus of a hare.
- To speed up childbirth: eat snails or drink sow's milk with honey wine.
- To prevent miscarriage: rub the woman all over with hedgehog ash mixed with oil.
- To relieve swollen breast pain after giving birth: rub with mouse dung diluted in rainwater or rub the breasts with sow's blood. If the milk has dried up, drink sow's milk to bring it in again or sip earthworms mixed with honey wine.
- For a woman who has passed childbearing years, eating a foetus taken from the uterus of a hare will bring renewed fertility.
- If a Roman baby is teething, goat's milk, butter or butter mixed with honey can be rubbed on their gums. Mentioned next to this is something no mother would surely want to rub into her baby's gums, but here it is: hares' brains.
- To settle a restless baby: make an amulet with some goat dung wrapped in a piece of cloth.
- To soothe infants suffering from nightmares: an ass's skin laid on the bed will keep night terrors away. A wolf's tooth tied on as an amulet does the same thing.[74]

---

74 For more Roman contraceptive advice, see the work by second-century AD Greek physician and doctor to Rome, Soranus, *Gynecology* I.61. See Pliny, XXVIII.77 for the hare to increase fertility; XXVIII.78 on babies; XXX.43 on conception and childbirth. (Please don't follow any of this advice: a bit of wool and olive oil won't prevent pregnancy and if you offer a new mother mouse dung to help with breast pain, you deserve what you get.)

Talking of amulets, getting hold of an amulet was another way of protecting your health. They would hopefully ward off your medical troubles and were made of all sorts of objects: the dust a hawk had rolled in wrapped in a linen cloth and tied up with a red thread to keep fevers at bay; the longest tooth of a black dog for the same affliction; a little stone taken from a swallow's nest worn as protection against epilepsy. Or perhaps you might buy a piece of snake skin wrapped in bull's leather, or a hyena's tooth worn as an amulet to cure night terrors and a fear of ghosts. (Pliny, XXVIII.27 & XXX.28–30)

Below the Waist

A prolapse of the anus is reduced by applying snail juice. Chaffing of the anus is eased by the ash of a field mouse mixed with honey, or the bile of a hedgehog mixed with the brain of a bat. If you can't get hold of these, apply some goose grease or a mixture of pigeon dung and honey. Oh, the simplicity of Boots the Chemist. Swan fat is said to cure haemorrhoids. Genital warts? Rub a spider on the affected area after removing its feet and head. Quite fiddly all round really.

Trouble with your testicles? Dust them with the ground-down bones of a horse's head. If one of your testicles hangs down, fear not: it can be remedied with the slime of snails. The shed skin of a snake also does the trick. If you can get it, snake skin burnt to ash and mixed with vinegar will also help your dangling testicle to buck right up again. (Pliny, XXX.22)

Here's a remedy based on superstition for afflictions to the groin. First, find a spider's web. Take a thread, tie it in seven or nine knots and, as you do so, name a widow at each knot. Attach it to your troublesome groin and let it do its work. (Pliny, XXVIII.12)

Got diarrhoea? Burn some snails alive and add the ash to a dry wine. Suffering from terrible wind? Snails are also good for flatulence. (Pliny, XXX.20)

ANIMAL VIVISECTION

Vivisection: from the Latin *vivus* (living) and *secare* (to cut).

Before we look inside the bodies of Roman animals, we need to take a look at the man who cut them up. The 'father of vivisection' Galen (AD 129– *c*.200) was a Greek philosopher, an author and a successful physician. So successful, in fact, that he influenced medicine for over 1,000 years after his death.

He was the head surgeon at the gladiator training school in Pergamon (an ancient Greek city in modern-day Turkey), which was great for his learning of the human body, either by treating a wounded one or observing the damage done to a dead one. He then settled in Rome where he went on to become the personal doctor to several Roman emperors, beginning with Marcus Aurelius.

The taboo of cutting up a human corpse was a hindrance to the study of anatomy, but Galen made good use of any opportunities that he came across: an ulcer, which had rotted the flesh down and exposed the bone; or an anthrax epidemic, giving a chance to observe patients who had parts of their body stripped of skin and flesh by the disease. But there was nothing as good as coming across a decomposed or badly damaged human corpse: the ripped-up bodies of humans thrown to wild beasts in the arena; the skeletons of babies left 'exposed' to die; a river that had flooded a hastily buried body, washing up the corpse that had lost its flesh, revealing the skeleton; a robber who had been killed during an attack and whose body had been left to decay on the side of a road – after birds had picked off the flesh, eventually a complete human skeleton was left, perfect for Galen's scientific examinations or demonstrations.

The bad news for animals was that ancient anatomists soon discovered that human skeletons had a similarity to ape skeletons. Galen made serious scientific headway by examining the bodies of animals, dead or alive, and would carry out public demonstrations of his experiments in vivisection where audiences could learn and be entertained all at the same time.

Galen was an absolutely prolific writer and wrote book after book on everything from bones, muscles and semen, to philosophy and pharmacy. His work *De Anatomicis Administrationibus – On Anatomical Procedures –* refers, amongst other things, to animal dissection and vivisection. Want to learn how to cut into a thorax or strip a membrane with your fingers? Galen's book reads like an ancient university lecture. But take a deep breath and hold onto your hat if you're a modern-day animal lover. Before we move onto the live ones, let's start with some of Galen's instructions on working with dead animals first:

- If you don't have the luck of coming across a human skeleton then use an ape. If you're working on a dead animal, the ape should be drowned rather than choked to death as strangling damages the neck.
- If you're working on apes, try and get a species that looks the closest to humans; for example, those that walk as upright as possible. Particularly for experiments on the brain, apes with round faces are the best as they resemble human beings the most.
- Newborn apes are not the best subjects. The muscles of newborn apes are soft and their ligaments don't have a lot of strength. Old apes aren't good either, but if it's a choice between old and fat or newborn, choose the newborn as too much fat obscures the fibres.
- If you can't get an ape, use other animals such as goats, pigs or dogs.
- Results are not as good if the animal you are dissecting has been dead for a long time as muscles and tendons dry up and tighten.
- You can get ox brains from local butchers in larger cities. If there's too much bone attached to them, get the butcher to remove it. Otherwise, do it yourself with a strong knife or carpenter's adze (an ancient tool a bit like an axe).

Galen's experiments on animals included examinations of the spinal cord, live dissections on apes, dogs, pigs and goats, and notes on which part of the animal was paralysed by what, or which severed vertebrae resulted in the animal losing its voice completely. He advised on what surgical tools to use; for example, if you want to dissect the very bottom of the brain stem where it connects to the spinal cord (the medulla), use the long 'palm-leaf knife', which is nice and strong. Make the incision, then stick your hand in and wiggle to make sure the spinal medulla is completely severed. In young dogs, goats and pigs, you don't even need to cut through bone if you use this method.

His experiments on live animals also showed the workings of the heart, the lungs and the brain. To show the lungs in action and demonstrate the air in them being expelled more clearly, get the animal to run before dissecting it so that it's panting when you cut its rib out. If the heart was exposed, he told his students their job was to keep it functioning. If the wound was compressed and tied off with ligatures, the animal should still be able to cry out, and still eat and drink. Galen noted that a non-rational animal is, in his opinion, far less sensitive than a human being and really doesn't suffer from such a wound.

A Few Tips on Ancient Animal Experiments

- For vivisection, small animals are better.
- Use the right tools; for example, the very sharp and pointed scalpel knife for the vivisection of piglets who are just a few days old.
- You need a board with holes in it. The live animal should be on its back, cords passed through the holes and the assistants should tie the animal down by its limbs.
- Cut deeply, without compassion or pity, just as you would if the animal were dead.
- Nothing ruins an operation more than haemorrhage, so when you cut into a live animal arteries need tying off to stop blood spurting. There's no need to stop a haemorrhage if you're not aiming to keep the animal alive.
- When you are excising ribs, thin animals are best for observing how the ribs move and change position when an animal cries out.

How to Entertain Your Audience During a Science Experiment

(Sensitive readers turn the page now.)

Galen had a famous experiment where he demonstrated the functioning of the brain by cutting the intercostal nerves in the spinal cord. He could prove paralysis, and he could prove loss of voice. His demonstrations were a big hit with spectators who were astonished at how an animal cried out in pain, but when the intercostal nerves were tied off the same animal would make the motions of crying out but emitted no sound at all. Untie the cords and the audience were even more amazed when the animal cried out and could be heard again. Galen found that strong yarns of wool made the best ligatures for these types of experiments.

The Benefits of Keeping Quiet

Galen discovered that the faces of apes had an unpleasant expression when they were being cut, since they really could look very like human faces. In fact, Galen specifically mentions how in his experiments on the thorax in live animals, where the skin is peeled off and the thorax cut into, he no longer used apes as it was such a terrible spectacle to see. Not only this, but if he was demonstrating the effects on the vocal cords, apes didn't cry out as loudly as pigs or goats. Pigs in particular made a lot of noise and so were perfect for this type of experiment, which was good news for the apes because, with other animals putting on a better show, it meant getting the ape, hopefully, literally off the hook.

Experiments on animals' brains were also part of Galen's work and demonstrations. His advice to students was to carry out the procedure first on young animals and then do the same experiment on old ones. The brain was exposed, the animal cries out and the brain rises upwards. In an old animal, Galen pointed out that the brain is too small to fill the skull and wasn't even big enough to rise over the bones around the dissected head of the animal.

If your own brain can bear to read on, Galen's live animal experiments proved absolutely how the brain sends messages to the body. The animal's head was tied down along with its limbs and he used hooks to pull out and examine different parts of the brain. He instructed his students to get to work with the hook and then observe whether the animal still had a voice, whether it had become paralysed in any part of its body, and whether its breathing or sensation had been affected. The result was always the same: all of these functions were affected and then the animal died.[75]

There's no doubt that Galen made huge discoveries about how the body worked, but if you found reading the details tough and would prefer to hear about a parrot whose brain is left intact and some beloved Roman dogs, then let's leave the world of vivisection and move along to the world of pets.

75 All this gory information on animal experiments is taken from Galen's *On Anatomical Procedures* books I, IV, VI, VII, VIII and IX. You can find this whole work online at wellcomecollection.org/works/udyqryja.

PETS

Delicia.

The Roman word for pet; literally a 'darling' or 'beloved'.

In AD 104, a Roman senator called M. Aquilius Regulus lost his son who was just 16 years old. Regulus was so grief stricken that he made a dramatic gesture at the boy's funeral. Gathering all the pets his son had loved during his short life, the animals were led to the funeral pyre. It is here that Regulus made a display of his grief, slaughtering several Gallic ponies that his son had ridden and driven, different kinds of dogs, and the boy's pet nightingales, blackbirds and parrots. (Pliny the Younger, *Letters* IV.2)

A ROMAN PET SHOP

Which animals made it into the world of Roman pets? We know that the friends of the first-century poet Martial kept, amongst other pets, a talking magpie, a snake, a lapdog, a dove and a nightingale (not just any nightingale, but one which was mourned and buried). Jackdaws, ducks and quails were just some of the animals the children of the elite might have, but if birds weren't your thing, why not tuck a pet monkey inside your toga when you were out and about in Rome?

Trust the cat to be elusive though. Cats aren't going to pad about much in this chapter, but as the cat turned up in Roman reliefs and mosaics – a cat playing on its hind legs with birdy treats dangled above it, or in the arms of a child on a grave relief – it does deserve a mention; it was certainly valued for bagging vermin, but it just might have managed to curl up for a bit of petting now and then too. For now, let's start with some monkey facts.

Monkeys

Gaul dresses you in a Santonic[76] overcoat: it was recently the cloak of a monkey. (Martial, *Epigrams* XIV.128)

The emperor Augustus didn't think much at all of people who walked about Rome carrying puppies or baby monkeys in their arms. But clearly, as you'll see from the list below, monkeys were one of those animals that could delight a Roman pet owner:

- Animal encyclopedist Aelian recorded seeing a monkey in a chariot holding the reins, and noted that a baboon is quite happy to drink wine but a bit nervous of wearing clothes (quite right). We also know of Roman monkeys dressed up with shields and helmets. Prolific Roman writer Cicero tells one of his best friends, Atticus, that he'd met up with Pompey's pal, Vedius Pollio. Cicero didn't think much of Vedius Pollio but, seeing as he had friends in high places, Cicero had to be polite. He didn't think much of Vedius's choice of pets either, as Cicero writes how Vedius Pollio, 'a bit of a good-for-nothing', turned up with a baboon riding in one of his chariots. (Aelian, V.26 and Cicero, *Letters to Atticus* VI.I.25)
- There's a record of a monkey playing draughts (but was he any good?) and being able to tell the difference between real nuts and nuts made of wax.
- Tame monkeys who were kept in the house were considered even more entertaining when they had had babies. They would carry their baby about the house showing it to everyone and didn't mind people stroking their offspring. (Pliny, VIII.80)
- A monkey skeleton, probably a macaque, was excavated from Pompeii in southern Italy and paintings were discovered there of monkeys – one dressed in a white jacket and the other sitting in a cart pulled along by two pigs.

---

76   The Santones were a Gallic tribe from modern-day France.

Birds

He is clever and has a good nature, even though he is obsessed with birds. I killed three of his goldfinches just recently and said that a weasel had eaten them. (Petronius, *Satyricon* 46: a father talking about his son)

Who doesn't love a talking bird? The Romans trained all sorts of birds to speak, even corvids like magpies, crows and ravens. Animal studies have proven now just how intelligent birds from this family are. Their sharp brain power did not go unnoticed in Roman times, with writers recording how a raven had been observed dropping stones into an urn of water in order to raise the water level high enough to be able to drink.

We know of a first-century knight in Rome who had a handsome pet crow from southern Spain. He'd taught his tamed bird to speak short sentences and the crow was learning new words all the time. The big bonus with birds like crows and ravens was that you didn't have to be rich to get hold of one. Some academics believe this could be one of the reasons raven and crow bones have often been found in excavations of Roman camps. These tameable birds may well have ended up becoming the pets of Roman soldiers.

The magpie was classed as a very articulate talking bird by the Romans with one writer noting that this bird had one voice for fun and another for more serious moods (a bit like a BBC news reader). Another wrote that if you couldn't see the magpie and heard it speak, you would have no idea it was a bird doing the talking but think you were listening to a human being. (Martial, *Epigrams* XIV.76)

Here are a few Roman magpie tips, all of them observed by the first-century living encyclopaedia Pliny:

- Train your magpie when it's young because they learn best up to the age of 2.
- They absolutely *love* learning new words, and if they forget a word and hear it spoken they cheer right up.
- Magpies who feed on acorns are the best learners.
- If a word is too difficult and they just can't get it, they die.

Any old soldier could find a raven or crow to tame in his cold military camp, but only the well-off could afford a nightingale – all the better if you could get it to sing to order or trill along with a musical instrument A nightingale could cost as much as a human slave and the emperor Claudius's wife, Agrippina, is said to have owned a white one – very unusual – as well as a thrush, apparently trained to mimic the human voice. (Pliny, X.59)

How to Train Your Parrot

Above all, birds imitate human voices. (Pliny, X.58)

Birds were taught to talk by trainers whose job was specifically to sit with the bird, ply them with titbits and encourage them to repeat words. ('Hail Caesar!' was a favourite phrase.) Parrots, *psittaci*, were a popular Roman pet. The Romans were most familiar with the parrots imported from India, a colourful bird with its green body and red around the neck. Even though the grey West African parrot is a much better talker than the Indian, there is no evidence for them turning up to delight the Roman people, although the green African parrot may have made it to Italy.[77] Pet parrots would greet their owners and repeat words back to them, but according to the Romans, they were even more fun with a bit of wine inside them. How do you teach your parrot to speak? According to Pliny's notes on this subject, you hit it on the head with an iron bar.

Despite all the head banging, it seems the pet parrot was much loved. The first-century Roman poet Statius immortalised his friend Melior's parrot in a poem, which tells us the pet bird had an ivory cage with silver bars and walked about the table at dinner parties, collecting titbits from guests. It even had a proper funeral when it died (too much wine?). (Pliny, X.58 and Statius, *Silvae* II.4)

ELITE PETS FIT FOR AN EMPEROR

Animals were a great way for a Roman emperor to advertise his status, power and wealth – after all, owning exotic animals such as lions or bears certainly helped highlight the fact you were someone special. However, it

---

77 Another insight from George Jennison, late author and superintendent of Belle Vue Zoological Gardens in Manchester, taken from his book *Animals for Show and Pleasure in Ancient Rome*. See Bibliography for more details on this jam-packed and well-researched book.

wasn't all about showing off, as we have evidence that some Roman emperors cared for their pets and enjoyed them just as we do today. Caligula wasn't the only emperor to have a favourite horse (remember Incitatus the chariot horse?) and the emperor Claudius had a little white lapdog, most likely a Maltese. Read on to see what we know about animals who shared their lives with the elite rulers of Rome:

- Tiberius had a pet snake, which he used to feed by hand himself. One day when he went to give his snake its food as usual, he discovered it covered in crawling ants and dead. This had to mean something – but what? Tiberius took it as a warning: beware of the power of the mob.
- A starling and several nightingales trained to talk in Greek and Latin were the childhood pets of Nero and his adopted brother, Britannicus.
- Why have a little white dog like Claudius, when you can have lions like the emperor Caracalla? (Remember: he was the 10-year-old who used to turn away with a tear at arena shows when people were executed by wild animals.) His favourite, whom he liked to caress and have around him in public, was called Acinaces – after a Greek sword – and ate and slept with him.
- There's nothing like writing a bad story about an emperor to give him a terrible reputation that will last thousands of years. Yet maybe the following tale is more fact than fiction, as we've learnt by now how some humans really do love to show off with a high-status dangerous animal for a pet. Teenage emperor Elagabalus (AD 203–222) was said to have his own rhinoceros, hippos, a crocodile and several Egyptian snakes. He particularly liked to be driven about by lions, tigers and stags in harness. Perhaps any teenager in charge of an empire would make the most of it, and certainly Elagabalus sounds like he did. He was driven around his royal residence in a chariot harnessed by four huge dogs and entertained himself by using his personal pet animals to frighten the hell out of guests. The story is that he kept tamed bears, lions and leopards, and that he sometimes liked to feed them with parrots and pheasants. These wild animals would have been very well trained but crucially they were *exarmati* – detoothed and declawed.[78] (No doubt those wine-drinking baboons at the top

---

78   This was still done to exotic pets more than two thousand years later: Salvador Dali, for example, had his pet ocelot's teeth and claws removed.

of this chapter might have suffered the same dental treatment.) Elagabalus loved to turn his exotic pets loose in guests' rooms at night or have the animals surprise them at dinner parties, because there's nothing like a bit of panic and terror for a great night out. (*Augustan History: Elagabalus* XXI.1)

- Emperor Valentinian I (AD 321–375) had his own bears. Their names were Mica Aurea ('Golden Grain') and Innocentia ('Innocence'). He kept their cages near his bedroom and made sure they were well looked after. Sounds sweet? Not really. Mica Aurea and Innocentia were actually kept as savage as possible, as Valentinian used them in the arenas where they carried out man-eating duties. The emperor must have felt something for his bears though, because after he'd seen them tear plenty of people to pieces he had Innocentia rehomed in the forest in the hope that she would go on to have cubs just like herself. (Ammianus Marcellinus, *History* XXIX.3, 9)

- Let's end with the emperor Hadrian, who you may remember loved his horse Borysthenes so much he wrote a poem about the animal when it died. Borysthenes may have been the emperor's favourite, but he wasn't the only horse or animal whom the emperor felt affection for, as history records that he loved his dogs and horses so much that he gave them burial places after their deaths.

DOGS

Dogs have run and barked through a whole section earlier on, but we can't leave them out of a chapter on pets. Although one Roman writer commented that a dog is so helpful around the house if it's trained, that for a poor man it's as good as a slave, and Regulus *did* sacrifice his son's dogs at his funeral pyre, there's no doubt Romans definitely formed bonds with their canine companions. We've seen the paw prints left in Roman tiles and the dead guard dogs of Pompeii, but what about a posher pooch? The emperor Claudius wasn't alone with his love of a Maltese dog, as we see here.

- The earliest record of these diminutive animals was an image found on a Greek amphora around 2,500 years ago, about 500 years before Claudius had his own little white dog.

- Upper-class Roman women in particular were fond of a Maltese, carrying them around in their togas. If you were a wealthy Roman, the dog of choice would be this breed; expensive enough to signal how well-off you were and just right for cuddling on your lap.
- Not only were they a high-status pet, but they also doubled up as a cure for a belly ache. Just lie with a lapdog on your stomach and you'll get some relief.
- A third-century AD Maltese was excavated from Roman Carthage. This little dog was buried at the feet of its teenage owner. The dog had spinal deformation, a dislocated hip, tooth loss and osteoarthritis. Despite all this, someone must have loved the dog as it lived until its mid-teens.

Issa, the Famous Roman Lapdog

Issa, the lapdog of Roman governor of Malta, Publius, has gone down in history starring in book I of poet Martial's epigrams. Martial immortalised his friend's pet in a poem, which proves Issa was pampered just as much as dogs are today, 2,000 years later. She snuggles up on Publius, sleeps on the bed, asks to get down when she needs the toilet, and there's even the ancient equivalent of a framed pet photograph of this little lapdog. (You can decide for yourself if Martial meant every word or if he was rolling his eyes when he wrote this.)

Issa is naughtier than Catullus' sparrow,
Issa is purer than the kiss of a dove,
Issa is more charming than all the girls,
Issa is more precious than Indian gems,
Issa the little dog is Publius' darling.
If she whines, you will think she is speaking.
She feels both sadness and joy.
She lies across him leaning on his neck and falls asleep
so that not a breath is heard
and when her bladder is pressed by an urge to go
not one drop soils the covers,
but she nudges you with her soft paw from the couch,
warns you to put her down and asks to be lifted.
There is such great modesty in this chaste little pup,

She knows nothing of Love, nor do we find
a mate worthy of so tender a girl.
So that the end of life does not carry her off completely,
Publius has portrayed her in a picture
In which you will see an Issa so like herself
that not even herself is so similar to herself.
In a nutshell, place Issa next to her picture:
either you will think that one is real
or you'll think the other is painted.

(Martial, *Epigrams* I.109)

In Loving Memory

If you didn't hang out with famous Roman poets who could immortalise your pet in verse, there were other ways to remember a beloved dog. Dogs certainly appeared on grave monuments as they were a symbol of death and of fidelity, but some of those dogs were likely to be images of real-life dog companions, just like the little dog on the first-century AD marble funeral altar for Anthus. It is dedicated by his father to the 'sweetest son' he lost too soon and shows the boy's pet dog at his feet.

What about memorials to dogs themselves? Found on a Roman-era tombstone is the inscription:

Behold Aeolis, a jolly little dog, taken by swift fate, whose loss pained me beyond measure.

If people had the money, they might pay for an inscription on a tombstone for their pet dog like the first- to second-century AD one above dedicated to the cheerful pooch Aeolis and found in modern-day Palestrina in Italy. Sometimes there might even be a portrait of the dog itself. There are lots of examples of these memorials to dogs – a watchdog who 'never barked out of place' and who was loved enough to deserve a cremation and an epitaph, for example.[79] But one of the most famous, from Salerno in Italy, left to the second-century dog Patricius will ring true for any twenty-first-century dog lover:

---

79 From the *Corpus of Latin Inscriptions* IX.5785.

A dead son and his little pet dog. Funeral relief: 'To the departed spirits of Anthus [set up by] his father Lucius Julius Gamus to his sweetest son'. (The Metropolitan Museum of Art, New York)

Drenched in tears I carried you to the grave, our little dog, just as I carried you home in happier times fifteen years ago. So my Patricius now you shall not give me a thousand kisses, nor shall you lie cosily across my neck. Grief-stricken I have placed you in the marble tomb that you deserve and I have forever united you to myself when my own spirits depart this world. You were just like a human in your clever ways. Ah, we have lost such a beloved pet. Sweet Patricius you used to join us at the table and cutely beg for food on my lap, with your eager tongue licking the cup which my hands often held out for you and so many times, when I came home exhausted you met me with a wagging tail.

(*Corpus of Latin Inscriptions* X.659)

SLITHERY PETS

Now dry your eyes because there's nothing sweet about this example of a Roman using their pet for sinister ends. Remember Vedius Pollio, who turned up with a baboon riding in his chariot? This first-century BC Roman equestrian and friend of the emperor Augustus kept quite a few animals at his estate. Lurking amongst his fishponds was a pond full of *murenae* – moray eels. Now, moray eels – whose skin was used to make whips for flogging the errant sons of Roman citizens – have very strong jaws and very sharp teeth, which gives you a clue about where this story is going.

Pollio had a reputation for treating his slaves cruelly and was quite happy to prove as much when Augustus was dining at his house. A slave accidentally broke one of Pollio's fancy cups. What to do? Obviously the slave should be thrown in with the moray eels. Plenty of other unfortunate people had met their end under Pollio's version of throwing a human to the beasts. The slave turned to Augustus for mercy, pleading for any death but this. Augustus, who was appalled by this particular punishment, called for all of Pollio's expensive cups to be brought to him and broke the lot. According to writer and philosopher Seneca, Augustus said to Pollio: 'If your cup is broken, a man's entrails are torn apart? It pleases you so much that you order a man led to his death, even with Caesar present?' (Seneca, *On Anger* III.40)

Not everyone used their pet eels for gruesome executions. An orator called Hortensius had a moray eel that he loved so much he wept when it died, and the second- to first-century BC Roman orator Lucius Licinius Crassus actually buried his moray when it died. His eel was said to recognise his voice and swim to him for food. Never mind a collar for your dog, Crassus's moray was adorned with earrings and small jewelled necklaces – and Crassus wasn't the only person to dress up their pet eel like this. Clearly, if you wanted a pet who was a talking point, no doubt a moray eel wearing earrings was quite the catch. (Aelian, VIII.4)

Off to a dinner party? Take your pet snake to coil around your neck like first-century Roman lady, Glaucilla. Or just enjoy the tame snakes slithering around the tableware like Seneca had to on a night out. Snakes could be kept as household pets and one Roman writer even talks about the tameness of the Egyptian asp: you can snap your fingers and out it comes; they become so gentle and so tame that you can feed them along with your children – they wouldn't harm anyone and just slither out of their lairs to coil up next to you. (Aelian, XVII.5)

A FAMOUS ROMAN SPARROW

With epitaphs for dogs and poetry for dead pets, if there's a chapter of this book where the Romans tell us themselves about the presence of animals in the Roman world, then this is it. So let's hear another Roman voice, with a poem about the most famous and long-lasting pet sparrow in history: the dead bird of the first-century BC poet Catullus's girlfriend, Lesbia.

> Grieve, oh Loves and Cupids
> and all you men of grace.
> My girl's sparrow is dead.
> Sparrow, my girl's darling
> whom she loved more than her own eyes.
> For he was sweet as honey and knew her
> as well as my girl knew her own mother,
> nor did he stir from her lap,
> but hopping about this way and that way,
> he would constantly cheep to his mistress alone.
> Now he flies off on his shadowy journey
> from where they say no one returns.
> But woe to you, evil shades of Death
> you who gobble up everything beautiful!
> You've robbed me of such a pretty sparrow.
> Oh evil deed! Oh poor little sparrow!
> It's your doing that now my girl's swollen eyes
> are red with weeping.
>
> (Catullus, *Carmina* III)

ANIMALS IN RELIGION AND PHILOSOPHY

Let's start with a fiery fox to light up the world of Roman religion, portents, prodigies and sacrifice. There's a Roman story that at a town in Italy called Carseoli, a farmer's son caught the fox that had been killing the family chickens. To punish the animal, he wrapped it in hay and straw and set it alight. Jumping free, the burning fox ran through the fields of corn, the wind setting the crops alight. Things get even worse for the fox because now it needed to be punished for burning the crop sacred to Ceres, goddess of agriculture. Every year on 19 April, as part of the *Cerealia* – the festival dedicated to Ceres when chariot races were held in the Circus Maximus – lighted torches were tied to the backs of unfortunate foxes and the burning animals were set loose to run in panic about the Circus, bringing death to the fox and luck to the harvest. (Ovid, *Fasti* IV.679)

RELIGIOUS FESTIVALS

Burning fox tails lighting up the night sky are just one example of animals playing a part in Roman religious festivals. Whether boys were running around in the skins of sacrificed goats and lashing women with strips of the bloodied hide (said to make the women fertile) in the annual *Lupercalia* festival every February, or a farmer was leading a pig, a sheep and a bull around the boundaries of his land, offering a prayer to Mars and sacrificing the animals in the *Suovetaurilia*[80] procession, which would purify the land, animals had important roles to play on special days:

---

80 *Sus* was Latin for 'pig', *ovis* for 'sheep' and *taurus* for 'bull' = *Suovetaurilia*. Three animals in one name.

A Rusty Dog: The Robigalia

It wasn't a common animal to sacrifice, but on 25 April, if you were a Roman dog and lived in the countryside, you'd be right to worry – even more so if your fur was at all red, in which case you should leg it as soon as possible. This is the day a red-furred dog was sacrificed to Robigo, the goddess of blight and red rust (if your survival depended on the harvest, the last thing you wanted was for your tools to go rusty or your crops to get mildew). Not any old dog, but an unweaned puppy, along with a sheep were the animals you needed to keep on the good side of Robigo. The entrails of the two animals were thrown on a fire together with wine and incense – incense would have helped mask any nasty smells from the blood and guts. Finally, a prayer was offered up to the deity beseeching rough Robigo to protect the crops of Ceres, nourish them with a friendly sky and stars, and keep the blight away until it is time for the harvest. (Ovid, *Fasti* IV)

A Festive Pig: The Saturnalia

In the month of December, the Romans celebrated the Saturnalia. Shops and schools were closed, the law courts shut down, people stuffed themselves, played games and gave each other presents. Best of all, if you were a slave you were given time off, got to sit at the table and enjoy the role reversal of your masters actually serving *you*. We could easily swap the word Saturnalia for Christmas, except it wasn't a turkey you needed at the table but a live pig. On 17 December, the Roman tradition, for those who could afford it, was to have an early bath, and then sacrifice a baby pig at the family altar. On 21 December, it was the turn of a pregnant pig who was sacrificed and offered, along with bread, to Hercules and Ceres.

A Horse's Head: The Equus October

Imagine a riot at a game of rugby, only with more blood. The *Equus October* – October Horse festival – involved a special sacrifice made to Mars, the Roman god of war, on 15 October, during a horse racing festival at Rome's Campus Martius. On this day, at the end of a *biga* – a two-horse chariot race – the leading horse of the winning chariot wasn't given a prize and a pat on its back but was speared to death by the *Flamen Martialis* – the 'priest of Mars'. The dead horse's tail and head were cut off, and the tail was carried to the Regia, the office of the forum, where the dripping horse's blood was smeared over the altar fire's hearth. The head received somewhat rougher attention. After being garlanded with bread loaves in order to thank Mars for watching over the harvest, the bloody head became the prize in a free-for-all between the male youth of two of Rome's districts: the Subura and the Sacra Way. Winning meant storming the opposing faction's side of the city and nailing the horse's head to either the wall of the Regia or the tower of Mamilius.[81]

PRODIGIES

Stories of portents from all around disturbed the minds of men with superstitious fears. (Livy, *The History of Rome* XXX.2)

The Romans were always looking out for prodigies, which were signs from nature that you should take as a warning of something bad about to happen, so that you could appease the gods accordingly with a rite of atonement: purify the city, sacrifice some animals, dedicate a statue to a goddess. When the Roman author Livy recorded his history of Rome's war with Carthage, he wrote about the fear that rose in Roman minds when they realised prodigies were happening from all over: crows pecking and eating gold ornamentation in the Capitol, mice gnawing a gold bracelet, swarms of locusts in Capua in southern Italy, or a foal born with five feet.

Here are a few more prodigies for the years 43–42 BC, when Julius Caesar was at war with his future assassins Brutus and Cassius. They all suggested these particular Romans needed to get those gods on side as soon as possible as there was trouble ahead:

- A mule giving birth in Rome at the Twelve Gates.
- The dead dog of a temple priest dragged off by another dog.

---

81 The October Horse was the only example of this animal being sacrificed by the Romans. The usual victims were goats, cattle, sheep and pigs.

- A wolf snatching a sentry's sword from its sheath and running off with the weapon.
- When Brutus and Cassius were getting ready for battle against Julius Caesar and Mark Antony, a swarm of bees settled in Cassius's camp.
- The legion's standards were seen to be covered in spider webs.
- In Caesar's camp at dawn, an eagle settled on the roof of the headquarters. Then, agitated by smaller birds, it disappeared from sight.

Don't Ignore a Prodigy

- In 77 BC, Roman general Pompey's staff officer, Decimus Laelius, must have had a bad feeling when two animal prodigies suggested his future was not looking good. At Rome, a pair of snakes were spotted slithering in two different directions from his wife's bed, and while sitting with Pompey at camp, a falcon swooped above Laelius's head. He was later ambushed and killed with his legion in the Roman civil war against Sertorius. (Julius Obsequens, *On Prodigies* 58)
- In Germany, in the camp of Roman military commander Drusus, a swarm of bees settled in such a way on the tent of Hostilius Rufus, the camp's prefect, that the whole of the front guy rope was covered in bees, as was a spear, thrust into the ground in front of the tent. All of Drusus's men were slaughtered in an ambush. (Julius Obsequens, 72)
- It doesn't matter how small an animal is, it could be a portent of something big. In the first century BC, Gnaeus Paprius Carbo failed to pay attention to the fact that his sandals had been gnawed by mice, the same animal which had predicted the war between Republican Rome and the tribes of Italy some years before when the rodents had gnawed through soldiers' shields at Lanuvium. Although white mice were considered a good sign, the little rodent was not to be ignored where bad portents were concerned as Carbo and his dodgy sandals were indeed defeated in his battle against fellow Roman statesman and general Lucius Cornelius Sulla. Carbo was eventually captured and led in chains to his execution in Sicily.[82]

---

82 The Latin for 'little mouse' is *musculus*, which is where we get our word 'muscle' from.

Look to the Birds

The owl is associated with funerals and is a terrible omen ... that's why when it is seen in cities or in daylight it is absolutely a sign of ill-boding. (Pliny, *Natural History* X.16)

Augurs (soothsayers) interpreted whether the gods were happy or unhappy with what humans intended to do. Should a military plan go ahead right now? Look to the sky at the thunder and lightning, and look to the birds.

- *Alites* were birds that gave omens by their flight: look to the eagle, the vulture, the hawk, the osprey.
- *Oscines* gave omens by their voice: listen out for the crow, the raven, the owl.
- It's a terrible omen if a raven makes a croaking sound as if it were choking.
- Woodpeckers were an important bird in auguries and were observed for both their flight and their calls.
- What did the Romans do when an eagle owl flew into the shrine of the Capitol in Rome? They held purification rituals in the city to appease the gods and protect against the dire events the owl had suggested were coming their way.

(Pliny, X.16)

Fowl Behaviour

If you were in the Roman Senate and had to make a big decision about going to war, which animal would you consult as a matter of the highest importance? A great serpent? A lofty eagle? ... Or a chicken?

The bird, which has become a symbol of fast food in modern times, meant something sacred to the Romans in the world of auguries – the art of interpreting the behaviour of birds to look for omens. Known as 'taking the auspices', the priests would feed the sacred chickens and then watch. The birds' behaviour would signal whether the gods approved of a course of action or not. Did the chickens peck happily at their grain? Did they eat so much that food actually spilt from their beaks – a *tripudium* and the best omen of all. Or did they refuse the grain and strut off elsewhere?

Sometimes the chickens were starved beforehand in their cages just to make sure of a good outcome from a hungry hen. The whole ceremony could be done again if the chickens weren't producing a good enough omen, and the results only counted for one day. If the signs were bad, try again tomorrow.

In 249 BC, during the First Punic War against the Carthaginians, Roman general Publius Claudius Pulcher ruffled everyone's feathers by disrespecting the sacred chickens. As he prepared for a battle at sea with the Carthaginians, he asked for the auspices to be taken. The grain was thrown and out came the chickens but they refused to feed at all. Well, said Claudius, if they don't want to eat, they can drink, and he ordered the birds to be thrown overboard and into the sea. You can't ignore the sacred chickens' signs and you can't mock the gods like that. What happened to Claudius Pulcher? His fleet was destroyed in one of the worst naval defeats Rome had suffered so far, and Claudius was tried for incompetence and fined for every ship lost. (Cicero, *On the Nature of the Gods* II.7)

Never Trust a Rooster

The Roman emperor Aulus Vitellius was the subject of some terrible omens. The equestrian statues which were being put up for him collapsed, breaking all the legs, and a laurel wreath put on his head fell off into a stream. It was a rooster, however, which sealed his terrible fate. The bird landed on his shoulder and then hopped up and perched on his head. Vitellius did not escape this bad omen. In AD 69, along with his brother and his son, he was tortured, killed and dragged by a hook to the River Tiber. The man who killed him was Antonius Primus who, as a young man, had the surname *Becco*, meaning 'Rooster's beak'. (Suetonius, *Vitellius* 9.18)

How to Make a Good Sacrifice

Examining the entrails of a sacrificed animal would tell those who asked whether the omens were good or bad. But what do you need for a good sacrifice?

- A healthy animal
- Decorations, ribbons, etc. to hang over your victim
- An axe, a sledgehammer and a knife
- Some salted flour
- Wine
- Incense
- A flute player
- A *popa* – the priest's assistant who felled the animal with a blow to the head with the back of the axe or sledgehammer
- A *cultrarius*, who cut the animal's throat

The animal sacrificed has to be the right one for the god or the goddess. It has to be the right species and the right sex, the right age, the right colour and have the right tail length. If the animal for sacrifice is a calf, the tail

From Pompeii, the altar of the temple of Vespasian. A relief showing the sacrifice of a bull. Spot the flute player in the background. The priest stands at the tripod, head covered while the popa *– priest's assistant – has his mallet at the ready. (Universal Images Group North America LLC/Alamy Stock Photo)*

must reach the joint of the hock; any shorter and it's just not a good offering for the god or goddess. The sacrificial animal should be worthy of a god – not sick and not blind. It's not an acceptable offering if the calf has to be carried to sacrifice – the animal shouldn't be lame and limping, and it shouldn't try to get away from the altar; any manhandling and dragging of the victim or the animal actually running away will undermine the whole sacrifice and is a terrible omen.[83]

Now that everything is ready and your animal is in place, here's how to sacrifice your victim:

1. There might be some background noise. This is not the right atmosphere for a sacrifice so drown it out with loud flute music.
2. Pour some salted flour and some wine over the animal's head.
3. Choose the right tool for killing your victim and make sure the death is quick and clean; hopefully this will happen as your *popa* and your *cultrarius* should be highly skilled. Starting at the victim's head, pass a knife along the length of its body to its tail.
4. Make your prayer to the god or goddess. Don't make *any* mistakes in your prayer. A reader will have dictated it to you from a script, so get it right as it doesn't bode well to have a word out of place.
5. Take out the animal's entrails and have the *haruspex* (diviner) examine them. The *haruspex* knows how the inner organs should look and where they should be. They can tell by their examination whether your prayers will be answered.
6. Cut up the rest of the dead animal: offer the entrails by burning them on the altar to the god or goddess; cook the rest for your feast later (boil cattle, or roast pigs and sheep) and sell any leftover meat at market.

Checking Out the Entrails

Now that the *haruspex* had those entrails in front of him, he had to get stuck into his work. How did he interpret what he saw?

- It bodes well if the heart is fatty.
- Pay special attention to the liver. If part of the liver is accidentally cut during a sacrifice, it is a bad omen.

---

83   Pliny, VIII.70, 183 and XXVIII.3.

- It does not bode well if the liver has blocked veins or is discoloured.
- If anything goes wrong, or if the signs are not good when your *haruspex* examines the entrails, get another victim and start again. Keep going until you get the results you want from the entrails.

Just before Julius Caesar was assassinated, the heart could not be found in the sacrificial ox and the next day part of the liver was missing from the sacrificed animal. All clear portents from the gods that Caesar was going to lose his life. (Cicero, *On the Nature of the Gods* I.52)

On the first day Augustus was in power, the livers of six victims were found to be folded inwards: this was a sign his power would double before the year was out. (Pliny, XI.73)

GODS AND ANIMALS

The king of the Roman gods Jupiter, his wife, Juno, and the goddess of wisdom, Minerva, had a special temple on the Capitoline Hill of Rome. They and their three birds, the eagle, the peacock (it wasn't just the goose that was sacred to Juno) and the owl, were known as the Capitoline Triad. All three of the birds ended up together on Roman coins. Here's a list of animals associated with different goddesses and gods:

- Jupiter: the eagle
- Juno: the peacock, the goose, the cuckoo, the lion and the cow
- Minerva: the owl
- Venus: the dove
- Mars: the wolf, the wild boar, the vulture and the woodpecker
- Neptune: the horse
- Apollo: the snake, the mouse, the dolphin, the raven and the swan
- Diana: the deer and the she-bear
- Ceres: the pig
- Vulcan: the quail
- Mercury: the ram, the rooster and the tortoise

A TINY BIT OF PHILOSOPHY

Let's end with some Roman voices. What did they actually think about animals? Here are some thoughts that have come down to us from thousands of years ago.

The worst kind of philosopher for an animal was a Stoic. This philosophy said: animals can't speak, they can't rationalise and they don't have any kind of kinship with man. They just don't have a sense of morality like humans do. What does this mean? It means we can do what we like with them, they don't deserve any rights and they don't deserve any justice. (Cicero, *On the Nature of the Gods* II.64)

Animals are a threat to man, they are the enemy and they don't deserve either sympathy or kind treatment. They are also more destructive than men. This absolute ferocity means they are doomed to be killed by us. (Seneca, *On Mercy* I.26.3–4)

ANCIENT PHILOSOPHICAL QUESTIONS

> For what do sheep bring to the table, except that by the production and weaving of their hair, to dress us?
>
> (Cicero, *On the Nature of the Gods* II.63)

Cover your dog's ears before reading out the ancient answers to these philosophical thoughts on why animals exist:

- What's a sheep here for? To provide us with wool for clothing.
- Why do pigs exist? To feed us with their flesh.
- What's the point of an ox? To labour for us. Look at its neck — it's perfect for the yoke and its shoulders were built to draw heavy loads.
- Why are dogs so good at guarding us? Why are they so affectionate to us? Why is their sense of smell so good at helping us hunt? Because they were created for human convenience.

- Why are animals here at all? Only for our use because everything in the universe was made for the sake of men.

ANIMAL RIGHTS

We should not treat living creatures like shoes or pots and pans, casting them aside when they are bruised and worn out with service, but, if for no other reason, for the sake of practice in kindness to our fellow men, we should accustom ourselves to mildness and gentleness in our dealings with other creatures.

(Plutarch, *Parallel Lives: Life of Cato the Elder* 5.5)

If you liked those lines from Plutarch, you will be pleased to know that we do have proof of some kinder ancient beliefs on animals. The Stoics would narrow their eyes and shake their heads at the words from the Roman poet Ovid in his lines on the teachings of the famous ancient vegetarian philosopher Pythagoras: how can you remove the yoke and raise your axe to kill the ox who has helped you plough the hard earth? How can you lead a victim to the altar decorated in ribbons and gold and watch it listen to the prayers and look at the corn it has helped you produce and then see it struck down with a bloodied knife? How can you see its lungs ripped from its chest just for men to look at and find out the will of the gods? And feed on this? Use the ox for ploughing, keep warm with the sheep's wool and keep your goats' udders full with milk for you to drink but don't trap the animals, don't bait them, don't kill them:

> Kill them if they harm you, but even then just kill,
> Let your mouth be free from blood and eat more kindly food.
> (Ovid, *Metamorphoses* XV.60ff.; 453ff.)

Some Platonist philosophers said that animals did deserve justice. We won't invite them all to this chapter, but let's hear from two of them.

Porphyry, from Roman Syria, who studied philosophy in Rome, said if speech is so important then how about this: animals *can* speak, we just don't understand their language. Animals should be given rights, it's not their fault we can't understand them.

If there is one ancient writer who has left us a defence for animals, it's philosopher, historian and biographer Plutarch. Here are some Plutarch facts from the three treatises he wrote on animals, one of which was devoted entirely to vegetarianism:

- We can learn a lot from the cleverness of animals. We learn weaving from the spider, home making from the swallow, music from the sweet song of the swan and nightingale.
- We can learn how to care for ourselves and each other. See how dogs know how to purge themselves by eating grass? How lions lay still after filling themselves with meat? Cretan goats rush to find wild hop marjoram whenever they are wounded and elephants help each other by carefully pulling out javelins or arrows that have injured other elephants.
- Animals have memory and emotion; they are sentient beings who deserve to be treated well.
- Being kind to animals might lead to more kindness towards human beings. If you fill yourself with compassion, it can only be good for mankind.
- Animals just kill to survive, man does it for pleasure. It is man who is cruel, not animals!
- If you want to eat animals, kill them yourself. And if you are eating meat, don't leave anything on the table to be cleared away. *So the beasts died for nothing!* Nature has given us plenty to keep healthy without eating meat and we don't even eat the animals that harm us! We eat the tame ones. When pigs are slaughtered and cry out, they are crying for justice.
- If you really do have to eat animals, kill them with pity, not with torture.[84]

THE LAST WORD GOES TO PLUTARCH

It is not those who make use of animals who do them wrong, but those who use them wastefully and cruelly.

(Plutarch, *On the Intelligence of Animals* 965B)

---

84 Plutarch, *On the Intelligence of Animals* 974 and 959F and *On the Eating of Flesh* 994B and 997E.

ANIMALS IN
THE MILITARY

The horse knew his master. With pricked ears and neighing loudly, onto the ground he threw his captor Bagaesus who was riding him across the battlefield. Galloping with speed ... he drew up by the face of his fallen master. Then with neck bent and dipping his shoulders, he bent his knees as he had been trained to do to let his master climb upon his back; and full of anxiety he trembled with an affection all his own.

(Silius Italicus, *Punica* 458–66)[85]

From their skins to their hooves, as inspirational emblems, baggage carriers or physical weapons of war, animals were a part of the Roman military world. Even a small white fawn could be useful as a battle tactic for getting your soldiers on side.

In the first century BC, Roman general Quintus Sertorius was gifted a white fawn, which little by little he tamed. The white deer used to accompany him on his walks and came to him when he called. Knowing the barbarian troops in his army were superstitious, he told them the deer was a gift from the goddess Diana. Whenever a messenger came to him with intelligence of enemy plans or news of a victory, he would use the white fawn to deliver the news to his men. Hiding the messenger, Sertorius would bring out the deer dressed in garlands saying the animal had spoken to him in his dreams and told him what to do. Believing the animal to be divine inspiration, the barbarian soldiers obeyed Sertorius's commands. How much

---

85 A faithful warhorse taken from Silius Italicus's epic poem on the second Roman war with Carthage. With his Roman master, Cloelius, speared and dying on the bloodied battlefield, the loyal horse throws his captor and gallops back to Cloelius.

better to think the gods were behind the military decisions of your general when you marched into battle. (Plutarch, *Parallel Lives: Life of Sertorius* 11)

Sertorius wasn't the only leader to use animals to influence his soldiers. In the Dacian[86] war against the Romans, the Dacian king Scorylo used dogs to show that even though the Romans were at civil war with one another, attacking them would make the Romans forget their political differences and unite as one against the Dacians. He pitted two fighting dogs against one another and as they fought he released a wolf. The dogs immediately stopped fighting each other and turned to face the wolf in a united attack. (Frontinus, *Stratagems* I.4)

HOW TO USE ANIMALS AS A BATTLE STRATEGY

All sorts of animals were used by the Romans and against the Romans in battle bluffs, tricks and tactics. Need to get a message past the enemy? Write your intelligence on an animal skin and sew it onto a sheep carcass. Need to get that message into a besieged town? Do what the first-century BC Roman general Lucius Lucullus did in the war against Mithridates in Asia Minor: sew your messages up inside two inflated animal skins and send one of your soldiers to float the information across the seven-mile strip of water into the besieged town.

Just as clouds of dust in the distance signalled the approach of a marching army, observing the behaviour of animals could be an important indicator of what the enemy was up to. Here are some examples of animals becoming part of a battle strategy:

• Birds often gave the enemy position away. In the Etruscan War, the Roman army was on the verge of descending into a plain near the town of Vetulonia (in modern-day Tuscany). Suddenly, great swathes of birds rose from the forest below and burst noisily into the sky. Scouts were sent to investigate and learnt that 10,000 enemy soldiers were lying in wait for the Romans. The birds' behaviour resulted in the Roman legions attacking from a different direction with great success. (Frontinus, I.2)

---

86   The Dacians lived in Dacia, modern-day Romania.

- In 203 BC, Roman general Scipio Africanus had the chance of sending an embassy into his enemy's camp. How could he use this opportunity for gathering intelligence? Some of his men purposefully let a horse loose and chased it around the enemy camp, secretly noting everything they could about their adversary's fortifications. Scipio used their findings to later destroy the camp by fire. (Frontinus, I.2)

- When the Carthaginian general Hannibal was camped in an area with little wood for fire, he knew the Romans were in the same fireless situation at their own camp. He abandoned the area but left some herds of cattle behind. The Romans seized the cattle as booty and took advantage of a chance to fill up on some meat, but with no firewood the meat was raw. Knowing his enemy was stuffed with raw and indigestible flesh, Hannibal returned under cover of darkness and made a successful attack on the Roman soldiers who were gorged with raw meat. (Frontinus, II.5)

- How about using an animal to fool your enemy into believing your situation is better than it really is? Have your pack horses crowd on a hilltop with as many people from your baggage train as possible to make it look as if your cavalry is bigger than it is. If you are in a siege, gather wheat from anywhere you can, feed it to just a few sheep and then send the sheep off in the direction of your enemy. When they slaughter the sheep they will find them full of wheat, think you actually have *surplus* food supplies if you can afford to feed precious food to your animals and give up on the siege. (Frontinus, III.15)

- A last animal trick from Carthaginian general Hannibal again. When Hannibal was on his mission to invade Italy in the second century BC, he found his army trapped in a valley at Ager Falernus in modern-day Campania. How could he get his army out through the heavily guarded pass? Gathering up heaps of dried twigs and kindling, he herded together as many oxen as he could find, had the kindling fixed to their horns and, as soon as night fell, set the torches alight. With flames blazing into the darkness from their heads, the terrified cattle began to run and as the Roman army rushed to deal with what they thought was a Carthaginian charge, Hannibal was able to slip away.

And their very fear of the flames blazing from their heads and the heat that stabbed at the quick at the bottom of their horns incited the cattle into a frenzy. Suddenly running to and fro, every bush around them was burning, as if the woods and mountains had been set on fire; the shaking of their heads fanned the flames and gave the impression of men running about in different directions. (Livy, *The History of Rome* XXII.17)

ANIMAL EMBLEMS: THE MILITARY EAGLE

Gaius Marius in his second consulship assigned the eagle exclusively to the Roman legions. From then on it was noted that there was hardly ever a legion's winter camp where a pair of eagles did not appear.

(Pliny, *Natural History* X.5)

The wolf of Julius Caesar's Sixth Ironclad Legion was not the only animal to become an emblem for a Roman legion. The *VI Victrix* legion – The Victorious Sixth – and the *IX Hispana* – The Ninth Spanish – (both stationed for a time at York in Britain) used the bull as their emblem. *Legio IV Flavia Felix* – The Lucky Flavian Fourth Legion – used a lion, while the emblem for *Legio III Italica* – Italian Third Legion – founded by the emperor Marcus Aurelius, used an animal totally opposite in image to a fierce lion or a raging bull: the stork. But there was one animal which soared above the rest and became *the* animal associated with the Roman military.

Just like the horns, bugles and trumpets, which blared and signalled across the battlefield, flags, banners and standards communicated orders in battle. Follow your standard, rally round it. Is it raised? Is it swaying? Standards could signal soldiers to retreat, to attack, to wheel and turn, to advance. Infantry legions had always used particular animals on their own military standards: wolves, minotaurs, horses, boars and eagles. But in 104 BC, under the consulship of Roman commander Gaius Marius,[87] the *aquila* – eagle – became the most important military standard for every

---

87 Marius (157–86 BC) was the Roman commander who completely reformed the Roman army, turning it into a professional force that changed the future of Rome forever.

legion and this was the animal image a legion carried into battle with the greatest reverence: the eagle was the legion's pride, it was Rome itself and it should be protected at all costs.

- The *aquila* standard was made up of a silver- and later gold-plated eagle, with Jupiter's thunderbolts clutched in its talons and wings spread, atop a long pole.
- Believed to protect the military camp and bring about success in battle, in times of war this important and divine symbol was housed at camp in a consecrated shrine known as the *sacellum*.
- As each legion had its own eagle, the *Natalis Aquilae* – 'Birthday of The Eagle' – was a celebration for the day a legion had been founded.
- The job of carrying the eagle into battle was an honour only given to a soldier of the highest merit. Known as the *aquilifer*, the eagle bearer was an intimidating and imposing sight: his face was often masked and over his helmet hung the stuffed head of a lion, a bear or a wolf, the animal's skin slung over the *aquilifer*'s shoulders, its fur hanging down his back and its paws tied together at his front.
- Soldiers would gather around the standard before battle, getting up blood and morale for what lay ahead, and bonding together in a situation where counting on the man by your side was a matter of life or death.
- Capturing a legion's eagle standard was a huge military coup for the enemy and an utter catastrophe for the legion who lost it. Such a disaster had to be rectified at all costs, even if it meant getting those standards back years later. In 53 BC, during the Battle of Carrhae (in modern-day Turkey) Roman general Crassus lost the battle, his life and the treasured eagle standards to the Parthians. This military humiliation could not be forgotten; it was a blow to national pride and was seen as a terrible omen for Rome. Thirty-three years later, diplomacy and a treaty saw Augustus bring the legionary eagles back to Rome, along with the captives taken prisoner all those years ago. A silver coin was struck to commemorate the event: Augustus's head on one side of the coin and Mars – the god of war – bearing the eagle standard in his right hand on the other.

A first-century AD *Roman relief of soldiers from the emperor's elite Praetorian Guard. The aquilifer (standard-bearer) holds the military standard. The eagle sits on top, its talons clasping the thunderbolts of Jupiter. (Granger, Historical Picture Archive/Alamy Stock Photo)*

Why should the eagle get all the military glory? The vulture was more than just a corpse-eating scavenger to the Romans. In the myth of the founding of Rome, it was the sight of twelve vultures soaring over the Palatine Hill that signified to Romulus: this is where to found your city. So when two vultures were seen hovering over the army of famous Roman general Marius, the soldiers took it as a sign. They got to work and forged two bronze collars, caught the vultures, put the collars round their necks and set them free again. Whenever they were on the march, the two collared birds could always be seen flying above them. Morale boosted, the soldiers would greet the vultures who were seen as a sure sign of victory to come. (Plutarch, *Parallel Lives: Life of Marius* 17)

MILITARY ANIMAL PRODUCTS

Skin, Fat, Fur and Feathers

What would the military do without animals? The world of war bellowed with animals: mules to carry the baggage, oxen to pull heavy artillery, honey from bees and the grease from sheep's wool to use in medical tents – a tent, by the way, which was made from animal skin. Soldiers' boots were made of leather (sometimes soldiers would stuff raw wool into boots or sandals to keep their feet warm), tunics made of wool, helmets lined with leather or felt on the inside, and decorated with feather plumes or horse hair. Intimidating bear skins could be slung over the top of helmets, the bear's head and teeth on top of the helmet to face the enemy, the rest of the bear skin hanging over the soldier's shoulders. If you were a *hastati* (infantryman) in the Roman Republic, you might wear a circle of feathers on your helmet with three upright purple or black feathers sticking up and adding an intimidating extra foot and a half (nearly half a metre) to your height; all helping to strike a bit of terror into the heart of your enemy.

The last thing you wanted in battle was a slash to the back of your heel or your shin bone. Greaves – bronze leg armour – protected that vulnerable part of the body and were held together with leather ties, with more animal product inside the armour in the form of a soft leather or felted wool lining. Wax protected armour and animal fat kept it shiny, which was good for morale. After all, according to Vegetius, the Roman writer of military matters, no soldier is going to look warlike if his equipment is covered in mould and full of rust. When you're feeling the hot breath of an enemy in battle, you want to look as terrifying as possible and glittering armour is one way to intimidate. Mix the animal fat with sand or ground pottery to really get a shine on.

Recruits may have started their training with wicker shields, but legionaries fought with wooden shields covered in animal skin – a bull's, calf's or sheep's, for example. When those shields weren't defending a man in battle or looking their best on a military parade, they were encased and protected with covers made of leather. There's even a record of how at one point in Roman history the skin of the hippo could be used for shields and helmets, providing an 'impenetrable' material that couldn't be pierced unless it had been soaked in water. Leather was used in the slings of larger catapults for the battlefield and slingers used slings made of flax or animal hair.

Siege Sinews and Animal Fire Blankets

In siege warfare, it was important to have a good supply of animal sinews, perfect for making the ropes strung onto catapults and other torsion engines. (During one of Rome's civil wars a besieged town ran out of animal sinew and the women had to cut off their hair to be used as the strings on catapults.) Animal horns and hides were also stored up for sieges as these materials were used for making war machines. (Vegetius, *On Military Matters* IV.10 and Caesar, *Civil Wars* III.9)

Goat hair was perfect for military use, especially the long hair from Cilician goats, which was good at withstanding wet weather. Blankets of goat hair were flung over horses' backs and goat hair tents dotted military camps. It was woven into ropes and cloth used by the navy, and as 'mats' placed along the top of walls to take the impact of missiles during siege warfare. Any skins, hides and fleeces could act as barriers against swarms of arrows, and freshly flayed hides made the best fire barriers. Double the hide over, stuff it with seaweed or straw, sew it up and then steep it in vinegar and you have an ancient fire blanket. Animal hair mixed into clay and then spread as a layer over siege machines could also act as protection against fire. Hang these over city gates in case the enemy try to set them ablaze. (Vegetius, IV.6 and Vitruvius, *On Architecture* X.14–15)

The Emperor's New Clothes

How's this for making use of animal products for your military needs? The Sarmatians[88] were said to make their body armour with scales made of horses' hooves sewn together with horse or oxen sinew. The emperor Domitian copied this ancient foreign fashion in a special *lorica* – breastplate – of his own. If you were important enough, these pieces of body armour were often decorated with impressive designs – Jupiter's thunderbolts across the shoulders, for example, embossed lions or mythological creatures. Domitian's high-status breastplate was, according to the poet Martial, made from the polished hooves not of horses, but of wild boars, and gave him more protection 'than the hide worn by Mars'. (*Epigrams* VII.2)

WEAPONS AND STRATEGIES

Animals didn't just contribute to the world of war with their physical bodies turned into materials for military use. They also gave their names to some Roman military techniques and devices. Let's start with the hard shell of the tortoise and end with a kick from an ass.

The Tortoise: Testudo

The tortoise was a wheeled mobile structure made of timber and covered with goat hair mats and fire blankets. Not only could the wheels move forwards and backwards, but there are accounts of them moving sideways too. The tortoise gave protection to the soldiers underneath 'the shell' and then protracting beams ('the head of the tortoise') would do different jobs. One tortoise's beam might have a hook on the end, perfect for ripping out stones in a wall; another type would have an *aries* (battering ram) with an iron head for smashing down and weakening structures. (If you don't want your wall to fall too easily, don't build your city walls in straight lines: put in lots of angles and build your wall in a winding fashion.)[89]

---

88 Sarmatia spread across areas such as modern-day Ukraine, parts of Russia, the Balkan states and parts of central Asia.

89 Vegetius, *On Military Matters* IV.14.

The tortoise was also a Roman shield formation where soldiers packed tightly together, holding their shields over their heads, the front row and even side and back rows facing their shields outwards so that every man was protected beneath the shield 'shell'. Here's the Roman historian Tacitus writing about Roman soldiers using this shield formation to attack the enemy walls.

> They weren't delayed by blood and wounds any longer but undermined the walls and battered the gates, the tortoise was formed again and climbing on shoulders they mounted its shell and seized the weapons and arms of their enemy. (Tacitus, *Histories* III.28)

The Scorpion: Scorpio

> There was a Gaul in front of the town gate who was hurling lumps of fat and pitch into the fire in the direction of the towers: he was hit by a scorpion bolt on his right side and fell unconscious. (Julius Caesar, *Gallic War* VII.25)

The scorpion was a crossbow that fired arrows, which got its name because the stinging missiles and bolts it shot inflicted death just like a scorpion tail.

The Wolf: Lupus

In a siege, a *lupus* – wolf – might be hung down on a rope to hook into a battering ram and overturn it or hook it up in the air. Alternatively, you could sling your hook into the body of an actual human being who was climbing up your wall.

The Hare's Burrow: Cuniculus

A *cuniculus* was a military mine or tunnel dug underneath a besieged town. Soldiers then snuck in under the cover of darkness and opened the town gates, or they dug to the wall foundations and tore out the strongest part, packed it with timber and brushwood, and set it alight.

The Raven: Corvus

What do you do if you're up against the superior naval powers of the Carthaginians? Invent the *corvus*, a wooden 'bridge' with a hook on the end like a giant deadly bird's beak. Get near the enemy ships, slam your ravens down, then let your soldiers surge across the bridge to turn a sea battle into a hand to hand one.

The Hedgehog: Ericius

'A hedgehog barred the gates.' So said Julius Caesar when he was writing about his defences against Pompey's army during the civil war. Not a brave hedgehog helping out Julius Caesar, but a beam studded with spikes.

The Wild Ass: Onager

A large catapult with the kick of a wild ass. Trying to get into a besieged town? Load your *onager* up with massive stones, cover them in pitch or animal fat, set fire to them and shoot. Horse hair from the tail and mane could also be used for catapult ropes. The *onager* was drawn, ready armed, on carriages pulled by oxen.

HORSE SKILLS

We can't look at the place of animals in the Roman military without giving the horse a section to itself.

- The Roman *decurion* was the commander in charge of his own *turma* – squadron of cavalrymen. This *decurion* had to be able to mount his horse fully armed, be highly skilled in using the lance and the bow while on horseback, and keep an eye on how well his men were looking after their equipment. It wasn't just his horsemen who needed constant practice to hone their skills, but the horses too.
- Military horses had to be familiarised to the sounds, sights and smells that were going to surround them in battle. Training meant getting them used to loud noises, fire, the smell of elephants (more of that to

follow) and it was useful if they could even get in some swimming practice. Who knows when a river might need to be crossed, when a sudden snow melt or heavy fall of rain might cause flooding? In the centuries before the Roman Empire, while it was still a republic, training used to take place at the Campus Martius, the 'Field of Mars' in Rome. Right next to the River Tiber, it meant that soldiers could have a clean-up after training as well as a swim in the river and it was a chance for the horses to get in a bit of swimming practice too.

- We know from the historian Polybius that Roman general Scipio (with whom Polybius travelled during his historical research) made sure his cavalry were well practised in the art of wheeling a horse to the left, to the right, in a quarter circle, in a half circle and so on. Horsemen were to practise dashing out at full speed from the wings or from the centre and then reining in to reform their troops or regiments sharply and efficiently. They had to be skilled in charging in every kind of formation, and whatever speed they were galloping at, each man should be able to stay in line and never fall out of his column. For Scipio, nothing was worse or more dangerous in battle than a cavalry which had become disordered and broken its squadron's formation. (Polybius, X.23)

- If there was a skill a Roman cavalry soldier had to master, it was vaulting the horse. In battle it was vital to be able to mount and dismount your horse quickly. This was so important that practice took place whatever the weather and in winter the cavalry drilled under cover in purpose-built riding areas. The same essential skills would be practised over and over: mounting and dismounting the horse from both sides; doing this unarmed, then with lance or sword, sword in its scabbard or sword drawn. Cavalry practised vaulting on wooden horses, then repeated their drills with the real thing. Horses were put through their paces too, getting used to their rider leaping on them from all sides until both man and animal were proficient in this essential battle skill. With constant practice the Roman cavalry could indeed mount their horses in an instant, weapons in hand and ready to fight. (Vegetius, I.18)

- If a river was wide or had a strong current, baggage animals and people could be drowned on the crossing. If it wasn't too deep, cavalry on horses would stand in two lines in the water, forming a channel for the baggage train to cross. On the one side, they acted as a barrier against strong currents, and on the other, they were there to catch anyone who was swept away.

- Rivers were also crossed by horsemen taking off their equipment, building small floats from dry reeds or rushes and tying a leather thong to the float. They could then swim their horses across the river with them and pull the floating equipment behind them.

- Cavalry didn't just train with their horses on flat ground but trained the animals on steep inclines and on ground full of ditches. In short, the aim was that nothing unfamiliar should surprise the riders or their horses in battle.

- If foot soldiers were going to face enemy horse, the best battle terrain to meet them on was rough, uneven and especially mountainous ground – not good for the horses. On the other hand, if you were sending your own cavalry in to meet the enemy, you wanted your ground to be higher, open and hopefully without loads of trees blocking your charge. (Vegetius, III.7)

- Part of being a skilled cavalryman was making sure your horses were protected. The midst of a battle was not the only time your horse was vulnerable. Horses needed to be guarded night and day whenever they were put out to pasture, or any time they were unsaddled and danger least expected. When men and animals were eating, when soldiers let their guard down at rest, when horses and soldiers were exhausted after a long march – that was when a surprise attack might happen.

- The first-century Greek writer and philosopher Onasander wrote a military treatise on how to be a good general, which he dedicated to a certain Quintus Veranius Nepos, Roman consul and one-time governor of Britain. Amongst his advice on matters of war were tips on how best to position a javelin on horseback. Every man should hold the javelin in the same position: directly between the horse's ears. This will look incredibly impressive, give the appearance of numbers and strike fear into the hearts of the enemy. How can I not tell you Onasander's advice on having men who love each other fight next to one another in battle? Whether they are friends, brothers or lovers, the love they feel will make them fight harder and feel all the more strongly that they should return any favour they have received in battle.

CAVALRY GAMES

What a sight it must have been to see the *Hippika Gymnasia*: a performance staged by the most practised and elite amongst the Roman cavalry, where displays of horsemanship gave the audience a chance to see the best of the best put through the most impressive of horsey military manoeuvres. Luckily for us, the Greek writer Arrian, Roman citizen and friend of the emperor Hadrian, left us a second-century AD description of the *Hippika Gymnasia* in his work on the art of warfare *Ars Tactica* – 'On Tactics':

- Teams competed against one another in exercises that tested the riders on their sling skills, firing crossbows, hurling javelins, or shooting heavy spears. They also competed in vaulting onto the horse in every way possible, including leaping on a moving horse in full armour. There were displays in hitting targets, mock battles, chasing down the enemy or facing an enemy attack. Riders would prove their expertise in swinging their shields over their heads, wheeling round to face an oncoming enemy with their lance, or making the *testudo* – tortoise – defence, keeping in formation with fellow riders and moving in on the enemy.
- Spectators could watch horsemen riding in formations such as the Cantabrian manoeuvre – a cavalry tactic where riders would move in a continuous single-horse circle, each man firing his javelin or arrows at the enemy when he had rotated round towards the front of the circle. The horses and riders would maintain a constant pace round and round, the weapons pouring out in a continuous and morale destroying attack.
- The competitive element of these cavalry games meant the whole event was a chance for cavalry to gain a stronger bond with those men on their teams – men who, more importantly, they would be riding into battle with and needed to rely upon. Riders would have practised hard for the tournaments and the displays would have been awe-inspiring with superior horsemanship performed by riders in polished, gleaming and shining helmets, backs straight and wearing spectacular costumes to take your breath away.

What was so spectacular about the appearance of these cavalrymen?

- Shields were heavily decorated to make them look as impressive as possible. They were much lighter than those for active service; after all, this was a display and the aim was to carry out manoeuvres as fluidly as possible.
- Each rider wore tight trousers and a tight leather tunic embroidered in bright scarlets, yellows or blues.
- Horses were in armour too, including head armour.
- As for the riders' helmets, think Hollywood film set. The most skilled or high-ranking horsemen wore helmets made of bronze or iron. These helmets didn't just cover the head and cheeks as they would for actual battle, where it was important to be able to see what was going on around you as quickly and as easily as possible; what made them so intimidating and glamorous was that they fitted, like a mask, over the whole face, leaving only eye holes.
- Helmets were polished and glittering, with bright yellow plumes hanging from them. Arrian writes that as the horse moved, the plumes would flow behind the rider, adding to the beauty of the appearance.
- Some of these helmets would be designed with female faces, long hair shaped from the iron or bronze making the riders look like the mythical Amazonian warriors, the perfect effect for when horsemen fought in mock battles as a 'Greek' team at war with an 'Amazon' team.[90]

ANIMAL WEAPONS

We've seen poisoned honey bring down an army, scorpions flung from city walls and snakes lobbed onto the decks of ships, so let's end this chapter with a trip somewhere dark and uncomfortable and see which animal is going to meet us there.

Imagine you are crawling down a tunnel towards a besieged city, pumped up and ready to attack the enemy. What could be a better deterrent to your mission than finding the tunnel buzzing with huge swarms

90   All taken from Arrian's *Ars Tactica* (*On Tactics*) 34–43.

of wasps and bees? This was an effective ancient technique in repelling the enemy and King Mithridates employed it in 72 BC when the Romans were digging their way through to the besieged citadel at Themiscyra.[91] Some of these tunnels were big enough to have actual battles in. Remember I asked you what could be a better deterrent than swarms of wasps and bees? The answer: bears.

The besieged citizens cut holes in the tunnels and not only shoved nests and hives of the stinging insects, but sent several bears and other wild animals into the subterranean hell holes for a combination of animal weaponry designed to induce Roman panic and retreat. (Appian, *Mithridatic Wars* XI.78)

You didn't need to be a powerful animal like a bear to bring an army down. Mice were the tiny animals which put the Roman army in peril in Spain in their first-century BC Spanish campaign in Cantabria. There were such plagues of the rodents that disease and a scarcity of grain became a real problem for the Romans. In the end, a proclamation was sent out offering mouse-catchers a bounty which increased with the number of dead mice collected. (Strabo III.4.18)

Finally, there is one animal who's been absent from these military pages and it's the largest animal of all. In fact, it takes up so much room it has a whole chapter to itself. So take a deep breath and buckle up, because the battle elephant is rampaging your way.

---

91   On the shores of the Black Sea, Themiscyra is said to be the mythical home of the Amazon warriors.

THE WORLD OF THE BATTLE ELEPHANT

> When the cavalry has surrounded them they pull back into the middle of their herd the weak, the exhausted and the wounded, and take turns going forth into the front line of battle as if they were acting under instruction and using reason.
>
> (Pliny, *Natural History* VIII.7)

In 55 BC, Julius Caesar stood on the banks of the River Thames and prepared to cross the waters with his men. As the British king, Cassivellaunus, eyed his foreign invader, it wasn't only the sight of Julius Caesar's great cavalry and chariots that faced the Britons. At the head of the oncoming Romans, a spectacular – and unknown – beast emerged from the water. A great armoured elephant clad in iron scales, a tower on its back with archers and slingers stationed atop, was enough to send the Britons and their terrified chariot horses to flight. One animal had seen off the enemy and the Romans crossed the river untroubled.

The story of Caesar's armoured elephant reveals a lot about the animal and its impact in war. The first sight of such an animal, armoured or carrying men in towers on its back, was a huge advantage in the days when fighting was up close with bloody hand-to-hand combat. Army commanders who used elephants in battle knew the value of the fear they could invoke in the enemy. More than any man, horse or chariot, it was the elephant which had the power to crush enemy morale.

ELEPHANTS FIGHTING FOR ROMANS

Did the Romans actually use battle elephants themselves? We know that elephants trumpeted on the Roman side of the battlefield during the conquest of Greece, campaigns in Spain and at that last battle with elephants between Caesar and Scipio at Thapsus in 46 BC. All of these campaigns were pre-Roman Empire, with the animals first charging for the Romans in 200 BC. Masinissa, North African king of Numidia, sent ten war elephants to them three years later and, it turned out, Masinissa was pretty handy at supplying the Romans with elephants against their enemies over and over again. The battles of Thermopylae (191 BC) and Magnesia (190 BC) followed, when the Romans faced their Syrian enemy Antiochus III. At Magnesia, the Romans positioned their sixteen elephants at the rear of their battle formation and, after causing Antiochus's elephants, camels and scythe chariot drivers to panic, it was a victory for the Romans. Fifteen of Antiochus's war elephants were captured from the field. Antiochus later had to hand over all of his elephants to Rome as well as 1,231 ivory tusks.

Move forward to 168 BC and the Battle of Pydna in Greece. Lucius Aemilius Paullus commands the Roman army and twenty-two war elephants. King Perseus of Macedon has trained his horses to face battle elephants by placing men with trumpets inside great model elephants and smearing these dummy pachyderms with foul-smelling ointment. Unfortunately, this has little effect when faced with the real thing. The Roman army and their war elephants create panic and disorder amongst Perseus's army and smash the Macedonian left wing. After a huge battle in the centre, the Romans are, once again, victorious. When Paullus marches into Rome in his victory procession, he brings with him 2,000 elephant tusks from Perseus's treasure chests. At the games in Rome to celebrate this victory, Paullus copies a Carthaginian custom and foreign deserters from the Roman army are thrown amongst elephants where they are trampled to death in front of the onlooking crowds.

All of these battles resulted in a victory for Rome, so you might think that war elephants would become a regular part of Roman military strategy. But elephants never did become a set piece on the Roman battlefield. It would seem Rome preferred their legions of men to the might of the elephant.

HOW TO GET THE BEST FROM YOUR ELEPHANT

Several strategies could enhance the chance of success with elephants in battle:

- Take advantage of the fact that elephants are the perfect psychological weapon in close-up warfare. This works best when your opposing army have never seen an elephant before. Deploy your battle elephants right at the front of your army. This is the best place to put the wind up your enemy as they are fully on display. The animals should have room behind them to retreat without trampling their own troops, and there should be space for men to part and leave a way for the animals to run through.
- If you have enough elephants, your front-line elephants can extend and curve towards the wings of your army. This is a powerful position for dealing with enemy cavalry – it's where the great Carthaginian general Hannibal deployed his elephants at the Battle of the Trebia. Horses are scared of the sight of elephants and terrified by the smell of them; if the horses scatter in fear, the cavalry positions crumble.
- Depending on how many elephants you have, the space between the animals should be about 100 feet. Men should fill these gaps. Elephants are large targets, so these foot soldiers should be archers, slingers or javelin throwers whose one task is protecting the animals in battle. Train some of these foot soldiers alongside individual elephants beforehand.
- Fix towers to the backs of your elephants and place men (*mahouts*) in the towers armed with weapons such as javelins.
- Avoid battle on hilly terrain. Elephants are best deployed on flat ground.
- Dress your elephants in armour. Supply them with crests to shield the drivers on their backs from missile attacks. Protect the elephants' legs from 'hamstring' attacks with leg armour. All this armour has another advantage as it makes the animals look even more intimidating, particularly to soldiers who have never seen an elephant before. It will take a lot of courage to stand and face such a spectacle in battle.
- Recognise the point at which your elephant corps might become uncontrollable and withdraw them or deploy them elsewhere. To be fair, this is incredibly hard and there's only one example of it from the Roman

historian Livy, who describes the Carthaginian general Hannibal rede-
ploying his elephants against the Gallic cavalry after pulling the animals
away from the missiles of the Roman light infantry, before they panicked and turned on their own men at the Battle of the Trebia.

- Elephants are not stupid. Pliny, Roman expert on all things animal,
  called them 'the nearest to man in intelligence' and writes how the
  elephant 'obeys orders, remembering duties it has been taught'.[92]
  These intelligent animals will not willingly walk towards javelins and
  missiles, so make sure you have thoroughly trained your elephants as
  losses through 'friendly fire' could be colossal.

- Elephants are notoriously unpredictable weapons. If they are
  spooked they can run amok and trample their own men. Make sure
  the *mahout*, who rides the elephant and drives it forward, has a stick
  with a spike on it. Should he lose control of his elephant and the
  animal starts going berserk and trampling its own troops, the *mahout*
  can hammer the spike through the elephant's brain to bring it down.
  Here's Livy again, describing how this tactic, invented by Hannibal's
  brother Hasdrubal, was used at the Battle of the Metaurus (in Italy)
  in 207 BC, between the Romans and the Carthaginians:

  > More elephants were killed by their own drivers than by the
  > enemy. They used to have a carpenter's chisel and a mallet
  > and when one of the beasts began to lose control and run
  > amok amongst its own troops, the mahout would position
  > the chisel between the ears at the point where the head joins
  > the neck and hammer it in with as much force as possible.
  > This was the quickest way that had been discovered of killing
  > an animal of such size when there was no hope of controlling
  > it. (Livy, *History of Rome* XXVII.49)

- Failing this, when the Romans faced the elephants of the Persian
  army, the elephant drivers carried knives tied to their right hands.
  If it looked like an elephant was going to turn and trample its own
  army, this knife could be used to slice through the animal's vertebra,
  which separates the head from the neck, bringing the elephant down
  before it could damage its own side.

---

92   Pliny, VIII.1.

THE FIRST ROMAN BATTLE WITH ELEPHANTS

It was in the ancient Italian province of Lucania that the Romans first saw and faced the elephant in battle, which is why the Romans also called the animals 'Lucanian oxen'. In 280 BC, the great general and mighty opponent of Rome, Pyrrhus king of Epirus (Greece) led his army into Lucania and became the first person to bring the war elephant into Europe.

Here, in Lucania, at the city of Heraclea, the Romans confronted war elephants for the first time in their military history. Pyrrhus lined up his twenty Indian war elephants, each one armoured, with a tower and battlements on its back, two fighters sitting atop the animal and a *mahout* to drive the elephant into the fray. As the Roman cavalry began to push back Pyrrhus's men, he gave the signal for his elephants to charge.

When the Romans laid eyes on elephants for the first time, the animals must have been a terrifying sight, their great hulks placed on the wings of Pyrrhus's army. As they charged towards the Roman cavalry, the smell, size and power of them scattered the panic-stricken Roman horses. With the horses 'screaming', as we know they do in traumatic circumstances, they reacted in terror to the elephants, and riders were thrown from the backs of their mounts or carried away as the horses bolted. The shockwave of Pyrrhus's elephants resulted in defeat for the Romans.

HOW TO FACE AN ELEPHANT

Thus the elephant of Libya, overpowered by constant weapons,
breaks every javelin rebounding from his craggy back
and with a twitch of his skin, shakes off those which cling.
His guts hide safe inside,
the weapons pierce him and stick fast in the beast
but no blood.
Wounds from so many arrows, so many javelins cast
do not cause a single death.
(Lucan, *Pharsalia* VI.208–13)

The description of the battle elephants above comes from the creative mind of the first-century Roman poet Lucan. Lucan's animals in his epic poem

243

about Rome's civil war sound immune to battle wounds, but in reality the war elephant must have suffered terribly. It is generally accepted today that elephants form incredibly strong bonds with one another and are known to mourn the loss of family members. Their capacity for feeling and emotion would have made them vulnerable to suffering on a psychological level, besides the physical dangers they were forced to face in the chaos and violence of close-up ancient warfare. There are accounts of battle elephants being burnt to death in an attack on enemy camps, and we know that if an elephant faced an enemy elephant, fights could ensue between them. A female elephant would not have left her calf at camp as she would have wanted to be near it, protecting her baby. This meant that calves were sometimes caught up in battle alongside their mothers. Elephants could be drowned in storms at sea when they were transported across the ocean for war or, during battle, suffered the blows of weapons set alight with burning pitch.

The Romans were going to have to learn how to deal with elephants on the battlefield. Here's a list of some anti-elephant strategies, some of which show us how vulnerable the animal could be:

- If the enemy has an elephant corps, avoid battle on open land as much as you can since flat ground is where elephants are most effective.
- If the battle takes place on flat ground anyway, look for the advantage: the elephants are exposed and even with foot soldiers to protect them, the animals are easier targets.
- Dig some ditches like the Roman consul Lucius Caecilius Metellus did at the Battle of Panormus (251 BC), when the Romans were facing Hasdrubal's Carthaginian army in the First Punic War. Ditches will confuse the elephants and stop their advance. This confusion could have the added benefit of elephants wheeling round and rampaging amongst their own side. If they fall into the ditch, they'll be trapped and easier to kill or to capture. This tactic resulted in a Roman victory for Metellus.
- Fire javelins and flaming arrows.
- Use the Roman *gladius* – short sword. This means you have to get up close, but the short sword is perfect for severing an elephant's trunk as it is designed for slashing and cutting. If you are really brave, use your *gladius* to hamstring the elephants by slashing the

back of their 'knee' area so that they will be unable to stay upright or walk at all.

- If you can isolate an individual elephant, it will be easier for you to kill. The animal can then be attacked from all sides and brought down.
- Arm your foot soldiers, and fix spikes on their arms, shoulders and helmets to stop an elephant from seizing a man with its trunk.
- Use pigs. If possible you could dangle a pig in an elephant's face. In AD 544, when the Romans were holding the city of Edessa in Mesopotamia, the Persians attacked the stronghold, positioning their biggest and most intimidating elephant right up at the city wall. The Romans quickly tied a pig to a rope and dangled it over the side where it proceeded to wriggle and squeal right in front of the elephant's face, sending the great beast into a panic, which infected the rest of the Persian army and resulted in a mass retreat.
- Remember Julius Caesar getting his troops prepared before the Battle of Thapsus? Do what he did and familiarise both men and horses with the sight and – for the horses – the smell of elephants. This will help to neutralise your horses against the terror of the animals when they face them in battle.
- Make good use of your *velites* – light infantry – as the Romans did at the Battle of Lucania when they faced that great ancient general Pyrrhus, king of Epirus. These soldiers are usually young, lightly armed and highly skilled in throwing weapons from horseback. Keep your *velites* near the elephants and have them continually fire their javelins at the animals. Attack 'as one' with these javelins and lances and you may be able to completely bring down an elephant.
- Open your ranks. Let the elephants pass through amongst your men and then surround them.
- Make good use of your bolt-throwing *ballistae*. You will need large *ballistae* and the heads of the bolts should be bigger than usual. Two horses should transport these in carriages to the rear of the line and when the elephants come near, these heavier bolts should be fired into their bodies. These kind of artillery weapons will have a big effect on enemy morale as well as killing their elephants.
- Confuse and frighten the elephants with noise. Use trumpets like the Roman commander Scipio Africanus did at the Battle of Zama.

- Aim for the men on the elephants' backs and any who are guiding the animals. Stones and rocks hurled by a skilled slinger are a powerful weapon. If your slingers are particularly skilled, they can aim for a particular part of the face, such as an eye.[93]

How could a stone be a good weapon? The Roman slingers were highly trained, practising on targets of bundles of branches or straw and slinging their stones from enormous distances reaching as far as 600 feet – that's way further than the length of a football pitch. Target practice was an important military exercise whatever the weapon. An ox skull found at the *Vindolanda* fort, just south of Hadrian's wall in northern England, was thought to have been used for exactly this purpose. An expert slinger could hurl stones at speeds of up to 100mph and researchers have shown that these ancient bullets had nearly the same impact as a hit from a .44 magnum gun and could fly with such force that they were capable of taking off the top of a man's head. Some of them even had holes in them so that as they flew through the air they let out a terrifying hissing sound. On top of this, the friction from the rush of air as they flew towards their target heated them up, helping them to penetrate a body. Violent, efficient and a formidable weapon against a man or an elephant.

THE ROMAN LEARNING CURVE WITH ELEPHANTS

Ausculum, southern Italy, 279 BC, and the Romans are confronted by Pyrrhus's elephants again. By now, they have devised some strategies for facing the animals. The ancient historian Dionysius of Halicarnassus tells us that the Romans came up with a piece of battle equipment that was designed specifically to take out these huge battlefield beasts: 300 wagons with upright beams on each and poles attached to each beam. These poles could swing round and hit out at the animals. Each pole had spikes protruding from it, cutting scythes of iron or iron tridents. Added to this

---

93 Several pieces of this advice were taken from Vegetius's work on the Roman military written in the reign of the fifth-century Roman emperor Valentinian. Vegetius thought it was important to make a note of anti-elephant strategies in the event the Romans were ever faced with the animals again.

were grappling hooks, which had been wrapped in flax and then covered in pitch. At the signal, men were at the ready to light the pitch and the burning hooks were to be aimed at the elephants' trunks and faces. Just to make sure, slingers and bowmen were positioned by the wagons to attack the elephants and the men who rode and guided them. These wagons were placed on the wings of the Roman army and there they waited for the elephants to come at them as they had in the first battle of this Pyrrhic war a year earlier at Heraclea.

The Romans may have been more prepared to deal with the war elephant, but Pyrrhus still won the battle. Pyrrhus's elephants didn't charge the wings as they had done before but were deployed at the end of the line where they didn't get close to the Roman anti-elephant wagons. A great swell of archers and slingers marched between the elephants with Pyrrhus's heavy infantry in front of them. As the elephants charged, once again the Romans were forced to retreat. Here's the writer Plutarch writing about the Romans facing Pyrrhus's elephants at Ausculum:

> But the greatest havoc was wrought by the furious strength of the elephants, since the valour of the Romans was of no avail in fighting them, but they felt that they must yield before them as before an onrushing billow or a crashing earthquake, and not stand their ground only to die in vain, or suffer all that is most grievous without doing any good at all.
> (Plutarch, *Parallel Lives: Life of Pyrrhus* 21.5)

Pyrrhus may have beaten the Romans at the Battle of Ausculum, but it's this Greek king who is the root of our phrase 'a Pyrrhic victory' since so many of his men were killed that day he was heard to say to someone who had congratulated him on his success: 'If we are victorious in one more battle with the Romans, we shall be utterly ruined.'

Move on to 275 BC and the Romans met Pyrrhus again at the Battle of Beneventum (in southern Italy). Pyrrhus deployed his 'most warlike elephants' and at first it looked as if they had the better of his enemy. How did the Romans put their lessons into action?

- The Roman troops had a bit of familiarity with the elephants at this point and were not so easily terrified by the sight of them, meaning they were better able to harass the animals, confuse them and send them on the rampage.
- The Romans retreated into deep ditches, which the elephants couldn't negotiate. The animals were thrown into chaos as the Romans fired missiles at them.
- An elephant calf, which had accompanied its mother into the battle, took a blow to the head from a Roman javelin. The calf cried out and wheeled around. Its mother recognised the cry of her calf, turned and began to run headlong into her own troops, causing panic amongst the other elephants who did the same and trampled their own men.
- Historians still argue about this, but it's likely a weapon was released against the elephants at Beneventum, which catapulted them into even more chaos. After all, 'The elephant is terrified of a horned ram and the squealing of a pig'.[94]
- Like living hand grenades, pigs were released onto the field, their squealing cries terrifying the elephants, who broke rank, turned into friendly fire and rampaged amongst their own men.
- Some historians believe the Romans went a step further and turned the pigs into the burning incendiary bombs that the Megarians of ancient Greece would go on to use in 266 BC in their battle against Macedonian ruler Antigonus Gonatas, when they coated the pigs in pitch, set them on fire and sent them squealing in agony towards the terrified elephants.

Beneventum resulted in a victory for the Romans. Learning how to cope with Pyrrhus's elephant corps was an important lesson in dealing with

---

94 Aelian, I.38.

This early form of money, an aes signatum *from the period of Pyrrhus, shows an elephant on one side. On the other is a pig – two animals you would never imagine might meet on the battlefield. (Granger, Historical Picture Archive/Alamy Stock Photo)*

the enemy. When Pyrrhus was finally defeated, some of his elephants were captured and transported to Rome. What better way to display your victory than parading these huge animals which the Roman army had faced and beaten? This would have been the first time the Roman people had seen elephants and here they were, towers on their backs, following behind the horses which had conquered them.

THE MOST FAMOUS ELEPHANT
COMMANDER OF ALL

The huge black beasts were brought forward and the Romans were confronted with the monsters. For Hannibal rode before them and ordered the Moors who controlled the Lucan oxen in battle with their sharp spears, to goad their animals and hurry the herd of elephants onwards. Trumpeting wildly, driven on by frequent stabs, the battle elephants ran forward at a pace. With towers atop their shadowy backs armed with men and javelins and fire, a hail of stones assailed the soldiers from afar and the Libyans, high up on their swaying ramparts, poured a shower of missiles far and wide.

(Silius Italicus, *Punica* IX.570–83)

The commander most associated with battle elephants and the great North African thorn in Rome's side was Carthaginian general Hannibal Barca. We can't examine the history of elephants in ancient military warfare without giving this famous figure the attention he deserves. Here are some Hannibal facts.

- Hannibal Barca was born in 247 BC in Carthage (modern-day Tunisia). His father, Hamilcar Barca, had fought the Romans in the First Punic War.
- His surname 'Barca' meant 'lightning' or 'thunder'.
- Practically growing up in an army that had its own elephant corps for nearly twenty years, and surrounded by military strategists and the skilled elephant handlers brought in from the East, Hannibal was primed for the business of war and steeped in a knowledge of the elephant's pros and cons in battle.
- By the time he was 25, Hannibal had been put in charge of the Carthaginian troops and would go on to lead the Carthaginians against the Romans in the Second Punic War (218–201 BC).
- Like the Carthaginian generals who had gone before him, Hannibal was willing to take risks as a military leader; after all, this was the Carthaginian way in war. Despite everything he knew about elephants turning into friendly fire on the battlefield, Rome would have to face his elephant corps just as it had faced the war elephants of Hannibal's predecessors.

HANNIBAL'S ELEPHANTS

The Carthaginians trained the elephants,
Lucanian oxen,
Towers upon their bodies,

Hideous, serpent-handed,
To suffer the wounds of battle
And assail with fear
The mighty soldiers of Mars.
(Lucretius, *De Rerum Natura* V.1302–5)

The bravest of Hannibal's elephants, called *Surus*, 'the Syrian', was most likely from the East. Indian elephants are larger than the species of African forest elephant which was used by the Carthaginians,[95] and Surus would have given Hannibal a good view over the battlefield. The elephant had only one tusk and it's said that Hannibal felt an affinity with the animal as he had only one eye. Surus is the most famous of ancient war elephants, getting a mention by both Roman senator, historian and soldier Cato in his *Annals* and by Pliny in his *Natural History*.

In fact, Cato, although he removed the names of the generals in his Annals, recorded that the bravest battle elephant in the Carthaginian army was called Surus, the Syrian who had one tusk missing. (Pliny, VIII.5)

ELEPHANTS OVER THE ALPS

The Romans believed that they would be squaring up to Hannibal in either Spain or North Africa; after all, no one could reach Italy across the impassable barrier of the Alps. But Hannibal was willing to take risks, remember, and had decided on a different strategy. Along with his elephants, he famously crossed the River Rhône and began to traverse the Alps with the aim of taking the war to Italy itself. Why would Hannibal take thirty-seven elephants across the Alps with him? Hannibal knew that elephants were most advantageous in battle when they faced men who had never seen them before. The Roman army might have fought elephants in

---

95   African bush elephants are, of course, larger than Indian elephants but Hannibal's elephants – supplied from the Atlas mountains of north-west Africa – were the much smaller and now extinct North African Forest elephant *loxodonta africana pharoahensis*. This now extinct species could grow to about 2.5 metres at the shoulder.

the First Punic War, but that war had ended over twenty years ago. The Roman troops he was going to face now in this second war with Carthage would have had no experience with the animals. This was a new chance for the elephants to have full impact, and Hannibal must have seen it as a gamble worth taking.

THANKS TO POLYBIUS

What was Hannibal up against? The Greek historian Polybius has left us an account of Rome's war with Hannibal. Polybius wasn't writing down stories passed on after hundreds of years. Born around two years after the end of the Second Punic War, he was close enough in history to do some excellent research. Crucially, he was able to interview survivors of the battles and visit sites himself. Researching the actual geography of the land, Polybius examined documentary evidence and visited the Alps in person, questioning the people who lived on Hannibal's route. The fact that he was able to gather first-hand accounts and evidence, even meeting with the Numidian king Masinissa, who had fought with the famous Roman general Scipio against Hannibal in Africa, makes anything he can tell us about Hannibal and his elephants all the more interesting.

So, how did Polybius describe Hannibal and his elephants crossing the Alps?

Hannibal travelled for five months, leading his animals and men from Carthage to the plains of northern Italy. Fifteen of these days he spent walking his army across the Alps. Elephants weren't the only animals to make this journey with his army: horses and pack mules also endured the trek.

Alpine tribes lived at various locations along Hannibal's route through the Alps and some of them were ready and waiting for Hannibal's army. The Allobroges, in particular, were a threat to Hannibal's troops. At one point the enemy harassed Hannibal's advance party along a narrow pass, resulting in the Carthaginian horses and baggage mules suffering heavy losses as they panicked, lost their footing and fell over the steep drops. As horses were wounded in the attack, they would either surge forward along the narrow path, throwing the whole line into confusion, or wheel around in pain, crashing into the pack animals behind them.

Polybius tells us that Hannibal's best resource in this situation were his elephants, as the barbarians were too afraid of them to come anywhere near the column where the elephants were stationed. When Hannibal finally got to the top of the pass, he rested his army for two days and many of the mules that had run off in panic re-joined him, making their own way along the trail of his march. But now Hannibal had to make his descent.

Hannibal had not anticipated just how steep his descent would be and a landslide had made the path way too narrow for the animals – particularly the elephants – to pass.

Some snow had fallen, making a firm foothold very difficult, not just for Hannibal's men but for his contingent of elephants and horses. In fact, new snow had fallen on a layer of older frozen snow beneath. Men and baggage animals who lost their footing fell over the precipices. Elephants and horses who slipped over onto the path and went through the top layer of new snow found their weight froze them to the older layer beneath.

Hannibal spent days digging out wider paths for his mules and horses to cross and three days building up a path for the elephants, who eventually made it across. Provisions of food for troops and fodder for the elephants were in short supply and by the time his elephants made it through the pass, they were in pretty poor condition.

However, despite all these challenges, Polybius records that Hannibal didn't lose one elephant out of the thirty-seven that accompanied him on this journey. Quite a feat! (Polybius, *Histories* III.53ff.)

WHAT HAPPENED TO HANNIBAL'S ALPS ELEPHANTS?

Hannibal's thirty-seven elephants may have survived such an arduous journey, but eventually they ran out of luck. Surus is thought to be the one elephant who survived as the rest went on to die either facing the Romans at the first big battle of the Second Punic War at Trebia in northern Italy, or from the bitter cold of a subsequent winter storm, which also killed off many horses and men.

With only one elephant left, and having lost the sight in one eye, Hannibal battled on, riding his surviving elephant and urging his men onwards in a four-day journey across the Apennines, through flooded marshes and terrible hardships.

The Battle of the Trebia (218 BC), fought after his crossing of the Alps, was the only Carthaginian–Roman battle in Italy in which Hannibal fought with elephants. Hannibal and his elephants won despite the losses to his elephant corps. He went on to defeat the Romans at the Battle of Trasimene and the Battle of Cannae. Cannae was the biggest defeat for the Romans in their military history. But next came the Battle of Zama on African soil. And the elephants were back.

ELEPHANTS AT THE BATTLE OF ZAMA

In 202 BC, fourteen years after the Battle of Cannae, the Second Punic War still raged on and Rome took the battle to North Africa, meeting the Carthaginians again at Zama. Two of the most famous generals in military history faced one another: the Carthaginian Hannibal Barca and the Roman Publius Cornelius Scipio. Scipio was only 25 when he was put in command of leading the Roman army against the Carthaginians, and by the time of the Battle of Zama he knew that dealing with Hannibal's elephants was going to be an important part of his military strategy.

Before the battle, incredibly, the two generals held a face-to-face meeting. In a scene which could be taken straight from a Hollywood screen, each rode out with a few horsemen and then, leaving these behind, met they one another with only their interpreters accompanying them.

HANNIBAL'S ARMY

Hannibal had about 50,000 men. In his very front line, he stationed his elephant corps, which comprised over eighty war elephants, the highest number he had ever fought with. This would have been a considerable force and it would have taken a *lot* of skill to mass such a number of animals in an organised line of battle. Hannibal's strategy was for the elephants to charge, throw the Romans into confusion and scatter their army.

Behind the elephants were Hannibal's 12,000 mercenaries. Hannibal saved his veterans for the rear lines, where he could draw on his most experienced men at a crucial moment. The front-line mercenary troops were most likely considered expendable. They were the men who would tire out the enemy and blunt the Roman short swords.

Next came the native Libyans and Carthaginian soldiers, and in his last line, the troops Hannibal had brought with him from Italy. Hannibal placed his cavalry on the wings, the Numidian horse on the left and the Carthaginians on the right.

The great general rode along the lines of his own troops and stirred up their courage and spirit, reminding them of the seventeen years they had fought together and the many battles they had fought against the Romans. They had faced Scipio's father at the Battle of the Trebia, they had fought them at Lake Trasimene, and they had defeated them at the great Battle of Cannae. (Polybius, XV)

SCIPIO'S ARMY

Scipio's army numbered about 34,000 men plus 9,000 cavalry. Normally, the Roman formation had no spaces left between the blocks of fighting men. At Zama, Scipio organised his soldiers in their cohorts (roughly 480 men per cohort) with crucial gaps left between each cohort. These gaps would prove to be vital in Scipio's handling of the elephant corps.

In between the gaps at the front line Scipio placed his *velites* – his light infantry. These men were ordered to begin the battle and if they were forced back they were to escape down the gaps that Scipio had organised or move quickly to the left or right. The plan was for the elephants to fill the gaps Scipio had left for them and leave the animals vulnerable to enemy fire on both sides of that gap.

At the front of each cohort, Scipio positioned his Roman legionaries with iron spikes about 3 feet long. These men had the task of hurling their weapons at the elephants and of hamstringing the animals with their short swords when the elephants got close enough.

The horses were positioned at the rear. Scipio's 9,000 cavalrymen took their positions on the left wing (Italian horse under Gaius Laelius) and the right wing (the Numidian horse under Masinissa) way back in the rear of battle. Each Roman horse and cavalryman was given a foot soldier next to him. This man's job was to fire weapons at the elephants to keep the animals at a distance from the horses.

When Scipio's army was in position, he rode amongst the ranks and delivered his address to the men: when they faced the enemy on the battlefield, their choice was to conquer or to die. He told them that keeping that spirit inside them as they faced their enemy would mean they would always end up vanquishing their adversaries, for when they took to the field of war they had already chosen to sacrifice their lives. (Polybius, XV.10)

SCIPIO'S ANTI-ELEPHANT STRATEGY

It was Hannibal's war elephants that began the battle with a mighty charge. Hannibal's plan was for the huge battle animals to throw the Roman army into confusion. Scipio had devised an anti-elephant strategy. When the battle began, every trumpeter in the Roman army began to blow his trumpet or horn. As the elephants stampeded towards the Roman front line, every man in Scipio's army began to scream as they had been ordered by their general. The terrible noise from the horns, trumpets and screams unnerved the elephants, and some of them about-turned and ran to the rear of their own army, colliding with Hannibal's Numidian cavalry.

The rest of Hannibal's elephants carried on their charge. These animals, undeterred by the terrifying noises surrounding them and described by the Roman historian Livy as the elephants who 'showed no fear', rushed on into the gaps that Scipio had left between each of his cohorts. The Roman light infantry sprang back out of the elephants' path and as the animals charged they were attacked by a continuous crossfire of javelins and spears. With missiles hitting them from all sides, as they ran, some of these elephants did indeed kill Scipio's *velites*, trampling them and gorging them with their tusks while the riders on their backs fired their arrows and javelins at the Roman enemy. But the number of Roman deaths was nothing like it would have been without Scipio's tactics, and the Carthaginian elephant corps suffered heavy losses themselves. The elephants were eventually driven out of the gaps into their own army where they rampaged against Hannibal's men. Attacked with volley after volley of javelins, the animals finally stampeded off the battlefield. (Livy, *History of Rome* XXX.33)

Laelius, in charge of the Roman horse, saw the chaos amongst Hannibal's battle elephant corps and knew it was the right moment to charge. The Roman horses thundered down. The Carthaginian cavalry, already in confusion from their own elephants' friendly fire, crumbled under this attack and fled as the Roman horse – and Scipio's Numidian cavalry – stormed after them in pursuit.

Despite his horse being gone, Scipio still had his disciplined and well-trained men. As Hannibal's front-line troops tried to push the Romans back, the Romans stood firm and didn't give way until, finally, they were able to charge the Carthaginians. As Polybius says, with swords clashing against their shields and screaming their war cries, they forced Hannibal's men back. (Polybius, XV.12)

The Battle of Zama was the end for Carthage. The Romans had lost about 1,500 men, but the Carthaginians had seen 20,000 killed and an equal number taken prisoner along with 11 elephants who had survived the battle. Part of the reparations that Carthage had to pay to Rome was not just the handing over of its war ships but the handing over of any other battle elephants in its possession, as well as bowing to the ruling that Carthage was forbidden to train any more of these animals.

Rome's greatest enemy had been defeated and it was Scipio's handling of the elephants which was a key part of his strategy. Rome had shown she could subdue the great Carthaginian war machine and Scipio had proved the superiority of the Roman soldier. The great Carthaginian enemy was crushed. Now Rome would go on to conquer the world.

Publius Cornelius Scipio took on the name that would go down in history: Scipio Africanus. The tactics of both Scipio and Hannibal would continue to be studied by the military for century upon century, and Hannibal's elephants have been associated with his name and gone down in history with their great Carthaginian general for more than 2,000 years.

We started with the elephant and here it is at the close, raising its trunk towards the sky and beseeching the heavens at the end of its life. As we read these words from Roman author of all things animal, Aelian, we can't help but reflect on the experiences of these gentle giants who found themselves at war in bloodied fields assailed by swords and clashing shields:

> When elephants are dying of a wound, either from battle or from the hunt, picking up any nearby grass or any dust by their feet, they look up towards the sky, cast the dust and grass and trumpet a lament as if sorrowfully beseeching the gods to witness how unjustly and undeservedly they are suffering. (Aelian, *On the Characteristics of Animals* V.49)

EPILOGUE

The space between us and the Romans reaches backs thousands of years. We shield our eyes and squint into the distance at these long-dead people from the past, these Romans who have nothing to do with who we are today.

It's true, we don't live in the same world as the Romans did – hopefully your idea of a good day out is not watching a man being ripped apart by bears, or hundreds of lions speared to death before your eyes. Nor are you leaving home tomorrow to charge on horseback across a field, hurling javelins at the enemy or dodging a whirling ancient bullet to the head. But perhaps the animals that paraded through the ancient world show us that, in some ways, the Romans are closer to us than we think.

Grinding down bones and reducing them to ash, mulching tonnes of pigeon poo onto their land or collecting sinews for ropes and catapults, the Romans seem so different to us. But animal bones are burned to ash and to make the fine bone china of our tea cups, cow intestines form the natural gut strings in top pro-tennis rackets, and ground-down animal bones fertilise our gardens. We boil animal carcasses, collect the fat and use it in foundations and lipsticks; lipsticks that in some parts of the world are dyed red from the crushed bodies of beetles in exactly the same way as the Romans used crushed insects as a dye for wool and leather. We also grab the genitals of musk deer, civet cats and beavers and extract a secretion from them for perfumes. We eat sweets made with gelatine from the boiled skins of pigs and the melted-down bones of cattle, and inject animal collagen into our faces to take the years off.

People still keep lions and tigers as high-status pets, wrap pet pythons around their necks and, in certain parts of the world, hunters still use eagles to help them catch their prey, just like the eagle hunters from thousands of years ago.

We might screw up our noses at Romans using animal dung, urine and blood in their beauty treatments and medicines, but slaughterhouse blood is used today as the adhesive in plywood, horse urine is used in some hormone medications, and nightingale droppings are the main ingredient in a Japanese facial popular with A-list celebrities (*that's* why they all look so young). At the moment, snail slime is the latest trend in skincare products, bull semen is the cool new treatment for dry and damaged hair in top Californian and London hair salons, and shark liver oil – squalene – is an ingredient in make-up (and not just from a few sharks, but enough sharks to fill up the Colosseum 1,000 times over).

A Roman emperor might deliver countless animals for slaughter in the arena and then write a poem for his favourite horse, just as some people might pamper dogs today with toys and winter jackets or bludgeon them to death in their thousands at summer festivals, depending on what part of the world they live in. We wag our finger at Romans pitting bears against Molossian hounds and bulls for a public show, but in parts of the world today detoothed and declawed bears (just like emperor Elagabalus's) are baited with dogs, while stallions are forced to fight one another to the death for sport.

Way back in history, the Romans drank parts of Africa dry to satisfy a greed for ivory, but 2,000 years later it turns out some of us are still just as thirsty for it. Flamingos everywhere are breathing great sighs of relief because the super rich don't eat flamingo tongues any more, but the wealthy still search for that high-status meal just like the Roman elite did: *fugu*, a poisonous Japanese puffer fish; *ortolan*, a bird that is kept in the dark, gorged and killed in a vat of brandy; or a top-quality beef burger sprinkled in gold leaf that any Roman emperor would be proud to serve at his table.

All those hamstrung elephants on the battlefields, the emperor Commodus striding round his raised platform and picking off bears and lions, the cattle with ribbons hanging from their horns sacrificed at temple altars; there's no doubt the Roman world was of its time and very different to our own.

But not completely different.

What do animals teach us about the Romans? That thousands of years might separate us, but animals bind us to the past with the glue we make from their bones, tie us together with their skins and wool and fur; we walk in shoes made of the same leather, rest our heads on the same feathers and soften our skin with the same animal fats. Horse lovers today may not get to name a city after their animal, but they are just as devoted to their horses as some of the Romans were. If you've ever gazed in wonder at the sight of dolphins at sea, saluted a magpie to protect against bad luck, watched a horse race, sat with a beloved dog on your lap or buried one with tears streaming down your face, then you have lived, for a moment, in some corner of the world the Romans lived in all those years ago.

APPENDIX

Roman Authors

It's the words of Roman authors who have filled the pages of this book. Here is a little about those ancient sources who offered up an insight into animals of the Roman world, with a focus on the particular works I have consulted. Although it's mostly in alphabetical order, despite beginning with a 'P', Pliny gets bumped to the top of any list for help with a book on Roman animals.

PLINY
Gaius Plinius Secundus

Also known as Pliny the Elder, if Pliny wasn't learning, he wasn't living. Sit next to him at dinner and he'd most likely interview you. Where are you from? What grows there? What's the wildlife like? Any good stories? Then he'd note it all down and file it away. Constantly curious, he was not just the writer of works on everything from histories to military matters – all lost to us – but the author of *Naturalis Historia* (*Natural History*): thirty-seven volumes on natural science covering animals, fish, gems, geography, you name it. Born in AD 23, Pliny was an advocate, a military man and commander of the Roman fleet at Naples, which meant he saw Vesuvius erupting in AD 79. Attempting to rescue friends (and no doubt unable to resist getting a closer look at a volcanic eruption), Pliny lost his life in this famous natural disaster. If you want to know about Roman animals, find some Pliny.

AELIAN
Claudius Aelianus

Aelian, born about AD 170, was a Roman author and rhetorician. He left us seventeen books under the title *De Natura Animalium* (*On the Characteristics of Animals*). Aelian was an excellent student of Greek and wrote his books in this language. (He spoke Greek so well he had the nickname *Meliglottis* – 'Honey-Tongued'.) Aelian did a lot of research from earlier works – Pliny in particular – and filled his books with stories and facts about animals, such as elephants covering their dead with grasses and dust or the bustard bird being the best friend of horses.

JULIUS CAESAR
Gaius Julius Caesar

Julius Caesar, soldier, politician, dictator, was born in 100 BC. The books that Caesar left to us on the civil war (*Commentarii De Bello Civili*) and his conquest of Gaul (*Commentarii De Bello Gallico*) are straightforward and direct, and great for giving us details on how Roman soldiering was carried out, written by a man who knew first hand. When Caesar writes about a Roman scorpion bolt taking someone out, it's clear he knows his business. Beware the ides of March: Caesar was assassinated on 15 March 44 BC.

CATULLUS
Gaius Valerius Catullus

Fancy a rude Roman poem? Leaf through some *Carmina* (poems) of Catullus and you'll find one. Born around 84 BC, Catullus was witty, sharp and let it all hang out on the page. We have over 100 of his poems, some of them starring his girlfriend Lesbia (and her pet sparrow).

CASSIUS DIO
Lucius Cassius Dio

Dio was a Roman senator, governor and eventually a consul. Born around AD 155, when Dio wasn't writing he was navigating a political career during the reign of the ostrich-decapitating emperor, Commodus. Dio's *Historia Romana* (*Roman History*) took the author twenty-two years to research and write, and was composed in Greek. He wrote an impressive eighty volumes but only nineteen of them survive in full.

CICERO
Marcus Tullius Cicero

Cicero was born in 106 BC, had a huge political career and was a star advocate in the Roman courts. If you wanted someone to plead your case or prosecute an enemy, this Roman knew how to nail a speech. Living through and being involved in a period of political turmoil when the Roman Republic was starting to crumble, after Caesar's assassination Cicero wrote a series of scathing speeches against Caesar's successor, Mark Antony, who promptly put the great writer and orator on a list of people to be killed. At 63 years old, Cicero was captured and beheaded, his head and hands nailed to the rostrum in the Roman forum. His works *Epistulae ad Familiares* (*Letters to Friends*), *De Divinatione* (*On Divination*), *Epistulae ad Atticum* (*Letters to Atticus*) and *De Natura Deorum* (*On the Nature of the Gods*) are all quoted in this book but they are just a tiny portion of Cicero's output. You'd need wide bookshelves to display all of Cicero's works, which cover everything from philosophy to speeches and essays. He also left around 800 letters to his friends, most of them not written for publication, so they are a treasure trove of the real Cicero. They could cut his hands off and stop him writing, but Cicero's words live on.

COLUMELLA
Lucius Junius Moderatus Columella

Born in AD 4, Columella wrote twelve volumes of work on Roman agriculture, called *De Re Rustica* (*On Rural Affairs*). If you want to know how to build a good animal enclosure, tend to your bees, or what it means to see your horse run at the head of the herd, Columella is your man.

DIOSCORIDES
Pedanius Dioscorides

The father of pharmacy, born around AD 30–40, Greek physician and Roman army doctor Dioscorides collected and studied herbs and animal preparations, putting all his vast knowledge into a work on herbal medicine *De Materia Medica* (*On Medicinal Substances*). It was the main reference on pharmacy for 1,500 years.

FRONTINUS
Sextus Julius Frontinus

Born around AD 30, successful military man, magistrate, governor of Britain, tribe subduer, revolt suppressor, fort builder, Roman consul and skilled water engineer, Frontinus is another of those Romans who makes me wonder what I've been doing with my time. On top of all his other achievements, Frontinus wrote a work on Roman aqueducts, another on military matters (lost to us) and his *Strategamata* (*Stratagems*) – a whole collection of military stratagems from Greek and Roman history.

JUVENAL
Decimus Junius Juvenalis

Sarcastic, sharp and witty, this Roman poet's date of birth isn't known exactly, but Juvenal is dated to around the mid first to early second century. He left us sixteen *Satires* ripping into Roman society and targeting what was wrong with it, including all those ivory table legs. Quite a few of his phrases are often used to this day – what are the people interested in? 'Bread and Circuses', 'Who will guard the guards themselves?', and 'Healthy mind in a healthy body'.

LIVY
Titus Livius

Livy was born in 59/64 BC, a member of the literary elite in Augustus's reign. We don't have many details on his life but we know he dedicated a good deal of it to writing the major historical work *Ab Urbe Condita* (*History of Rome*), which includes Rome's encounters with Hannibal and those battle elephants.

LUCAN
Marcus Annaeus Lucanus

It's easy to imagine these Roman authors as old men, but Lucan was just a young man of 25 when he was forced to take his own life after being charged with taking part in a conspiracy against the emperor Nero. Born in Spain in AD 39, Lucan had been a friend of Nero's, but the friendship took a bad turn, the emperor banned Lucan's poetry from publication and Lucan was dead before completing his epic work *Pharsalia* about the civil war between Julius Caesar and Pompey. Even Nero wasn't able to stop the ten books of Lucan's poem living on and becoming perhaps the greatest epic poem of its age.

MARTIAL
Marcus Valerius Martialis

If Martial were still alive and you'd gone to a dinner party with him instead of Pliny, you might have choked on your food – unless you aren't fazed by a rude story and a bunch of filthy swear words. Born in AD 38–41 in Spain, Martial left for Rome in his twenties and began his career as a pithy poet. His first book, *Liber de Spectaculis* (*On the Spectacles*), was written to celebrate the opening of the Colosseum in Rome in AD 80. Thanks to these epigrams, we know, from someone who was there, about Rome's famous rhino, which animals were pitted against which, and much more. Master of the witty one liners, Martial went on to write his long-lasting books of epigrams. His poems can still make you blush.

OVID
Publius Ovidius Naso

Born in 43 BC, Ovid was a prolific writer of poetry, popular with Augustus until he offended him and was banished from the high life at Rome to the small town of Tomis on the Black Sea. He wrote erotic poems on love affairs and the art of love, left us the *Fasti*, a Roman calendar, which gives us all that information on Roman religious festivals, and wrote his wonderful *Metamorphoses* filled with mythology and stories of humans changing into other forms. Poor old Ovid eventually died on Tomis in his early seventies. If only he'd known his work would escape from the boundaries of his miserable exile and travel the world for thousands of years to come.

PETRONIUS
Gaius Petronius Arbiter or
Titus Petronius Niger

'He was a man whose day was passed in sleep, his nights in business and pleasure.' That's Petronius, according to the historian Tacitus. Yet somehow, this Roman night owl managed to leave the world one of its first ever novels, the witty work on Roman society *Satyricon*, which gave us that werewolf story. When he wasn't creating comic characters who would go on to live for several thousand years, Petronius was busy at the Roman court. He had such an eye for style and artistic elegance that Petronius became the emperor Nero's go-to friend for fashion advice and good taste. Appointed Nero's *arbiter elegantiae* – 'judge of elegance' – if Petronius gave it the thumbs up, it must be good. Sadly, Nero eventually ended up giving his friend the big thumbs down. Petronius was accused of conspiring against the emperor and took his own life in AD 66. He was as stylish in death as he had been in life, however. Slitting his wrists, bandaging them up, opening them again, Petronius eased himself out of this world, settling down at dinner, chatting with friends, listening to music, drowsing and reading poetry.

PLAUTUS
Titus Maccius PlautuS

A comedy playwright, born in 254 BC, Plautus left us some of the earliest Latin literature. His slapstick plays such as *Captivi – The Captives –* are where we find out a little of how real Romans spoke and get examples of all those animal terms of endearment. Thank you Plautus, my little hare.

PLINY THE YOUNGER
Gaius Plinius Caecilius Secundus

The elder Pliny's nephew, also called Pliny. Pliny the Younger was about 18 when he stood with his uncle looking out at Vesuvius erupting. He stayed behind at a safe distance and lived on to have a political career, as well as leaving us his *Epistulae*, ten books of letters, mostly to his family and friends, and a book of letters sent to and from the emperor Trajan. What a treasure trove!

PLUTARCH
Lucius Mestrius Plutarchus

Plutarch was a Greek philosopher born about AD 45. He spent several decades of his life as a priest at the Temple of Apollo at Delphi. A prolific writer, Plutarch wrote over 200 works and many of them were philosophical; we don't have most of them but we do have his *Moralia*, which include the three treatises on animals, their intelligence and their rights: *De Sollertia Animalium* (*On the Intelligence of Animals*), *Bruta Animalia Ratione Uti* (*Whether*

Beasts are Rational) and *De Esu Carnium* (*On the Eating of Flesh*). His most famous work is a historical one, *Vitae Parallelae* (*Parallel Lives*) – biographies of forty-eight famous men, half of them Greek and half of them Roman, mined by writers, including Shakespeare, throughout history. An impressive resource.

POLYBIUS

Now this is an interesting man. Born about 200 BC, Polybius was Greek but ended up being held hostage in Rome for seventeen years where he became good friends with, in particular, Scipio Aemilianus, the Roman general who destroyed Carthage in the Third Punic War. He was a hands-on researcher, travelling with Scipio during his campaigns, and was a witness to the fall of Carthage and the destruction of Corinth. He offers great material for the historian. Polybius used his experience, research and interviews to write his *Histories*, recording Rome's ascent to power over Carthage and Greece.

SENECA
Lucius Annaeus Seneca the Younger

Born about 4 BC, philosopher, playwright, tutor to the young Nero and advisor to him when emperor, Seneca ended up being accused of taking part in a conspiracy to assassinate Nero and was condemned to death with an order to take his own life, which he did, aged 68. He left us plays, letters, essays and treatises on all sorts of philosophical and ethical subjects: *De Ira* (*On Anger*), *De Brevitate Vitae* (*On the Shortness of Life*), *De Clementia* (*On Mercy*), for example.

STATIUS
Publius Papinius Statius

Statius was a Roman poet born in AD 45 and rival of Martial. He lived in Rome during Domitian's reign, became the emperor's court poet (no wonder he made Martial grit his teeth) and no doubt was an eye witness to the death of the lion who starred in his 'Leo Mansuetus' – 'The Tamed Lion' – taken from one of the five volumes of poetry in his great work *Silvae*.

SUETONIUS
Gaius Suetonius Tranquillus

Born about AD 69, a lot of Suetonius's work is lost, but we do have *De Vita Caesarum* (*The Lives of the Caesars*, often referred to as *The Twelve Caesars*) – his famous biographies of Julius Caesar and eleven Roman emperors from Augustus up to Domitian. This is the author who told us about Caligula and his favourite chariot horse Incitatus. If you want a good read full of scandals and juicy anecdotes, Suetonius is great at filling your imagination with lifelike scenes.

TACITUS
Publius Cornelius Tacitus

A close friend of the Younger Pliny, Tacitus was born in AD 55. He was an orator, senator, Roman governor and major historian. His *Histories* and his *Annals* are full of the lives of emperors and Tacitus's piercing insights into how politics and government works.

VARRO
Marcus Terentius Varro

Varro, born in 116 BC, was a Roman scholar who also fought in the civil war against Pompey. He wrote hundreds of volumes of work but we only have one which survived in its entirety. Varro's *De Re Rustica* (*On Agriculture*) – written for his wife – has lived on for over 2,000 years, giving us information on how to manage a farm and care for every kind of domestic animal, from sheep to fish. All those lost works were important sources for famous Roman authors to come, including Virgil, Cicero and Pliny. What a stamp of approval!

VEGETIUS
Publius Vegetius Renatus

We're skipping forward to the fourth century AD now. We don't know much about Vegetius's life but we do know he wrote a work on veterinary medicine and one on the military, *De Re Militari* (*On Military Matters*). Vegetius's commentary was studied century after century by those wanting to learn about military tactics, but for those of us not planning to go into battle, his *De Re Militari* is a great read for history lovers.

VIRGIL
Publius Vergilius Maro

Roman literature's most famous poet, born in 70 BC in northern Italy. How can a tiny paragraph say enough about Virgil? His great poems the *Eclogues* and the *Georgics* (the beautiful verse about the chariot race is from here) were followed by one of the most famous literary works in history. Written over the last ten years of his life, Virgil's epic poem the *Aeneid* follows the destiny of Trojan hero Aeneas. Before the poem was completed, 51-year-old Virgil caught a fever and lost his life while travelling home to Italy. The story is that Virgil wanted the *Aeneid* burnt when he died, but the emperor Augustus ordered it published – and here it is, thousands of years later, with stags and war horses galloping through it, still read, still translated by great poets, still studied and still number one.[96]

---

96   If you're interested in any of the books listed, the Loeb Classical Library has all of them: beautiful little hardback books with both the Latin and the translation.

BIBLIOGRAPHY

If you want to get instant access to the Roman world, Mary Beard's books such as *SPQR*, *Pompeii* and *The Colosseum* will open the door and take you right in. And if you love the Roman military, Adrian Goldsworthy has written several information-packed books. As for the language, if you've enjoyed any of the Latin words in this book and haven't had the chance yet to look at some Latin yourself, then I hope you might be interested in checking it out. If you want to sit down next to some Latin and get to know it, Peter Jones's book *Learn Latin: The Book of the Daily Telegraph QED Series* is a great way of making friends with the language. In fact, any of Peter Jones's books are a great way of making friends with the Romans in general.

Here are some of the writers who have helped me get to the (animal) bones of my book:

Alpers, Antony. *Dolphins*. London: Robin Clark, 1963.

Beard, Mary. *Religions of Rome*. Cambridge: Cambridge University Press, 1998.

Campbell, Brian. *The Roman Army, 31 BC–AD 337: A Sourcebook*. London: Routledge, 2006.

Christesen, Paul and Kyle, Donald G., ed. *A Companion to Sport and Spectacle in Greek and Roman Antiquity*. Chichester: Wiley Blackwell, 2014. (Specifically the chapter by Sinclair Bell.)

Coleman, K. 'Fatal Charades: Roman Executions Staged As Mythological Enactments', *The Journal of Roman Studies* 80 (1990): 44–73.

Dixon, Karen R. and Southern, Pat. *The Roman Cavalry*. London: Routledge, 1997.

Engels, Donald. *Classical Cats*. London: Routledge, 2001.

Epplett, Christopher. 'The Capture of Animals by the Roman Military', *Greece & Rome* 48, no.2 (October 2001): 210–222. Cambridge University Press on behalf of The Classical Association.

Fagen, Garrett G. *The Lure of the Arena*. Cambridge: Cambridge University Press, 2011.

Gager, John G. *Curse Tablets and Binding Spells from the Ancient World*. Oxford: Oxford University Press, 1992.

Goldsworthy, Adrian. *The Complete Roman Army*. London: Thames & Hudson, 2011.

Harris, H.A. *Sport in Greece and Rome*. New York: Cornell University Press, 1972.

Hopkins, Keith and Mary Beard. *The Colosseum*. London: Profile Books, 2011.

Hyland, Ann. *Training the Roman Cavalry: From Arrian's 'Ars Tactica'*. Stroud: Sutton Publishing, 1993.

Hyland, Ann. *Equus*. New Haven: Yale University Press, 1990.

Jashemski, Wilhelmina Feemster. *The Gardens of Pompeii, Herculaneum, and the Villas Destroyed by Vesuvius*. Cambridge: Cambridge University Press, 2002.

Jennison, George. *Animals for Show and Pleasure in Ancient Rome*. Philadelphia: University of Pennsylvania Press, 2005.

Kalof, Linda, ed. *A Cultural History of Animals in Antiquity. Vol 1*. Oxford: Berg, 2011.

Kyle, Donald G. *Spectacles of Death in Ancient Rome*. London: Routledge, 1998.

McLaughlin, Raoul. *The Roman Empire and the Indian Ocean*. Barnsley: Pen & Sword Military, 2014.

Majno, Guido. *The Healing Hand: Man and Wound in the Ancient World*. Cambridge, MA: Harvard University Press, 1975.

Mayor, Adrienna. *Greek Fire, Poison Arrows and Scorpion Bombs*. New York: Overlook Press, 2004.

Mitchell, P. 'Human Parasites in the Roman World: Health Consequences of Conquering an Empire', *Parasitology* 144, no.1 (8 January 2016): 48–58. Published online by Cambridge University Press.

Newmyer, Stephen T. *Animals in Greek and Roman Thought*. London: Routledge, 2011.

Scullard, Howard Hayes. *The Elephant in the Roman World*. New York: Cornell University Press, 1974.

Toynbee, J.M.C. *Animals in Roman Life and Art*. London: Thames & Hudson, 1973.

Turcan, Robert. *The Gods of Ancient Rome*. Edinburgh: Edinburgh University Press, 2000.

Special thanks to Bill Thayer for his advice, thoroughness, support and the incredible body of work on his site: penelope.uchicago.edu/Thayer/E/home.html.

All translations are by the author, with the exception of:

All Cicero quotes translated by David E.D. Freeman, author's brother and Cicero fan.

Curse tablets translated by the very helpful John G. Gager, with his kind and generous permission. For details on Professor Gager's excellent book on curse tablets and spells see the Bibliography.

Quotes from the following works, which are in the public domain:

Aelian: My translation of: Aelian. *De Natura Animalium*. Translated by Friedrich Jacobs. Jenae: F. Frommann, 1832.

Diodorus Siculus. *Library of History. Vol. III*. Translated by C.H. Oldfather. Cambridge, MA: Loeb Classical Library, 1935.

Lucan. *Pharsalia*. Translated by Sir Edward Ridley. London: Arthur L. Humphreys, 1919 edition.

Oppian. *Cynegetica the Chase* in *Oppian, Colluthus, Tryphiodorus*. Translated by A.W. Mair. Cambridge, MA: Loeb Classical Library, 1928.
  A quick note about Oppian: scholars still debate who actually wrote the *Cynegetica*. The only real information we have is from the writer of *Cynegetica* himself, when he states he is from Apamea in Syria. The lack of direct evidence means that *Cynegetica*'s Oppian is also referred to as 'Pseudo Oppian' or 'Oppian of Apamea'.

Plutarch. *Lives*. Translated by Bernadotte Perrin. Cambridge, MA: Loeb Classical Library, 1914.

Plutarch. *Moralia. Vol. XII*. Translated by Rev. William Watson Goodwin. Boston, MA: Little, Brown, 1878 edition.

Vegetius. *On Military Matters*. Translated by Lieutenant John Clarke. 1767.

INDEX

Note: illustrations are indicated by *italicised* page references; the suffix 'n' indicates a note

Aelian 23–5, 35, 50, 60, 64–5, 69–70, 106, 201, 209–10, 258, 263
Alexander Severus, emperor 65, 172
Alexander the Great 38, *39*, 102, 172
Alpers, Antony 52
amphitheatres *see* shows and games
Androcles 99–100
Antiochus III, king of Syria 34, 240
Antony, Mark 61, 97, 214, 264
ants 76, 185–7, 204
apes 195–6, 198
Apicius 173, 175, 177, 180
Apion 99–100
Argos (Odysseus's dog) 79–80
Armenia 95, 150, 159, 164
Arrian 236–7
Asclepius 91, 101–2
asps 107, 210
asses 141–2, 158, 182, 190–1, 193, 233
Augustus, emperor 22, 24, 102–3, 181, 184, 201, 209, 219, 227, 267, 271; shows and triumphs 22, 95, 104, 116, 124, 158, 163
Ausculum, Battle of (279 BC) 246–7

Bath 79
bears 27, 138, 155, 164–5, 167, 188, 204–5, 219, 227, 229, 238, 260; in shows 147, 149–50, 152, 154, 156, 158, 160–2, 164, 168, 172, 260
beauty treatments 140–6, 259–60
beavers 143, 189, 259
bees 8, 71–6, 185, 214, 237–8; wax 71, 73–4, 145, 187, 190, 229; *see also* honey
Ben-Hur (films) 111–12, 120

Beneventum, Battle of (275 BC) 25, 248
birds 8, 55–67, 72, 114, 145–6, 155, 219, 224, 229, 263; as food 64, 135, 172–3, 178, 182–3, 260; as pets 63–7, 200, 202–4, 210; and prodigies 214–16; and the weather 184–6; *see also individual species*
blood, animal 104, 143, 179–81, 187, 190–1, 260
boars 150, 158, 167, 175–6, 190, 219, 226, 231
bones, animal 20, 77, 82, 141, 181, 190–1, 194, 259
Britain 26, 53, 57, 77, 79, 84, 91, 98, 149, 154, 157, 173, 179, 181, 226, 235, 239
Brutus, Decimus 61–2
Bucephalus (Alexander the Great's horse) 38, *39*
bulls 27, 141, 144, 188, 191, 194, 211, *217*, 226, 260; in shows 84, 147, 151, 157–8, *161*, 164–5, 167
bustards 35, 263

Caesar, Julius 11–15, 27, 34–5, 38, 97–8, 107, 157, 175–6, 179, 213–14, 219, 232–3, 263; and elephants 11–15, *16*, 166, 239, 245
Caligula, emperor 20, 22, 114, 124, 139, 152, 204, 270
camels 152, 178, 182, 240
Campus Martius, Rome 116, 212–13, 234
Cannae, Battle of (216 BC) 254–5
Caracalla, emperor 114, 125–6, 154, 204
Carrhae, Battle of (53 BC) 227

Carthage/Carthaginians 74, 112, 115, 132–3, 187, 206, 233, 240, 250, 269; *see also* Hannibal; Punic wars
cats 8, *61*, 92–100, 189, 192, 200, 259
Catullus 66–7, 210, 263
cavalry 8, 13–14, 34–5, 68, 115, 225, 233–7, 239, 241–2, 243, 255–7; *see also* horses in warfare
Cerberus 90
chariots/charioteering 21, 40, 95, 201, 204, 211; in shows and triumphs 8, 22, 33, 111–34, 152, 156, 212–13; in war 34, 97, 239–40
cheese 182
chickens 7, *61*, 65–7, 86, 89, 103, 105, 186, 211, 215–16
childbirth 189, 192–3
Cicero 8, 64, 155–6, 166, 171, 185, 192–3, 201, 216, 219–20, 264, 270
Cilicia 135, 155, 230
Circus Maximus, Rome 25, 112, 114–15, 117–18, 125, 157, 165, 211
Claudius, emperor 26, 54, 103, 125, 148, 152, 176, 202–4
Claudius Pulcher, Publius (consul) 216
Cleopatra 104
clothes 76, 87n31, *117*, 119, 135–41, 229, 237
cockerels/roosters 133, 173, 178, 186, 193, 216, 219
coins 15, *16*, 27, *28*, 92, 158, 162, *168*, 172, 219, 227
Colosseum, Rome 8, 151, 153, 158, 162, 164, 167–9, 172, 267
Columella 29, 33, 40–1, 45, 72, 78, 85, 89, 174, 265
Commodus, emperor 7, 37, 114, 125–6, 153–4, 164, 264
cows 174–5, 182, 189–90, 192, 217–19, 230
cranes 65, 153, 172–3, 186
Crassus, Lucius Licinius 209
crocodiles 144–5, 162–3, 204
crows 65, 202, 213, 215
cuckoos 67, 219
curses 130–3

deer 84, 86, 137, 167, 172, 219, 223–4; health and beauty 104–5, 142, 188, 190–1, 259; in shows 150, 154, 164, 169
dice 20, *21*, 64
Dio, Cassius 37, 124, 152–4, 158, 163, 172, 264
Diocletian, emperor 44, 137, 167, 182
Diodorus Siculus 18, 94
Dionysius of Halicarnassus 246–7
Dioscorides 104, 188, 265
dogs 8, 32, 64, 78–91, 96, 160, 178, 196–7, 200, 220, 222, 224; guard dogs 8, 29, 60, 78, 80–2, *83*, 87–8; for hunting 80–5, 87, 91, 96, *148*, 150, 164, 169; Maltese 204–6; medicinal uses 91, 190–1, 194, 206; Molossian 81, 84, 169; as pets 8, 78–81, 86–8, 91, 200, 204–8; and religion 91, 102, 212, 213
dolphins 47–53, 185–6, 219, 261
Domitian, emperor 114, 125–6, 153, 168–70, 231, 269–70
dormice 8, 172, 177, 182
doves 62–3, 67, 189, 200, 219
Drusus 57, 214
ducks *61*, 64–5, 172, 186, 200
dung, animal 7, 63, 72, 89, 104, 144–5, 189–94, 259–60
dye 138–43, 167

eagles 55–6, 184, 214–15, 219, 226–7, *228*, 259
eels 172, 209
eggs 137, 143–7, 171, 189
Egypt 11, 18–19, 62, 92, 94, 112, 136, 155, 159, 162–3
Elagabalus, emperor 114, 125, 172, 178, 204–5
elephants 8, 11–26, 159, 188, 192, 222, *249*, 263; African 8, 11–15, 17–18, 25, 159, 243, 251; Indian 17, 19, 251; in shows 15, 22, 24, 147, 153–4, 157–8, 165–6, 240; in warfare 7, 11–15, *16*, 106, 159, 239–58; *see also* ivory
Engels, Donald 94

entrails 143, 173, 175, 178, 185, 212, 218–19, 260
Epidaurus 91, 101–2
Eumenes of Pergamus, king 105–6
executions 148, 151–4, 159–62, 205
extinctions 18, 159

fat, animal 41, 143–4, 188–9, 194, 218, 229–30, 259
feathers 62, 66, 135–6, 229
ferrets 93–4, 181
Fishbourne Roman Villa, Chichester 49, 181
fishes 49–50, 56, 64, 104, 143, 178–81, 260; see also individual species
flamingos 172, 178, 260
food, animals as 44, 171–83, 193, 218; birds 64, 135, 172–3, 178, 182–3, 260; fish 104, 178–81; pigs 86, 171, 173–5, 182–3, 218, 220, 222, 259
foxes 84, 141, 189, 191, 211
frogs 72, 82, 185, 191
Frontinus 61–2, 265

Galen 195–9
garum (fish sauce) 180–1
Gaul/Gauls 28–9, 40, 53, 60, 84, 91, 143, 157, 232, 241–2
geese 59–60, 103, 135–6, 143, 173, 186, 188–90, 194, 219
Germanicus 22–3, 57, 167n63
gladiators 23, 125, 128, 136, 139, 148–9, 153, 156, 163, 195
goats 64, 75–6, 97, 137, 150, 186, 196–7, 211, 213n81, 221–2, 230–1; fashion and beauty 135, 143; medicinal uses 182, 188, 189–93

Hadrian, emperor 7, 38–9, 141, 205, 236
Hadrumentum, North Africa 130–1, 133
Hannibal 26, 42, 105–7, 159, 225–6, 240–2, 249–57, 266
hares 37, 84, 142, 147, 150, 172, 182, 186, 190–1, 193, 232
hawks 56–7, 63, 67, 194, 215

health see medicinal uses of animals
hedgehogs 137, 193–4, 233
Heraclea, Battle of (280 BC) 25, 243, 247
Herculaneum 36, 87
Herodian 55, 154
Hippo Diarrhytus, Tunisia 51–2
hippos 154, 157, 159, 204, 230
Hirtius (consul) 61–2
honey 71–2, 75–6, 171, 173, 177, 193, 229; beauty treatments 143–5; medicinal uses 42–3, 187–94
hornets 71, 72, 77
horses 33–46, 219, 261; and emperors 7, 20, 38–9, 124, 126, 204–5; for hunting 7, 39, 84, 97, 150; medical care of 40–3, 127–8; medicinal uses of 7, 189–90, 194, 260; in shows 15, 22, 111–34, 156, 158, 172, 212–13; see also chariots/charioteering
horses in warfare 34–6, 38–40, 105, 223, 225, 233–7, 245, 252–7; elephants, reactions to 12–13, 233–4, 240–1, 243, 245, 249, 257; see also cavalry
hunting 7, 17, 19, 47, 56–7, 59, 63, 70, 106, 155, 159, 176, 259; for big cats 95–9, 156, 163; with dogs 80–5, 87, 91, 96, 148, 150, 164, 169; with horses 7, 39, 84, 97, 150; in shows 83–4, 147, 148, 150, 153–4, 163–4, 169
hyenas 137, 150, 194
India 17–19, 50, 53–4, 92, 95, 102–3, 150, 154, 172, 179, 203, 251
insects 68–77, 138, 143, 186, 259; see also individual species
ivory 17–21, 135, 141, 144, 165, 190, 203, 240, 260
Jerusalem 78
Juba I, king of Numidia 11–15
Juno 59, 102, 173, 219
Jupiter 55, 75–6, 184, 219, 227, 228, 231
Juvenal 18, 20, 113, 122, 142, 180, 265–6

Laelius, Gaius 255–6, 257
lanolin 128, 145, 188
leather 43–4, 54, 82, 117, 119, 120, 137–8, 145, 194, 229–30

leeches 142–3, 190
Lemnos 76
leopards 95–8, *99*, 138, 147, 150, 154–6, 158, 167, 204
Lepcis Magna frieze 98
Libya 69, 76, 97, 107, *161*, 170, 243, 255
lice 77, 142, 192
lions 95–100, 138, 144, 159, *161*, 167, 188, 204, 219, 222, 226–7, 259; in shows 8, 95–7, 99–100, 144, 147, 149, 151–2, 154, 157–8, 163, 168–70
Lippinus, Fulvius 176–7
liver, animal 143, 173, 178, 185, 218–19, 260
Livy 28–9, 106, 213, 226, 241–2, 256–7, 266
lizards 63, 145, 185
locusts 76, 213
Lucan 107, 243, 266
Lucania 25, 243, 245, 250
Lullingstone Roman Villa 79
lynxes 157, 190
Lysimachus, king 79

Magerius mosaic 98–9
Magnesia, Battle of (190 BC) 240
magpies 200, 202, 261
Marcus Aurelius, emperor 125, 153, 195, 226
Marius, Gaius 226, 229
Mars 27, 29, 58, 211–13, 219, 227
Martial 66, 121–3, 135, 138, 141, 147, 158, 162, 169, 171–2, 200–2, 206–7, 231, 266–7, 269–70
Masinissa, king of Numidia 240, 252, 255–6
medicinal uses of animals and animal products 7, 29, 71, 101, 187–94, 229, 265; dogs 91, 190–1, 194, 206; dung 89, 104, 188–9, 191, 193–4; eye troubles 128, 188–9, 191; honey 42–3, 187–94; horses 7, 189–90, 194, 260; skincare 141, 143–5, 192, 260; snake bites 103–5
medicine for animals 40–3, 70, 89, 127–8
Megara 97–8, 248

Metaurus, Battle of the (207 BC) 242
mice 8, 93, 186, 189, 193–4, 213–14, 219, 238
military, animals in the 223–38, 240; war elephants 7, 11–15, *16*, 106, 159, 239–58; *see also* horses in warfare
milk 58, 82, 141–2, 171, 173, 176, 182, 191–3, 221
Mithridates VI, king of Pontus 34, 75, 105, 224, 238
moles 135
monkeys 95, 150, 200–1
mosquitoes 41, 77
moths 72, 76
mules 36n11, 40, 43–4, 182, 213, 229, 252–3
mullet 49–50, 180
Mutina, siege of (43 BC) 61–2
'Muziris papyrus' 19
Myos Hormos, Quseir al-Qadim 93

Nero, emperor 23, 30, 103, 114, 120, 125, 139, 141, 160, 176, 204, 266–9
nicknames 8, 48, 56, 66–7, 93–4, 174, 179
nightingales 178, 200, 202–4, 222, 260
Numidia/Numidians 11–12, 22, 115, 170, 240, 252, 255–7

Onasander 235
Oppian 47–8, 84, 96–7, 165
Ostia 54, 150, 152
ostriches 7, 28, 65, 158, 164, 167, 172, 178
Ovid 53, 58–9, 86, 111, 141, 145, 173, 211–12, 221, 267
owls 67, 186, 215, 219
oxen 7, 137, 185, 196, 219–21, 225–6, 229, 231, 246, 249
oysters 171, 179, 182

Panormus, Battle of (251 BC) 25, 244
panthers 155, 158
parrots 172, 200–4
partridges 65, 102–3, 146
Paullus, Lucius Aemilius 160, 240
peacocks 65–7, 172–3, 178, 182, 219

Perseus, king of Macedon 240
Persia/Persians 18, 34, 68–70, 150, 242, 245
Petronius 30–1, 177, 202, 267–8
pets 8, 89, 200–10, 260–1; birds 63–7, 200, 202–4, 210; dogs 8, 78–81, 86–8, 91, 200, 204–8
pheasants 65, 178, 204
philosophy 8, 183, 220–2, 268–9
pigeons 7, 60–3, 194
pigs 7, 65, 158, 185, 188–91, 196–7, 201, 222, 245, 248, *249;* as food 86, 171, 173–5, 182–3, 218, 220, 222, 259; and religion 86, 211–12, 213n81, 218–19
Plautus 64, 66, 268
Pliny the Elder 16n3, 30, 135–7, 140, 160, 164, 174, 219, 226, 262–3; on beauty treatments 141–6; on birds 55–8, 61–5, 183–4, 202–3, 215, 226; on cats, big and small 92, 95–6; on crocodiles 144–5, 163; on dogs 80, 83, 85, 89; on dolphins 48–51; on elephants 16–18, 21, 23, 26, 157, 165–6, 173, 239, 242, 251; on food 173–5, 180–3, 189; on health matters 104, 188–9, 192n73, 193n74, 194; on horses 38, 115, 117–18; on insects 68, 71–2, 73n25, 75; on pets 200–3; on shows 23, 114–15, 117–18, 157, 164–6; on snakes 104–5; on the weather 184–5; on whales 53–4
Pliny the Younger 51–2, 114, 160, 171, 200, 268, 270
Plutarch 32, 45–7, 56, 60, 97–8, 103, 105, 183, 221–4, 229, 247, 268–9
Pollio, Vedius 201, 209
Polybius 90, 96, 234, 252–3, 256–7, 269
Pompeii 8, 36, 38, 48, *61*, 81, *83*, 87–9, 93, 181, 201, *217*
Pompey 11, 15, 22, 34–5, 105, 107, 157, 165–6, 201, 214, 233, 270
Porphyry 221
Praetorian Guard 36, 54, 69, 178, *228*
prices 44, 137–8, 167, 180, 182
Probus, emperor 151

prodigies and omens 56, 58–9, 65, 185–6, 213–19, 227
Prometheus 162
Psylli (African snake experts) 103–4, 107
Ptolemy, king of Mauretania 139
Ptolemy XII, king of Egypt 94
Punic wars 25, 90, 106–7, 159, 213, 216, 223, 225–6, 240–2, 244–5, 249–57, 269
purple 138–41, 167
Pydna, Battle of (168 BC) 240
Pyrrhus, king of Epirus 25, 243, 245–9
Pythagoras 183, 221

quails 64–6, 146, 182–3, 200, 219

rabbits 150, 181
rams 37, 219, 248
ravens 57–8, 67, 186, 202, 215, 219, 233
religion 20, 91, 101–2, 160, 211–19
rhinoceroses 18, 154, 157, 167–9, 204
Richborough, Kent 79, 179
Romulus and Remus 27, *28*, 32, 58, 229
Rudston, Yorkshire 98
'Rutupian' oysters 179

Sabinus, Titus 80–1
sacrifices 7, 174, 211–13, 216–19, 221, 260
Saturnalia 212
Scipio Aemilianus 234, 269
Scipio Africanus 90, 102, 225, 245, 252, 254–8
Scipio, Quintus Metellus 11–15, 240
scorpions 68–71, 189, 232
seals (animal) 7, 147, 184
Seneca 20, 66, 100, 105, 183, 209–10, 220, 269
Septimius Severus, emperor 55, 68–9, 149, 158
Sertorius, Quintus 214, 223–4
sharks 50, 260
sheep 64, 72, 82, 96, 136, 182, 185, 211–12, 213n81, 218, 220, 224–5, 230
shellfish 138–40, 144
shows and games 7–8, 28, 83–4, 117–18, 147–72, 205, 236–7; bears in 147,

149–50, 152, 154, 156, 158, 160–2,
    164, 168, 172, 260; elephants in 15,
    22, 24, 147, 153–4, 157–8, 165–6,
    240; horses in 15, 22, 111–34, 156,
    158, 172, 212–13; lions in 8, 95–7,
    99–100, 144, 147, 149, 151–2, 154,
    157–8, 163, 168–70; *see also* chariots/
    charioteering; gladiators
sinews 173, 230–1, 259
skin, animal 21, 54, 97, 103–4,
    160, 184, 193–4, 209, 211, 259;
    fashionable uses 135, 137–8; military
    uses 7, 29, 105, 224, 227, 229–30
skincare, human 141, 143–5, 192, 260
snails 171, 176, 194, 260
snakes 91, 101–7, 193, 194, 200, 204,
    209–10, 214, 219
Spain 90, 112, 115, 123, 150, 156, 164,
    179, 181, 184, 202, 238, 240, 266
sparrows 66–7, 210, 263
spiders 72, 186–7, 190, 194, 214, 222
Statius 169–70, 203, 269–70
storks 104, 189, 226
Strabo 53–4, 75n27, 102–3, 106,
    162, 238
Suetonius 38, 43, 102–4, 124, 139,
    152–3, 175–6, 178, 180, 184, 270
Sulla, Lucius Cornelius 154, 157, 214
swallows 114, 194, 222
swans 135, 183, 194, 219, 222
Symmachus 156, 163
Syria 34, 69n23, 76, 150, 188, 221, 240

Tacitus 44, 160, 232, 267, 270
Thapsus, Battle of (46 BC) 11–15, 245
Thessaly 104, 157, 159
Tiberius, emperor 57, 69, 175–6, 180,
    184, 204
tigers 85, 95, 147, 149, 158–9, 204, 259
Titus, emperor 7–8, 55, 153, 158–9, 172
tortoises 18, 102–3, 219, 231–2, 236
Trajan, emperor 8, 68, 159–60, 268
Trebia, Battle of the (218 BC) 241–2,
    253–5

triumphs 15, 17, 22, 25, 97, 104, 157,
    240, 249
Tyre 138–41

urine, animal 142, 189–1, 260

Valentinian I, emperor 205, 246n93
Varro 33, 62–6, 72–3, 81–2, 105, 176,
    177, 182, 270
vegetarianism 183, 221–2
Vegetius 34, 136–7, 230, 234–5,
    246n93, 271
Venus 38, 64, 93, 98, 165, 179, 219
vermin 72, 92–3, 200
Verus, emperor 114, 126
Vespasian, emperor 44, *217*
vinegar 7, 42–3, 104, 142–3, 188,
    190–4, 230
Virgil 46, 72, 134, 270, 271
Vitellius, emperor 114, 178, 216
vivisection 187, 195–9
vultures 64, 67, 215, 219, 229

wasps 71–2, 237–8
weasels 8, 104, 187
weather 184–7
werewolves 30–1
whales 47, 53–4
wine 49, 97, 173, 176, 201, 203, 212,
    217–18; beauty treatments 142, 145;
    medicinal uses 40–2, 71, 104, 188,
    191, 193–4
wolves 7, 8, 27–32, *28*, 58, 82, 137, 188,
    191, 193, 214, 219, 224, 226, 232
woodpeckers 58–9, 215, 219
wool 74, 87n31, 93, 128, 136–8, 145,
    188, 191, 193, 198, 220, 229

York 77, 149, 226

Zama, Battle of (202 BC) 245, 254–6